The True Story
of a Jewish Boy
and His Mother in
Mussolini's Italy

A Child
al Confino

Eric Lamet

Foreword by Risa Sodi, PhD

Avon, Massachusetts

A large portion of this material was previously published as *A Gift from the Enemy* by
Eric Lamet, published by Syracuse University Press, copyright © 2007 by Eric Lamet,
ISBN 10: 0-8156-0885-3, ISBN 13: 978-0-8156-0885-1

Published by
Adams Media, a division of F+W Media, Inc.
57 Littlefield Street, Avon, MA 02322 U.S.A.
www.adamsmedia.com

ISBN 10: 1-4405-0997-2
ISBN 13: 978-1-4405-0997-1
eISBN 10: 1-4405-1126-8
eISBN 13: 978-1-4405-1126-4

Printed in the United States of America.
10 9 8 7 6 5 4 3 2 1

Library of Congress Cataloging-in-Publication Data
Lamet, Eric
A child al confino / Eric Lamet.
p. cm.
ISBN-13: 978-1-4405-0997-1
ISBN-10: 1-4405-0997-2
ISBN-10: 1-4405-1126-8 (eISBN)
ISBN-13: 978-1-4405-1126-4 (eISBN)
1. Lamet, Eric 2. Jews, Austrian—Italy—Biography. 3. Jewish refugees—Italy—
Biography. 4. World War (1939–1945)—Italy—Jews. 5. Jewish children in the
Holocaust—Italy—Biography. 6. Italy—Biography. I. Title.
DS135.A93L364 2010
940.53'18092—dc22
[B]
2010038754

Photos from the private collection of Eric Lamet.

This book is available at quantity discounts for bulk purchases.
For information, call 1-800-289-0963.

Author's Note

These memoirs were inspired by a compulsion to give my children a glimpse of how their father grew up in what were arduous times, especially for European Jews. They were also written before the memory fades and the experiences endured by me and many others like me are forever lost to future generations. I have not attempted to gain the reader's sympathy, for none is deserved. I did, however, make a diligent attempt to depict, as objectively as I could, the lifestyle we experienced in Italy during the Fascist regime.

I am happy that not all that is written addresses itself to the ugliness of mankind. In the midst of all the horror of that period, there were glimmers of human goodness. Some even touched me personally.

I do not call myself a "survivor," for this term rightly belongs to those brave and remarkable individuals who endured the brutalities of the German death camps. I do consider myself a remnant of what once had been the large, culturally rich Jewish community of Europe.

My odyssey lasted sixty-seven months and represents a period in my life that I would not want to relive for all the fortunes in the world. Yet, sixty years later, I very much cherish the memories.

All the individuals portrayed herein are real persons and only in a few instances, mostly because of memory lapses, have their names been changed or omitted.

With gratitude so great that words fail to adequately express it, I wish to thank the following:

My loving agent, Sally Wecksler, whose belief in me and my work made this book a reality. Sadly, fate deprived her of rejoicing in this success and seeing that her trust was justly placed;

My editor, Peter Schults, for his indefatigable and enthusiastic attention to this work and his constant encouragement;

My dear wife, Cookie, for graciously enduring the countless times I compelled her to reread the same chapters or paragraphs and for the faith she continues to have in me.

Dedicated to Lotte and Pietro Russo, for all they still mean to me.

In memory of the millions of innocent human beings who suffered and who perished at the hands of the Nazi monsters.

Eric Lamet was born Erich Lifschütz on May 27, 1930, into an upper-middle-class Jewish family. Both of his Polish-born parents moved to Vienna before the first Great War.

On March 18, 1938, five days after the Anschluss, when German troops marched into Vienna, Lamet's family fled to Italy, where he spent most of the next twelve years. When World War II ended, Lamet settled in Naples with his family. He finished high school in that city and later enrolled in the Department of Engineering at the University of Naples.

In 1950, the family moved to the United States, where Lamet continued his engineering studies at the Drexel Institute of Technology in Philadelphia near his family's home. Deciding that business was more in keeping with his personality, he embarked on a business career. Over the years he became involved in a variety of enterprises and retired as a CEO in 1992.

Fluent in German, Italian, English, Spanish, and Yiddish, Lamet served as an interpreter for the U.S. State Department and taught Italian for several years.

Lamet has three children, two stepchildren, and seven granddaughters. He lives with his wife in Tamarac, Florida.

Contents

Foreword by Professor Risa Sodi

If you travel today to the southern Italian village of Ospedaletto d'Alpinolo in the Apennine Alps east of Naples, you will find a village perched 2,200 feet above sea level and ranging over 1,400 acres, half of them rocky cliffs. Its 1,639 residents make a living today as they have for centuries: from the hazelnut and chestnut forests surrounding the town. Its 643 dwellings are interspersed with pizzerias, restaurants, hotels, and shops that provide the amenities of modern life—including Internet access, as evidenced by the town's website.

Sixty-five years ago, however, when young Eric Lamet and his mother, Carlotte Szyfra Brandwein, were sent there to begin four years of compulsory internal exile, life in Ospedaletto was radically different. The terrain and the surrounding forests were essentially the same, only the population, with 1,800 inhabitants, was slightly larger than it is now. In 1940, the Fascist system of *il confino* (from the Italian verb *confinare*, meaning "to confine, to relegate") had forcibly brought to the village scores of foreigners, political activists, Jews, and sundry other potential enemies of the state

Il confino was a system of enforced internal exile devised by Mussolini quite early in his regime in order to marginalize those who could potentially cause it harm. Conceived as a measure halfway between a warning and incarceration, *il confino* was a police procedure that required no actual trial but, rather mere denunciation by local authorities. In the years preceding 1938, the *confinati* were usually vocal political opponents of fascism; indeed, the most prominent anti-Fascist thinkers of the day ended up in internal exile, mainly on Italy's countless small islands. There, they were divorced from political events, deprived of the means to communicate with the mainland and settled among generally indifferent or non-politicized local populations. The Communist theoretician Antonio Gramsci, the Socialist leader Pietro Nenni, and the liberal thinkers Giovanni Amendola and Piero Gobetti all were sent into internal (island) exile before 1938.

The mechanism of *il confino* was quite simple: Those affected were required to remain within a certain area (usually within the town limits) and to sign in daily at the local police station. They were responsible for finding their own housing and providing their own means of support aside from the stipend provided from the Fascist government. Correspondence was censored, and in many locales gatherings of *confinati* were banned. In1938, in an effort to appease Hitler and keep pace with his German ally, Mussolini promulgated a series of "racial laws" applied specifically to Italy's Jewish population.

The native-born Italian Jews, spread among several dozen central and northern Italian communities, worshiped in either the Italian or the Sephardic rite. They fell mostly into the middle class (though there were notable wealthy families, such as the Olivettis of Ivrea, as well as pockets of desperate poverty, especially in and around Rome) and were extraordinarily assimilated into Italian political, cultural, and everyday life. The Fascist racial laws directed at them were at once overarching and picayune, vexatious, and devastating. As of autumn 1938, for example, Jews were forbidden from marrying Aryans (non-Jewish Italians), from holding any sort of state job, serving in the military, or employing an Aryan domestic, or even from owning land over a certain value or a factory with more than a certain number of workers. Jews could not list obituaries in their local newspapers or own a radio. Jewish students were banned from public schools, including the universities and Jewish teachers, attorneys, doctors, and others were banned from their professions. Exemptions were allowed within certain limits; nonetheless, the impact on the Italian Jews—both psychological and material—was crushing.

Foreign Jews suffered to an even greater extent after Italy entered World War II in June 1940. A previous 1938 law had required them to leave the country, although few had obeyed; those remaining were subject to internment camps or *il confino*. Thus, in 1940, Eric and his mother, like thousands of Jews who had left Germany, Poland, Hungary, Austria, and Romania for the relative safety of Italy, were caught up in the Fascist regime's new policies. Thus far, Lamet and his mother's peregrinations—from Vienna to Milan, to Paris, to Nice, and to San Remo—had kept them one step ahead of the authorities. But in June 1940, all that ended with Italy's entry into World War II and their relegation to "confinement" in Ospedaletto.

The crux of *A Child al Confino* centers on young Lamet's and his mother's struggles in backward Ospedaletto. Urban sophisticates, they faced often-arduous adjustments to harsh new climes, new customs and cultures, and new language systems—the often impenetrable dialects of the Italian mountain communities. Once residents and part owners of a premier Viennese hotel, they were now straining to find suitable housing, to scrounge for food and to procure some sort of education for twelve-year-old Eric . . . all futile searches, as it turned out. Lamet echoes the observations of other internees, notably Carlo Levi and Natalia Ginzburg, both Italian-Jewish authors and former *confinati*; Lamet's memoir, like Levi's *Christ Stopped at Eboli* and Ginzburg's *It's Hard to Talk about Yourself*, notes that relegation to the primitive mountain *confino* villages was akin to stepping back in time.

Just as mother and son struggled, however, they also were favored with new friendships and new ties. Lamet's portrayal of the ragtag group of Ospedaletto *confinati* characters at times amusing, endearing, and maddening. It also introduces Pietro Russo, a fellow exile who had such a profound impact on Lamet's life that he dedicated this memoir to him.

In the fall of 1943, General Mark W. Clark and his Allied troops began Operation Avalanche, the long slog up the Salerno coast that eventually liberated southern Italy. Eric and his mother rejoiced at their liberation by American soldiers that October. At the time, they could not have known that in a strange twist of fate *il confino* had saved their lives, for had they been interned in northern Italy they would have come under the jurisdiction of Nazi troops and most likely would have found themselves among the 7,000 Italian and foreign Jews who were deported to Auschwitz and other Nazi *lagers*. Of those deported, only three hundred Italian Jews and five hundred foreign Jews survived.

Eric remained in Italy until 1950 when he, his mother, and her second husband—that same Pietro Russo—settled in the United States. His memoir traces a little-told story: of child refugees in Italy, of foreign Jews in Italy during World War II, of the hardships imposed by the *confino* system, of the southern Italian mountain villages, and of the mutual respect that often developed not only among *confinati* but also between unsophisticated peasants and urban intellectuals both struggling under adversity.

CHAPTER 1

Escape from Vienna

Stunned, peeking from behind the hallway wall for the longest moment, I watched my father rapidly pacing the four corners of the living room floor. I could tell he was very tense. Never changing his fast rhythm, he was mumbling in such a low tone I couldn't tell whether he was speaking German or his native Polish.

We had eaten our breakfast hours before, yet my mother was still in her silk robe. *Mutti's* hair lacked its usual neatness and her face was drawn and without makeup. She sat stiffly against the wall on one of the dining room chairs. While her eyes followed my father's every step, I could tell that her mind was far away, immersed in other thoughts. Never, until that awful morning, had there been such an upheaval in my well-ordered, carefree life of nearly eight years. *What did I do?* was the only thought running through my mind. *Did my teacher send home a bad report?* I was certain they were discussing what punishment I deserved, something they had never done before.

"What happened?" I asked meekly voicing words that had crossed my mind moments before, instantly sorry to have said anything and hoping not to have been heard.

Neither of my parents answered. Often I had felt bothered when my parents failed to notice my presence but, this time I was glad they hadn't. In my frightened state, I felt relieved not to have to cope with their answers.

That morning, for the first time, *Mutti* had not helped me to get dressed. She had come to my room at the usual hour and sat on the bed. "You're not going to school today."

"Why not?"

"Please, don't ask questions."

Now, my mother's nervousness of earlier that morning was more intense. I watched as her foot delicately tapped the parquet floor, her hands tightly clenched her knees, showing the white outline on her fair skin.

Millie, our housekeeper as well as my governess, walked into the dining room to set the table for the midday meal and my father stopped pacing. Millie always moved about the house with a bounce in her step, humming some Austrian folk tune; now she worked in silence. The sight resembled a movie scene in slow motion: *Mutti* sitting motionless and staring into space, Papa awkwardly standing still on the spot where he last had placed his foot, and Millie moving about as if unaware of our presence.

Though I was not quite eight, I had already learned to stay out of my parents' way when something unusual was going on. What was happening was more than unusual; it was downright scary. Perhaps it was best to make myself invisible. Creeping backward toward my bed-room all the while trying to guess what could possibly have happened to cause such gloom, a bizarre thought crossed my mind: I wished I could have been in school with the teacher I detested, doing assignments I liked even less.

From my doorway I watched as Millie left the dining room and Papa resumed his pacing. I quickly returned to my room and, cuddling my teddy bear, I lay on my bed and cried quietly.

Soon after, I heard my parents' loud exchange. Driven more by curiosity than fear, I walked back to the living room. They were shouting in Polish, a language I could understand when spoken slowly and calmly. And as they did neither, I understood nothing. But I could tell they were not fighting with one another, as they had done many times before and that was a relief for me.

"I'm glad you're here," *Mutti* said. "I was just going to call you. Come *Schatzele*. Lunch is ready." Her tone had none of the pleasantness I so loved.

As though nothing had happened to give rise to the strange behavior I had witnessed all morning, we sat at the table to eat the main meal of the day.

"Millie," *Mutti* called. "You may start serving."

Sullen, Millie entered, placed a silver-plated soup tureen on the table, then turned on her heels and left. Never had she acted like that before. My ever-smiling Millie had always served each of us. No one ever had to ask her. She had loved doing it. Papa was about to say something but, my mother looked at him and with one finger across her lips, motioned for him to be silent. Then she shrugged her shoulders and did the serving herself.

We sat in silence. I waited for the storm that was certain to come.

"Why aren't you eating?" *Mutti* asked.

Her words caught me off guard. Trembling, I started to cry. "I'm scared, *Mutti*. I don't know what's happening."

She placed her arms around me, pulled me close, and stroked my hair. "Erich, one day you'll understand." As she spoke, I saw tears well in her eyes. "Yesterday German soldiers invaded Vienna." It was March 14, 1938.

My mother was right. I did not know what it all meant. Still I felt threatened. What did it mean that German soldiers invaded Vienna? Who were these German soldiers? I wanted to ask these questions and more but, somehow did not dare.

We had just finished lunch when *Mutti* suggested I take my daily rest. "Go, *Erichl!*"

I usually loved it when she used the pet name *Erichl*, but this time it did not seem to matter much.

A blaring radio jolted me out of my nap. The noise had to be coming from neighbors across the courtyard. No one in our home would turn on the radio right after lunch when we were taking our afternoon naps. Nor would my parents, out of concern for the other tenants, allow the volume to be so loud. Strange music screeched from the speaker, mixed with a man's voice more loud than understandable. Crowds screamed in the background. I got up to see where the sound was coming from.

In her colorful Austrian *dirndl*, the costume she wore only for special occasions, Millie sat transfixed in front of our radio. She had pulled a dining room chair into the antechamber, next to the small table on which she had placed the much-too-large receiver. It looked dangerously close to the edge and almost ready to fall. And that chair? No one had ever moved those chairs out of the dining room. Millie knew it wasn't allowed. What was going on? She seemed hypnotized and unaware of my presence.

I walked up to her and placed two fingers on the volume knob. Without a glance, Millie grabbed them and pushed them away with such force as to crack the small bones and make my hand go numb. I was in shock. Was this the gentle and loving Millie in whose bed I cuddled many mornings before going off to school, preferring hers to my mother's? I wanted to cry out but, her meanness made me run away and look for safety inside my room, where I buried my face in the soft down pillow.

That evening the situation grew still more troubling. Millie was nowhere to be seen and my mother was left to bring dinner to the table herself. My parents hardly spoke and I, grasped by the fear of the unknown, did not dare utter a sound.

After dinner, *Mutti* moved our dishes to one corner and pulled her chair next to mine. She cleared her throat and I, though looking at my father, spoke to me. "Listen to me carefully, Erich. I don't want you to go out of the house. I don't want you to speak to Millie or anyone in the building. I don't want you to listen to the radio, and you will not be going to school for the next few days." From her tone and my father's nodding approval, I knew none of this was open for discussion.

Eric's father, Markus Lifschütz, in 1928.

Between 1930, the year I was born, and 1938, my family had enjoyed a comfortable lifestyle. Papa, with his younger brother Oswald—my Uncle Osi—managed the Hotel Continental. It must have been a first-class hotel since many rich and elegant foreigners came to stay. I thought the hotel was ours but, later learned it was owned by my granduncle Maximilian, who had made a small fortune when oil was discovered on his land in the Ukraine. From my parents I learned that Uncle Max, who was my grandpa's brother, was a generous man who shared his good fortune with members of his family. With the proceeds of the sale of his oil fields, he had purchased real estate in several European countries then let a number of his relatives benefit from some of the revenues these investments generated.

After my parents married and for the first four years of my life, we lived at the hotel, where my mother enjoyed many comforts: built-in babysitters, laundry service, daily maid help, and two restaurants with room service. Well-to-do families without children found it convenient to live in a hotel in those days. The Continental had suites with kitchenettes and living rooms and it offered services and comforts not found in private homes. A number of my parents' friends had taken up residence at the hotel.

Cooking and baking were my mother's loves, and since living in the hotel made it difficult to satisfy her longing for those passions, we moved to our own apartment in 1934. I had liked living in the hotel. It was the only home I had known. My friends were all there: the bell captain, the concierge, the waiters, the chambermaids, and some of the regular guests. I wasn't anxious to change. So I asked *Mutti* why we had to move. "Growing up in a hotel is not good for a child," was her answer.

We stayed in our first apartment for the year I attended kindergarten, but as soon as I was ready to start first grade, we moved again, this time to larger quarters on the Tabor Strasse. The hotel was on the same street, right on the corner intersecting the Prater Strasse, no more than 200 yards away. For Papa this was very convenient. He could walk to work, come home for lunch, take a short nap and be back at the hotel for the remainder of the day.

Mother's lifestyle was typically Viennese. In the afternoon, almost ritually, she met her friends at the Kaffee Fetzer where, after an exchange of gossip, she played bridge until evening. After dinner at home, many of these same women met again, this time accompanied by their husbands, to socialize in one of the many coffeehouses for which Vienna was famous.

Eric's mother, Carlotte Szyra Brandwein, in 1928.

Our first apartment was across the narrow street from the Kaffee Fetzer. Often I walked over to see *Mutti*, not out of any interest in her friends or the coffeehouse, but because I liked the candies one of her lady friends frequently brought with her. Once that friend sent me to the candy store around the corner.

"Please get one-quarter pound of chocolate-covered orange peels," she said.

Convinced the woman intended the candies for me, I asked the clerk to let me taste one before placing the order. I cringed. "Too bitter," I said.

"May I get you something else?" the clerk asked.

"Yes, I'll have those," I pointed at the pralines.

When I returned with the wrong candies, the ladies looked amused and I did not get scolded. Not even *Mutti* was annoyed. The lady, who had given me the money, took her change. "It is perfectly all right," she said. "You may keep the candies for yourself."

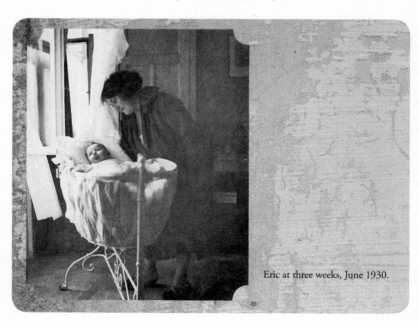

Eric at three weeks, June 1930.

Eric at age one with his mother in Semmering, 1931.

Mine was a happy, orderly life that revolved around my Millie, two-month-long Alpine summer vacations on the Semmering with Mother until I was about four, yearly visits with my grandparents in Poland, and weekly afternoons with *Omama*, my maternal grandmother. I also had many friends near my own age; we played in our courtyard and shared mutual birthdays. Oh, how I loved the chocolate pudding with sliced bananas, a favorite at any birthday party. Then there were our relatives, who made a great fuss over me, for I was the only child in the family's Viennese contingent.

During the four days following March 14, our lives changed dramatically. I stayed home with *Mutti* while Papa came and went more often than usual. My parents endured Millie's many disrespectful actions. Because of the disturbances on the streets, no one shopped for groceries that Monday and, since we had no means to keep food cold, by Tuesday we had little in the house to prepare for a meal.

"Millie, would you go to do the shopping?" *Mutti* asked.

Millie's tone was insolent. "I'm busy right now. I'll do it when I have time."

I couldn't believe my ears. What had happened to her respectful "Of course, madam, right away"? At twenty-two she had lost all her good manners. Mother would never have tolerated that tone from me.

The radio, the volume blatantly turned high to show Millie's newly asserted independence, blared throughout the apartment. In the streets people were chanting and marching, but I did not know what was happening because my ever-watchful mother made sure I did not look out the window.

Millie was allowed to take off more time than ever before. Well, not really allowed. She didn't ask, merely announced, "I will be going out for the day."

"When will you be back?" *Mutti* asked.

"Whenever I get back."

Mother never asked that question again.

Millie's absence gave my parents the freedom to talk openly. They would ask me to leave the room, but even though I did, I could not help but overhear when their voices rose. In their eyes I knew I was not old enough to be trusted with the gravity of our situation, yet I was old enough to sense it was really serious.

"They're rounding up Jews and taking them into cellars," my father said. "I don't know what they are doing, no one knows, but I hear horrible stories. Someone said they have stopped Jewish women on the streets and forced them to use their fur coats to wash the sidewalks." When I heard that, I thought of my *Mutti* and could not imagine her complying with such an order.

"We must leave!" *Mutti* said. She was a woman of action, always in charge of our family. "With our Polish passports, we'll be able to leave Austria without any trouble."

In spite of living in Vienna for more than twenty years, my parents had never given up their Polish citizenship.

We must leave? I repeated to myself. What did that mean and where would we be going? I spent most of the next four days in my bed whispering to my teddy bear and trying to read. I felt like a prisoner waiting for his sentence. The fear of the first day mounted with every passing hour.

On March 18, five days after the German troops had marched into Vienna, *Mutti* came to my room to tell me we were going to Poland. Her face was pale, her eyes swollen and red.

"Do we have to?" I asked.

With a forefinger placed on her lips, she signaled for me to remain silent. "*Opapa* is ill and has asked us to come visit him." Her voice was unnaturally loud. I couldn't understand why she had raised her voice so much when I was standing close to her in the same room.

"We were . . ." I started, but Mother placed her full hand over my mouth.

I had always looked forward to visiting my grandparents, but this time was different. The brand new sleigh I had craved for so long was finally mine, a surprise gift from my parents on Saint Nicholas Day, a day considered by many in Germany and Austria as a gift-giving day without religious connotation. The sleigh was leaning against the wall in one corner of my room. Every morning I could see its shiny wooden slats and bright runners. I had used it only twice. Going meant I would not be able to use it and the parks were covered with fresh snow. Nor would my teddy bear be allowed to come with me. *Mutti* had never allowed me to take him on previous trips. A family friend had bought the stuffed toy before my first birthday. When placed into my crib, the docile bear—larger than I was—provoked such screaming that my parents stored him in an armoire and out of sight for months. Now having to leave Teddy behind was the thing I disliked about our trips to Poland.

Through free-flowing tears, I tried to cajole my mother into relenting. "Just this time. Please, *Mutti*."

"The answer is no."

Although her voice had a determined tone, I was not deterred. "Why not?"

She looked tired, drawn and annoyed at my persistence. "Just do as I tell you. Please."

Dashing from the room to get away from her, I shouted, "I hate you!"

Millie kept sitting in the anteroom. In those last four days she had spent so much time listening to the radio that she had done nothing else around the house. Worse yet, she, who for the past three years had been my solace and comfort, was now coldly indifferent to my pain. Two months and thirteen days from my eighth birthday, in our own home, surrounded by the people I loved, I felt alone and abandoned.

Eric's grandfather *Opapa* with Uncle Norman in Lwow, Poland, in August 1939, less than one month before the German invasion.

Later that afternoon, my parents exited the bedroom. Father, in his fur-lined overcoat, carried two suitcases. Mother, wearing not her fur coat but her cloth overcoat, tried to be warm and friendly.

"Millie," she said, "we will be gone for only a few days."

The young servant never looked up. She seemed not to have heard.

My mother stood silently for more than a moment. "Here is money in case you need to buy something for the house. If you need anything else, you know you can call the hotel."

The woman made no attempt to reach for the money. Mother placed it on the table, near the radio. As she did, she spotted the daily paper lying on the floor. Staring at her was a full-page picture of Adolf Hitler. Abruptly my mother turned to my father.

"Get a taxi and make sure you find one flying the Nazi flag." Her voice had a slight quiver.

Papa was back a few minutes later. We were ready to leave and, as I walked backward toward the door, my eyes remained focused on Millie. Oh, how I loved her and I was certain she loved me. Why else would she have taken me to spend the past two summers at her parents' farm? I stopped and waited.

Very softly, hesitantly I called: "Millie."

She never raised her head to look at me.

Mutti grabbed me by the arm. "Let's go!"

Life was so cruel! I was leaving behind my Millie and my Teddy. I didn't know one could hurt so much inside. The taxi was waiting. Its front fenders flew two small red flags bearing a strange black cross similar to the Austrian cross. Once we were in the car, *Mutti* told me what a swastika was. The driver held the door for my mother. She stepped in, immediately lowered the side curtain and fell back onto the seat. I didn't know whether she wanted to avoid seeing what was going on outside or to prevent anyone else from seeing us inside.

During the ride I stole some glimpses of the outside world. A circle of agitated people surrounded two kneeling, well-dressed women washing the sidewalk.

"What are they doing?" I asked.

My father made a small opening in the curtain and glanced out. He leaned over to Mother and, with a hand cupped over his mouth, he whispered. "Just what I was telling you. They want those poor women to rub off the oil-painted Austrian symbols with their furs."

I remembered having asked my father why all those Austrian emblems had been painted on sidewalks and bridges. "To celebrate the new year," he had said.

The cab dropped us off at the main entrance of *Südbahnhof*, one of the city's train terminals. The driver lifted our two suitcases from the luggage rack and placed them on the curb. Papa looked around for a porter but none was in sight. "Take the bags and let's go!" *Mutti* said, nervously.

The railroad station, with its hollow-sounding interior, was not as I remembered it from our previous trips. Soldiers were everywhere. Prominent on the sleeves of their black uniforms was a red armband with the same funny looking black cross that I had seen on the taxi's flags.

"My God, we're surrounded by the SS," *Mutti* whispered. I noticed that she trembled.

"What is SS?" I asked.

Mother ignored my question. My father put the suitcases on the floor of the large hall. It was March, still winter in Vienna, yet perspiration had formed on his forehead. He had carried the luggage up the long stairway and halfway into the hall and now stood there out of breath. I had hardly ever seen my father lift anything heavier than a glass of water.

He used his breast-pocket handkerchief to wipe the sweat off his face, then walked away, leaving us standing there. Mother paced stiffly around the two valises. Soon Papa returned, escorted by a soldier in that sinister black uniform.

The man, apparently an officer, turned to my mother, clicked the heels of his highly polished boots and raised an arm in a snappy salute. "*Heil* Hitler!" he blurted.

My mother nodded and smiled.

"Follow me," he said. Walking with a distinct Prussian step, the soldier led us to a far corner of the station.

"Can you believe this?" *Mutti* mumbled. "Still trying to be chivalrous—even to a Jewish woman?"

"*Sai sha*," my father shushed her in Yiddish.

More soldiers than travelers filled the immense hall. Echoes reverberating throughout multiplied the harshness of each sound. Men and women wearing the same menacing black outfits constantly clicked their heels and raised their arms in that strange salute. Each click of the heavy boots bounced off the distant walls and the high ceiling, creating a deafening clamor. I felt like we were surrounded by a whole army.

"You go here and you there!" the officer barked. This was the same man who, only moments before, had saluted us so gallantly.

I cringed and took one step closer to my mother. With one menacing finger he ordered Mother and me toward one door and my father to another.

I held on to *Mutti*'s skirt as we moved quickly in the direction the man had pointed. We walked through the door and found ourselves in a small room, made tinier by a very high ceiling and white sheets, draped over metal frames, to partition the space into small cubicles. They reminded me of the oppressive prison cells I had seen in the movies. I looked to *Mutti* for help. She offered none. Her forlorn look—one I had never seen before—made her face seem very small.

"Undress. Take everything off. Everything!" a woman sitting at a small desk shouted. The tone of her voice was similar to the one I had heard in the hall. I was shivering. "*Schnell! Schnell! Ich kann nicht auf die Juden Schweine warten!*" she yelled, ordering us to hurry, hurry, for she could not wait for Jewish pigs.

The fear I had felt over the last four days was pale in comparison to my present terror. If only I could run away or maybe hide somewhere. How could so many people be so heartless?

I stood there, unprotected in that empty space. Catching an encouraging look from my mother, who was standing naked, bashful, and full of fear, I removed my clothes as well, laid them on the floor and waited. I, who once had refused to undress when Papa had taken me to an all-male Turkish bath, now stood stripped, while evil-looking men and women milled all around.

A large woman, wearing a black dress, high black leather boots, and the scary red and black armband on her sleeve, pushed the partition to one side. She seemed tall, perhaps taller than she actually was because of my nakedness. That hair pulled tightly to the back of her head, those thin lips held rigidly together, and her manly gait all exuded a ruthlessness that held me paralyzed. But what terrified me most was the icy, empty look in her eyes, a blank stare that cut through me. I was naked and cold and so frightened!

"Do you have any jewelry?" the woman bellowed.

"No, no! No jewelry, I swear," *Mutti* protested in a high-pitched voice.

As the big woman's hands searched all of *Mutti*'s body, my eyes turned away. I had never seen my mother naked and didn't want to be a witness to my proud parent's indignity.

Then came my turn. I heard the heavy boots hit the pavement and felt the woman's rough, large, sweaty hands grabbing me by the shoulders.

Without a sound, she forced open my mouth, looked into my ears, looked under my arms and last, pushed her cold finger into my rectum. I was too crippled by fear to scream and though the physical pain was intolerable, my mental anguish was even more so. Several times she rotated that large searching finger inside me. Dying at that very moment would have been a relief.

After what seemed the longest wait of my life, we were allowed to dress and join Papa. The strain on my parents' faces reflected the ordeal they had endured. I felt so helpless and wished I were big and able to comfort them. I wanted to say, "Don't be sad. It's all over." Instead I was just a little boy, not yet eight.

Leaving the vast hall, we walked toward the platform. Papa, bent over by the weight of the two suitcases. *Mutti* and I following close behind. As we reached the train's open door, my mother, breathing with great difficulty, stopped to dry the tears off my face with her pretty embroidered handkerchief. "I want you to forget what just happened."

"Why did they do this to us?" I asked, still trembling.

"Because we're Jewish. Just because we're Jewish."

My father lifted the suitcases on the train and boarded. "I'll find us a compartment. Wait here."

We waited and waited. No sign of my father. *Mutti* was wringing her hands. Finally, Papa's head showed through a partially opened window. "I found us a compartment."

Dad's find was already occupied by five other people. One of the men helped my father lift the suitcases onto the rack, freeing the wooden bench of the second-class cabin for us to sit on. We had removed our overcoats, which Papa had hung on one of the wall hooks.

The train was late leaving the terminal. My parents were nervous. Father looked at his watch every few minutes, almost as if he kept forgetting what time it was. "This train was supposed to leave twenty minutes ago. What's happening?" he asked. I didn't know to whom he was talking since no one responded.

German soldiers dressed in those ghastly black uniforms and those heavy boots, were everywhere. Each time one poked his head into our compartment, *Mutti*, as though hit by some electric shock, stiffened in her seat. Unable to follow her advice to forget, I cringed and broke into a cold sweat at the sound of their every step. After what seemed an eternity, the conductor whistled and the black locomotive, with a deafening blare, spewing white steam and dark smoke, began pulling the train out of the station to the screeching of its iron wheels. But the soldiers, stiff in their black uniforms, continued to mill in the narrow passageway outside our compartment, refusing to give our nerves a moment of rest.

By the time the long line of cars pulled over the maze of rails and onto the open tracks, the sky had become dark and the streetlights were turned on. I leaned out the window and watched as the distance increased between my city and me. Accompanied by the rhythmic clank of the iron rails as they bounced back on the passing wheels, we traveled through the night.

I sat immersed in my own thoughts while my parents, absorbed by their own fears, did not speak for the longest time. The snack cart passed our compartment and Papa bought three sandwiches and two bottles of mineral water.

Mutti broke her silence. "Go to sleep," she said. "I'll sing you 'Sonny Boy.'" Since my birth, Mother had put me to sleep with Al Jolson's famous melody. I loved that song and she sang it so well.

This time, however, the song held no appeal. My mind was so mixed up. Before I had wanted to escape; now I was determined not to shut my eyes, fearing that if I did fall asleep something might happen.

My eyelids kept closing, for I was exhausted, but I was too stubborn and afraid to give in.

"You'll be tired tomorrow," *Mutti* added gently. I could tell she was not going to insist on my going to sleep.

I didn't even know what time it was, for my beloved silver watch, a special gift my grandfather had given me for *Pesach* on one of our last trips to Poland, had been left behind.

It was still pitch dark when the train stopped and what sounded to me to be foreign-speaking soldiers boarded the train.

"*Passaporto, per favore,*" one said, asking for our passports.

"Why don't they speak Polish?" I asked.

Only after the men left and Mother realized we were no longer in Austria did she share the truth with me. She jumped from her seat. "We are in Italy!" she exclaimed. Then she looked at me, sat, took my hand and, in a soft tone, said: "We are not going to Poland."

Because I was unable to grasp what was going on, that bit of news had little impact on me. But I was excited just being in a new country and my anguish gave way to anticipation.

The border crossing had a big effect on the other passengers. Everyone, silent before, was now engaged in lively conversation. Dad ventured into the corridor, looked right, then left, and shouted with enthusiasm: "No Nazis."

"Not so loud," *Mutti* warned.

There was an air of jubilation in the compartment. All the lights were turned on and snacks were exchanged between passengers.

My father sat next to me and looking out the window, told me of his experiences during the war. "This is where it all happened. Some of the bloodiest battles took place right here. The Italian army tried desperately to push us back but with no success. We were at the top of the mountain and they were down below. You can imagine we made chopped meat out of them." Papa seemed to be reliving those days. "The Italians had mules to carry their big guns. We were set in place and our machine guns just cut them down. *Tat, tat, tat*. Even the animals were killed."

"Did you get wounded?" I asked.

"Oh, no. Never." Then he told me he had been kept from combat because of his flat feet.

"That was a blessing," *Mutti* said. "The Polish army was part of the Austro-Hungarian Empire and, if your father had been allowed to fight, the empire would have collapsed sooner than it did." Mother had regained her sense of humor.

Papa's words created all sorts of fantasies in my fertile mind. As he related stories of battles, I envisioned swarms of soldiers rushing from the dense foliage, surrounding the fast-moving train and shooting wildly at an invisible enemy. I could see bodies partially entombed under a thin layer of soil, their bloody limbs stretched upward toward the sky, the gruesome sights of death.

For hours my mind ran wild as my eyes followed, in the faint light coming from the window, the smooth up-and-down movement of the telegraph wires as the train raced from one pole to the next. In the end, overcome by fatigue, I fell asleep until the screech of the iron wheels, braking to a slow halt in the Milan terminal, awoke me.

As the train came to a full stop, excited passengers moved with a new charge of energy. Everyone in the compartment was standing, stretching limbs, loosening necks by turning from side to side, then reaching for items placed on the overhead racks the night before. There was no room for anyone to stand for the floor was covered with baggage. Papa was close to the window and pushed it down. A strange smell, a mixture of steam and burning coal, invaded the cabin. Mother was busy gathering the belongings we had pulled from our luggage during the night, while Papa, with the aid of a stranger standing outside on the platform, pushed our two valises through the open window and into the man's outstretched arms. Nothing about my father's dapper look betrayed that he had sat up all night. His hair was neat, his tie perfectly knotted and the white handkerchief in his breast pocket gave a finishing touch to his steel gray, double-breasted suit.

He grabbed his overcoat, then rushed down the corridor and onto the platform to claim the luggage gathered there. Mother looked around one final time to be sure nothing had been left behind, then, handed me my fur-lined coat and pushed me ahead through the corridor and down the three steep steps. The height of those steps made it impossible for a woman to get off the train in a ladylike fashion, for she needed to lift her skirt way above her knees. Standing at the top of the platform, her head outside the door, holding on to both side railings, Mother looked to either side, before lifting her skirt and stepping down.

Seeing my father's hand gesture, a wrinkled porter, who seemed older than any other person I had ever seen before, rushed up to us. He grabbed a thick and heavily worn leather belt that was holding up his pants and ran it through the handles of our two suitcases. He secured the strap to the buckle and then with a rapid jolt, draped the belt over his right shoulder, letting one suitcase fall in front and the other behind. After balancing himself under the heavy weight, mumbling words I could not understand, he led the way through crowds of passengers. We walked the full length of the platform under a steel and glass roof, blackened by years of smoke from the coal-burning locomotives.

The old man carried our bags to the side exit, from where he hailed a taxi. The driver rushed from the cab to place our luggage on the car's roof, then tied it down with a rope that was hanging there. The porter looped the leather strap through his drooping pants, gave them a yank to stop them from dragging on the ground and, respectfully removing his oily and sweat-stained cap, turned to my father and said, "*A suo favore*," leaving the tip to my father's discretion.

Papa pulled from his wallet a few Austrian Schilling. The porter, with a blocking motion of the hand and a smirk on his face, made it clear he wasn't at all interested in taking those bills. Papa had to find an exchange booth to bring the predicament to an end.

2

Poland—My Extended Family

Both my parents were born in Poland: my papa, Markus Lifschütz, in Krzywczyce on February 15, 1897, the oldest of three boys; my *Mutti*, Carlotte Szyfra Brandwein, in Nadworna on May 10, 1901, the youngest of four. When the 1914–18 war was nearing its end but before the breakup of the Austro-Hungarian Empire, my father and his two brothers moved to Vienna.

Vienna was a cosmopolitan city, and the three young men looked for a better future than what would have been possible in rural Poland. Moreover, their uncles, Simon and Maximilian, had already settled in the Austrian capital and become successful property owners.

I met both of my great-uncles, my grandfather's brothers. I visited Uncle Simon in his luxurious apartment with its thick Persian rugs, but Uncle Max, who was held in awe by the family, I only knew from a distance.

In 1936, my parents took me to Lwow, Poland, where most of the Lifschütz family had settled after leaving their *shtetl*. We stayed with

Papa's parents, and during that visit I spent much of my time meeting the more than sixty members of my father's large family. I couldn't believe I had so many cousins, aunts, and uncles. But of greater disbelief was the uncle who was younger than his own nephew.

"How can *Yankle* be older than his Uncle Morris?" I asked.

"Why do you always have a question?" She hesitated struggling to explain. "*Yankle* was five when his grandmother died. Her husband married a much younger woman and their first child was Morris. When he was born, *Yankle* was already eight; that's why he is older than his Uncle Morris."

I was only six years old. How did Mother expect me to understand such a *mishegas*?

When not visiting relatives, I played on the street with the neighbors' children.

One day a dirty, drunken, shabby, middle-aged man stood some distance from me. "You damn Jew," he screamed, as he hurled a heavy brick my way.

He may not have been too steady on his feet, but his aim was excellent. The missile sailed through the air. I saw it fly toward me and turned around just in time to save my face, exposing my back to absorb the full force of the impact. Crack! My thin shirt was little protection against that hard brick. In great pain and sobbing, I ran home to tell my grandfather, *Opapa* Moses. "*Opapa*, I wasn't d-d-doing anything to him."

He held me tightly to his chest while his white beard stroked my face and my freely flowing tears wet his shirt. "*Sha, sha, Kindele. Ikh veis. Got vert im shoin beshtrufen.*" "Quiet, child. I know. God will punish him," he said. When I asked what that meant, he told me it referred to the punishment that would befall the enemies of God's chosen people.

The next day, to get me off the street, my parents took me for a long walk. We traversed a city park, then climbed up a hill. The gently inclined serpentine road circled several times until the last loop brought us to the peak from which we looked at the town below. I saw people, horses, carriages, and even trolley cars that seemed real but were so small to fit in the palm of my hand. I was baffled. How could that be?

"Where do those small people live?" I asked.

"Down in the city," Papa replied. "It's called an optical illusion. You can only see them from here."

When we returned home, I was ready to explode. "*Opapa*, you have never seen people so small," I exclaimed. Then holding out the palm of my hand, I said, "I could carry them right here. Papa says nobody can get close to them. You can only see them from the mountain. Did you ever see them?"

He shot a questioning look at my parents.

"*Er redt auf di menschen man siht von oiben*," *Mutti* explained. "He's talking about the people you see from the top of the hill."

"*Opapa*, please tell me."

"When you see people from so far away, they just look small. You know when you look at the stars, you just see a small dot? But the stars are very, very large."

For Passover the following year we again visited Lwow. *Pesach* was a great celebration in my grandparents' home. In Vienna my mother observed the holiday with the traditional Seder and kept our home free from bread and other forbidden items, but in Lwow the tradition had a totally different flavor. Preparations for *Pesach* went on for days. Cleaning every corner of the house, removing all dishes and replacing them with special Passover ones was for me an unknown experience.

"Why are you changing all the dishes?" I asked my grandmother.

"For *Pesach* one must use special kosher dishes," she replied.

"But I thought your dishes were kosher."

At that moment my mother entered the kitchen, took me by the hand, and I never heard the rest of my grandmother's answer.

"Why is Grandma changing all the dishes?" I asked my mother.

"Because for *Pesach* religious people must not use the everyday dishes."

"How come we don't change dishes?"

She placed her hand on my mouth. "I'll tell you later."

A few days before the first Seder, *Opapa* asked me to recite the traditional four *kasche*. Although I was not surprised, for my father had alerted me, I was very excited. I knew that asking the four questions was a special honor.

The evening of the Seder I was running a high temperature but was not about to give up the momentous privilege that had been bestowed upon me. I argued about wanting to get out of bed so I could do my part at the table. "Please, *Mutti*, I have studied so hard. I know the four *kasche* well. I'll be good and will go to bed right after dinner. Please." I did not hear an immediate "no" and with my mother that was a good sign. "Are you sure you feel well enough?" she asked.

"I'm fine. I'm really fine." I was so overjoyed by her question I wanted to jump up and down.

"But back to bed right after dinner!"

Mutti was so good to me and how I loved her. First she placed her hand, then her lips to my forehead to check my temperature. Then, putting her arms around me, she gave me a strong hug and a kiss. "When you're ready to get dressed, I'll help you." She always helped me get dressed.

I adored my mother's attention but resented her constant worry that something was wrong with me. Whether I had just come home overheated from running with friends or awoken from a short nap, she always thought she saw the signs of some hidden sickness on my face. "You don't look good. Come here, let me feel your head." Had I really been ill each time my mother thought that I was, I would not have survived childhood.

Grandpa was a warm, loving, and incredibly tender man. Though modern in some small ways, he was a dedicated Talmudic scholar. The pocketless, floor-length black coat, the round fur hat, the long white beard, the side locks, and *tsetses* completed the portrait of this kind old man. Each morning before breakfast in the sitting room, he'd say his prayers while putting on the phylacteries. I liked watching my grandpa in his white shirt, the left sleeve rolled up, as he wrapped the leather straps around his bare forearm. One turn after the other, he placed one band close to the next, adjusting its distance as he went along, while his lips murmured the Hebrew prayers. He was meticulous and so absorbed in his ritual that I don't think he ever noticed my presence. My father, too, laid *tfilin* every morning, but *Opapa's* concentration and his visible devotion conveyed a more religious image.

Grandmother, by herself, prepared the elaborate Passover meal, while *Opapa* conducted the religious portion of the Seder. Dinner started with gefilte fish, which Grandmother made from scratch, just as my mother did. I would go with her to the fish store to buy a live carp, which we would dump into the filled bathtub as soon as we got home. When Grandma was ready to cook it, we began the difficult job of capturing the lively fish—no easy task for a young boy and an elderly lady. By the time we succeeded, the floor and our clothes were soaked from the many times the slippery fish slid out of our hands and splashed back into the water.

I would not stay in the kitchen to watch my grandmother kill the fish but came back in time to see her slit it open and clean the inside. The thin outer skin she placed to one side. The bones she discarded, while the flesh she mixed with vegetables and passed through a hand grinder. After cooking it, she put it back into the fish's skin. I looked in awe as she recreated the fish she had killed and taken apart.

But that was only a small part of the Seder. Grandma also prepared matzo balls for the chicken soup, boiled chicken, and boiled flanken with horseradish, vegetables, and desserts.

Before enjoying the Seder meal, we had to observe the religious traditions. First we washed our hands, then said the prayers, ate bitter herbs, and rinsed our hands once more. All this while my stomach rumbled and grumbled from hunger.

Soon my turn came. My knees were shaking. I was not quite seven. Rising in place at the table, I recited the traditional four questions in fluent Hebrew. "*Mah Nishtanah* . . . Why is this night . . ." begins the traditional prayer. Not one error. Not a hesitation. My knees were still trembling, clapping against one another, but I was beaming from ear to ear. I had done it! My parents' faces glowed. They were proud of me, I could tell.

Then *Opapa* called me to his side. In his hand he held a small tissue-wrapped package. His eyes had a warm glimmer and in a voice like a soft caress, he said, "Here! This is for you." I ripped the paper, lifted the lid of the small white box and there it was, shining brightly a silver pocket watch.

After overcoming my surprise, I flung myself at him almost knocking him off the chair. "Oh, *Opapa*! I've always wanted a pocket watch."

With a gentleness all his own, he placed one hand on the back of my head and held me against his face while I buried mine into his beard. How I loved my *Opapa*! I loved him so much that even kissing his coarse beard did not feel coarse to me at all.

"You did great credit to your parents. I'm proud of you," he said in Yiddish. The tone of his voice made me realize how much my recital meant to him.

Holding up the watch, I asked, "Is it silver?"

"Of course it's silver. Here!" With his hand he motioned for the watch. His smile radiated through the thick gray beard. "You see this? This is all engraved by hand."

I got the impression he had done the engraving himself. "Did you do it?" I asked.

His quiet laughter slid through the air. "No, no! But I know the man who did it. He is one of the finest in our community. Now, look here." He pushed the small button on the crown and the cover popped open. "Read this."

Engraved in Hebrew on the inside cover was my Jewish name and the date: "To David Mendel—Pesach 5697." From the corner of my eye I could see *Mutti*, Papa, and Grandmother quietly enjoying the scene.

As I had promised my mother, right after dessert I went to my room. That night I wanted to sleep with my new gift.

"You can't sleep with it," my father said. "You'll break it if you roll on it. Why not hang it on the wall?"

That was a good suggestion, I thought. Papa brought a hammer and a long nail and helped me hang the watch over the headboard. Three times I took it off the wall before falling asleep. For four days the watch remained on the wall while I stayed in bed waiting to shake off whatever was ailing me.

3

Milan

Nearly a year after that celebration in Lwow, my precious silver watch was gone, abandoned in Vienna with Teddy and almost everything else I owned. The morning of our arrival in Milan was bleak, the air saturated by fog so dense it was hard to see anything. Our ten-minute ride from the train station passed in total silence. The only details visible through the darkened air were some neon signs and the hazy form of the policemen directing traffic. The taxi dropped us off at an address written on a small piece of paper that my father had handed the driver.

Only after we got out of the cab did I dare say something. "Did you see the funny hats the policemen were wearing?"

Inside the building, where the driver had placed our two suitcases, we looked to see what to do next when *il portinaio* peeked his head from behind a door and asked us what we wanted: *"Cosa desidera?"* Papa handed the man the wrinkled piece of paper.

"*Un momento,*" the janitor said, then lifted a receiver and pushed one of the many buttons on the instrument. When he hung up, he turned to us. "*Piano secondo,*" he said, which would have meant nothing to me had he not shown two fingers and pointed up. The man helped place the suitcases in the small elevator, inserted a coin in the coin box, slid the gate closed, and sent the elevator up with Papa in it. *Mutti* and I were left to climb the stairs.

Standing on the landing we found Signora Rina Gigli wearing a full-length housecoat, slippers, and more makeup than I had seen on any face before. A gray cat rested in her arms. With a big smile lighting up her face, our new landlady welcomed us to her home. "*Buon giorno e benvenuti!*"

I did not understand a word of the melodic sounds, but in the first few moments the warmth of her voice introduced me to the romantic Italian language and to a new friend, her cat. Soon I was in love with the cat and infatuated with the landlady.

Eric holding Rina's cat on the balcony in Milan, Italy, 1938.

With enthusiasm we settled into our new home, a single bedroom with limited kitchen use. Gone were the Nazi soldiers, gone were the menacing sounds coming from the radio, gone was Millie with her change of heart. The first days I spent making the acquaintance of Rina's pets, the gray cat and a cute mutt that kept running from room to room. The events that had frightened me only days before seemed far away.

I was not old enough to understand how all the pieces had fallen into place—the slip of paper with the address, Signora Gigli waiting for us. It had all been prearranged. That was the beginning of what my parents called "the Jewish underground."

"What is the Jewish 'under something'?" I asked.

My mother tried to explain. "There are many good, decent people out there who try to help people like us, who have been forced to leave their homes and go to live in a foreign land. Don't forget, Erich, one day, when you get to be a man, you may be called upon to help someone less fortunate. I want you to remember what total strangers are doing for us now."

Because of my parents' Polish citizenship, we were allowed to leave Vienna but were permitted only two suitcases and very little money.

"Would you believe that they let us take out only two hundred *Schilling* per person? That would be enough to live one week. We weren't permitted to take our valuables or any of my jewelry," Mother said to an acquaintance.

At that time, the son of a wealthy Turkish merchant who was studying medicine in Vienna had taken up residence at our hotel. My father sent a letter to him and, luck being on our side, the young student received our plea for help. Through his parents, who lived in Turkey, my father bartered Italian lire for hotel lodging. Thus we received needed funds in Italy, and the Turkish student received paid accommodations at the Hotel Continental.

With the help of the same student, who passed through Milan once or twice, Mother was able to retrieve much of her cherished jewelry. She sold pieces one by one to help us survive in our new country. Parting with a ring or bracelet or earrings caused great tension between my parents, making me realize how much these objects meant to my mother.

In a short time, my life in Milan became almost normal, perhaps too normal. Within two weeks after our arrival, my parents enrolled me in the Hebrew school.

"Why do I need scholastic discipline?" I complained. "Why can't you leave well enough alone? Do I bother anyone?"

The school provided bus transportation. In Vienna I had had to walk. The bus came for me first, then, after crisscrossing the width and length of the whole city, it stopped to pick up the last child just across the street from where I had been standing an hour earlier. The same tedious route was repeated on the way home, keeping me a school hostage two hours longer than necessary. I asked the driver to let me off on the corner, which would have saved me one hour, but the answer was "no." I was convinced my mother had a hand in arranging the schedule. This was a devilish way for my parents to keep me away from them. Only the constant display of their affection convinced me otherwise.

The scholastic year ended two months after my enrollment and the lengthy bus rides were soon forgotten. But worse than those daily trips was adjusting to Milan's weather. The fog and humidity that greeted us on our arrival were a daily occurrence. Occasionally the fog lifted but only to make room for a heavy rainfall to make sure we would not miss the humidity. The weather was bad in winter and, as we soon found out, no better in summer.

"I can't believe a city with such lousy weather has attracted so many famous people," Mamma remarked.

"And to think it is Italy's largest city," Papa said.

We arrived in Milan on March 19. Winter was almost over, and yet, because the apartment did not have central heating, every night Papa had to load hot embers into a brazier, which he placed between the covers to dry the damp sheets.

We did have a short, but much too short, period of pleasant spring weather. Lying in a valley, surrounded by mountains, Milan had an oppressive and brutal summer. Almost every night my parents awakened me to take a walk to a city park, the beautiful Sforzesco Castle. There we could catch some breathable air. The idea was not original; thousands of the city's one million citizens did the same. The event, in fact, was so popular that the city authorities provided fireworks, imparting a festive mood to these nightly outings.

We stayed in Milan eight months, during which I enjoyed many firsts. Seeing an opera was one. My mother often spoke about her experiences at the Vienna opera when she was a young girl. She had heard the best of that era: Lotte Lehman, Jan Kiepura, Richard Tauber, Joseph Schmidt, Enrico Caruso.

"Do you realize," *Mutti* said, "except for Caruso, these were all Jewish artists? And Hitler calls Jewish artists degenerate."

She described the times when she had followed Jan Kiepura from the opera house back to his hotel, then waited with a crowd of hundreds for the singer to appear on the balcony and serenade his fans below. Or when, one winter, she stood all night for the ticket window to open in the morning. She had wanted a standing-room ticket to hear the great Caruso.

Through her vivid memories I relived the glorious moments of Vienna's past. Because she spoke with so much passion, I was able to feel the emotions she had felt many years before. Perhaps it was only how she remembered things, but I didn't care. Her stories gave me a great thirst to see an opera for myself. I was filled with curiosity.

"Did you ever meet any of these artists?" I asked.

"*Nein, mein Hasele.*"

Oh, how I loved the many terms of endearment my *Mutti* used for me, like *Hasele, Schatzele, Katzele, Puppale, Tatale, Stück Gold,* sometimes adding more schmaltz by prefacing them with *goldenes*.

One day after lunch, Mother said, "You take a nap and I'll have a big surprise for you."

"What surprise?" I asked.

"We'll take you to La Scala. Only if you take a nap."

I had heard of the famous opera house and decided that going to La Scala to see an opera was worth a nap, perhaps even two. That night, at the age of eight, dressed in my best Lord Fauntleroy suit, knee-high socks, and a black velvet ascot, I entered the portal of the greatest opera house in the world to hear *Turandot.* The red velvet parapets and overstuffed chairs, the gilded wall decorations, the huge crystal chandeliers, men and women in their flashy evening clothes, all made a lasting impact, putting me in a state of total ecstasy.

For days I told everyone I met of having been at La Scala, little realizing that, for those living in Milan, this was nothing unusual.

Another first was learning true woodworking. When I was five years old and still living in Vienna, with a small coping saw and a piece of thin plywood, I created a complete bedroom set that fit into a shoebox. But that had been child's play. In Milan I befriended a real cabinetmaker. Passing by his shop one morning, I stopped to watch. Cautiously, I moved into the sawdust-filled shop. The man stopped what he was doing and, shining a broad smile, greeted me and asked me something.

We had been in Italy less than two months and my Italian was not good enough to understand the question. In the best way I knew how, I asked the man to repeat what he had said. It took a few minutes and a great deal of the man's patience before I understood that he had asked me if I liked woodworking. I then tried to explain to him what I had done at age five, but only when I drew pictures to explain did he finally understand me.

This cabinetmaker did not work with coping saws and shoeboxes. He made full-sized furniture with full-sized tools. I was impressed by the large and deafening electric saw. As I prepared to leave his shop that first day, his arm around my shoulders and his warm squeeze made me realize I would be welcome back. His shop was just around the corner from where we lived and that made it easy to hop over any day I had time.

During that same period I became the little darling of some of the salesladies of the local Upim store located on Via Meravigli. What a perfect combination. The cabinetmaker supplied me with scraps of lumber, and the sales clerks were generous in letting me have batteries, lamps, wires, and everything else I needed to build my small projects.

So while most other kids played in the streets or the courtyards, I was in our room sawing, hammering, running wires, and building things. Despite the mess I created in our bedroom, my mother was proud of the scaled-down trolley car her little son had built—a copy of the real thing running through city streets. It had a seat for the conductor, two rotating controls (one the accelerator, the other the brake), a working headlight, and a bell.

I realized at an early age that my mother was a great socializer, and soon after we settled down in our new country, she made a great number of new friends. They must all have been refugees like us, for I never heard anything but German and Polish spoken. Mother had friends for bridge, others for sitting with at a coffeehouse, and others with whom she spent pleasant hours at home. Every time one of these friends came to visit, Mamma would ask me to sit in the trolley and show off my creation. She made it a ritual. They never stopped coming, and so biased was my *Mutti* that she failed to recognize what even I could see: her friends had little interest in her son's handiwork.

In going through my father's night table one day, I found a pair of glasses. With the find held high in my hand, I bolted out of the room in search of Mother. "Whose glasses are these?" I called out.

"They're Papa's," she answered.

"I've never seen him wear them," I said, stunned.

With her words still ringing in my ears, I dragged myself back to our room and broke into uncontrollable sobs. To me, only old people wore glasses and I didn't want my parents to get old.

My father was an impeccably elegant man. His tailor-made double-breasted suits, the white handkerchief folded into a perfect rectangle peeking from his breast pocket, and the knotted, thin-striped tie centered between the starched white collar were his personal trademarks. His hair, too, combed straight back without a part, was always perfect, thanks to the net he positioned with meticulous care before going to bed at night. He wore wing-tipped black shoes shined to a luster that, together with the squeaking soles, made them seem new.

Five feet ten inches tall, my father maintained his slim figure by devoting ten minutes each morning to his own version of gymnastic exercise. In boxer shorts, garters holding up the knee-high socks, his arms outstretched forward, he slowly bent his knees while his torso moved up and down a dozen or so times. On occasion, crouching next to Papa, I tried to imitate him.

The Giglis treated their cat and dog like children. Mrs. Gigli cooked special food for them, bathed them regularly, and each pet had a pillow at the feet on her bed. During our stay, the poor cat had to be put to sleep. It was a sad moment for everyone when we watched Mr. Gigli take the cat on its final trip to the veterinary.

I had adjusted to the cat's being gone when a few days later, to my consternation, Rina brought the stuffed animal home. She placed it on the living room mantlepiece where it sat taunting the dog by refusing to play with his old friend. Whenever my parents sat in the living room, they whispered about the dead cat sitting on the mantlepiece. "*Takke meshuge!*" *Mutti* remarked. Really crazy. One Sunday morning we were gathered in the living room with our landlords when the subject of religion came up.

"You don't go to church, Signora Lotte. Are you not Catholic?" Rina asked.

"No. We are Jewish."

"Jewish!" Rina shrieked. "*O, Madonna mia!* I would never have guessed. But you don't look Jewish."

My mother was bewildered by Rina's statement. "How does a Jew look?" she asked.

"Well, I thought. . . ."

Mutti was clearly impatient now. "You thought what?"

"I thought all Jews . . . had horns."

Both my parents burst into loud laughter. The subject never surfaced again, nor did Rina or her husband show any difference in their warm feelings toward us.

That year my mother came up with a great idea. She arranged for me to go to a summer camp in Switzerland. The camp had been organized and financed by a group of good-hearted Swiss ladies who had raised the necessary money to offer a slice of happiness to Jewish refugee children by selling home-baked goods on the streets of Zurich, Basel, and Geneva. I had turned eight, and the thought of my being allowed to travel to another country, away from my parents' strict discipline, was so exciting I could hardly sleep. "How many more days?" I kept asking.

Two days before the long-anticipated departure, Papa took me for a haircut. As we were walking down the stairs, Mamma shouted, "Short, I want him to be cool!"

A little with sign language and less in his poor Italian, my father tried to communicate with the barber. The man tapped my father's arm and indicated that he understood perfectly and proceeded to shave off my hair completely. Back home, at the sight of my bald head, Mother's eyes opened wide and from the lack of color in her face, I was sure she was about to faint. That haircut caused a long argument between my parents and, for most of the summer, it gave my camp playmates a reason to taunt me.

The day finally came when we all went to the train station for my trip to Basel. Embarking on my first real adventure alone put me beyond exhilaration. I wanted my mother to stop hugging me, so certain that each hug was delaying the train's departure. My father had already placed the suitcase on the luggage rack and was waiting to get me settled in the third-class compartment.

"I hope you have a very good time and I hope and pray that you will behave," said Papa as he placed his arms around me, lifted me off the floor, and covered my face with kisses. My father had kissed me many times before but never so many times. He stepped off just as the conductor whistled and the doors slammed shut. At the window I waved a final goodbye and, exhausted, fell into my seat.

The metal wheels squeaked. The excitement and anticipation that had caused me to pester my mother endlessly, turned into panic. I was alone in that large compartment built for eight, on a train going to an unknown city in some foreign country. I hated that stupid piece of cardboard hanging from my neck holding the documents. No one else ever wore anything like it. Maybe it was best nobody was in the cabin to see it. But thanks to the "necklace," I received extra attention from the Swiss border guards who had boarded the train and I didn't have to show my passport with that ugly photo.

"I will help you when we arrive," the conductor said. Good to his word, on arrival he guided me to an awaiting counselor.

The two months I spent in the Swiss chalet, nestled in a dense forest, surrounded by flowers and a variety of wild animals, was a delightful period. I enjoyed long walks through the woods, learned handicrafts, and made many new friends. Most of the children were from Austria and Germany, so language did not present a problem. The food was plentiful and delicious, and I was introduced to a variety of new dishes, such as venison and hare, which were served at least once a week and became my favorites.

We learned to make papier-mâché puppets, to milk goats, and to feed the farm animals living on the property.

My stay in this idyllic spot almost ended before its time when a counselor wrote to my parents asking them to take me back so the other children could enjoy the remainder of their summer. All because I poured cold water on the boy sleeping in the bed next to mine? It was only for fun. Protected by some unknown source, I was allowed to stay for the duration.

At the end of the season, I returned to Milan wearing the full regalia of an American Indian, complete with a spear and feathers, the costume I had created in a handicraft class.

Artwork by Eric sent to his parents in Milan from camp in Switzerland in the summer of 1938.

4

Settling Down

I learned much of what was happening from the conversations between my parents and their visiting friends. Italy had kept its borders open to many displaced Jews from Austria and countries of Eastern Europe, but by 1938 Mussolini was cultivating his alliance with Adolf Hitler. To appease his new ally, he promulgated a milder version of the German racial laws. Among other things, they barred Jewish children from attending public schools and Jewish men from serving in the military. And while the latter did not concern me at all, I was delighted about the former. But I was only eight and did not grasp the meaning of "racial laws."

So, that fall, my parents did not enroll me in school, leaving me to cultivate my friendship with the cabinetmaker and the young women at Upim. Now I could build and tinker and not have to worry about homework.

My father began working soon after we arrived from Vienna. He would buy silk stockings from a factory, then went house-to-house to sell them to other immigrants. I don't know how well he made out financially, but my mother had plenty of silk stockings and many of the premiums Papa used to give his customers.

Hardly a day went by that one or two salesmen did not come to our door peddling bolts of fabric, stockings, pens, or useless little gadgets.

"Why are so many people coming to the apartment door?" I asked.

"*Hasele!* The police will not give immigrants a work permit. This is their only way to earn some money," *Mutti* explained. "Not even Papa can get a permit."

By sleeping in the same room with my parents, I had become privy to many of their concerns and adult conversations. That's how I learned that a new industry had sprung up in Milan: the manufacture of furs made from remnants.

"Leave it to the Jews," Mamma remarked. "They always find a way to earn their bread."

Papa described these factories. They had been set up in old abandoned apartment buildings no longer suitable for human habitation. Cutting tables and sewing machines were crammed into poorly lit rooms, creating intolerable working conditions, especially during the hot summer months, when a few small electric fans were all there was to mix some outside air with the stale air inside.

"Those poor workers! Because they are illegals, would not dare complain," my mother remarked. "They are glad to earn some money. No one else will hire them. I ask how God could allow this to happen. I've met people who were wealthy men in the old country and now are laborers. They look like beggars."

One hot day my father took me along to one of these sweatshops. Just as he had depicted, the inside air was intolerable. I found it hard to breathe and wanted to leave, but Papa had to speak to the owner. While I waited, I watched a worker take a small piece of fur, not much larger than a postage stamp, place it on a table next to many similar squares, and painstakingly try to fit it into a matching pattern. Slowly he turned each tiny piece a full circle until his trained eye was satisfied with the fit. Then with a pin he fastened the new remnant to the others, picked up a new square, and repeated the process. After several fur pieces had been pinned together, he carried the large puzzle to a special sewing machine, where he fed it into a curved needle and sewed the many sections into one continuous pelt. As one hand was pushing the jigsaw puzzle through the fast-moving machine, two fingers of the other hand removed the no-longer-needed pins. When the last pin was removed, he lifted his finished masterpiece high over his head, displaying it first to himself, then to me. He had a sparkle in his eyes. I would never have guessed this was anything but a single pelt.

In spite of my many requests, Mother had never allowed me to wear long pants. After I celebrated my eighth birthday, I thought it was a good time to ask again.

"They're only for dressy occasions. Do we understand each other?" *Mutti* admonished.

With a military salute, I said, "Oh yes, sir!" I was ready to understand anything she wanted me to understand as long as I got my long pants. In the end, she relented. I wrapped my arms around her and covered her face with kisses. "Oh, *Mutti*, I love you."

"I love you too, *Hasele*. You're my whole life."

That week Mother took me to a tailor. There was a long conversation about the kind of pants before the man started taking my measurements. I was dancing around from being so excited. Annoyed, the tailor said, "Unless you stop moving, I won't be able to make your pants." I froze in my tracks. Around the waist, down my leg, then from the crotch, around the hip, and the thigh. I never knew pants needed that many measurements. Meanwhile, my mother had chosen a gray checkered fabric from the swatch book.

"Do you like it?" she asked.

I liked it a lot.

"Come back next week for the first fitting," the tailor said.

Back for the fitting we went, but all his measuring did not seem to help the pants fit my body. Perhaps he'd made a mistake and used someone else's measurements. Perhaps this was a plot to deny me my long pants. The man looked puzzled. He walked around me twice, pinched some loose material, circled me again, and marked some places with chalk while other spots he pinned.

"Come back next week," he said.

Although my mother had ordered knickers and, while not quite the long pants I had hoped for, they were more adult than anything I had owned before. I had to wait through one more fitting and two more agonizing weeks, but when I tried on the finished knickers, they fit and I walked out from the small shop wearing my first long trousers. I swaggered like a man instead of the boy I still was. I felt taller and certain everyone on the street was aware of the fine figure I cut.

The second time I was allowed to wear my new pants, I took a tumble on a stone sidewalk, causing an irreparable rip to my knickers. My knee was torn up also and bleeding badly, but my crying was not for the physical pain. It was for the loss of the long trousers I had wanted for so long.

Mother took one look at me then at the pants. "Well," she said, "I guess that's the end of your long trousers."

My initial infatuation with our landlady blossomed. Often Rina invited me to eat with her, developing my taste for a variety of Italian specialties. I loved being the center of her attention when her husband worked late and she and I were the only ones at the kitchen table.

Within weeks after our arrival, the going-to-bed ritual also required a goodnight kiss from Rina.

"Signora Gigli, you like children so much. How come you never had your own?" Mamma asked.

"I would have loved to but we couldn't. But you brought Enrico and he means as much to me as a child of my own could." I had cuddled up to her and she held me close to her bosom.

From the time I returned from Switzerland, I began spending more and more time with Rina. Mother was happy I was staying off the street, while Rina and her dog were delighted to have me around.

My papa and I had never spent much time together—a few minutes each morning just before I left for school and at mealtimes. On occasion, when I got home before he did, I waited on the street and, recognizing his characteristic waddle from a distance, I'd run and throw myself into his waiting arms.

Nor did I know much about the relationship between my parents. I saw many tender moments, but there were also many shouting matches in their impenetrable Polish. Once my mother threw a metal plate at my father, hitting the wall right over his head with a force that left a chip in the plaster. Judging from the spankings she gave me, I knew that Mother had a strong arm, but fortunately for Papa, not very good aim.

One day my father had just come home for the midday meal. Breathless, he tried to explain to my mother what had happened that morning. "I went to the police office and they sent me to another office. Lotte, they don't want to renew our permit."

"What do we do?" *Mutti* asked. Within days, my parents applied at the U.S. Consulate for an immigration visa. The Polish quota was much too small to accommodate the large number of applicants. At least a two-year wait, my father was told. We had to leave Italy.

Hearing talk about going to America, I asked, "Why do we have to leave? I like it here."

"We can't stay here any longer," *Mutti* said.

There was much discussion between my parents and lots of shouting, but I couldn't figure out what was going on.

One morning after breakfast, *Mutti* announced, "We are going to France and Papa is going to Lwow."

The news caught me off guard. "Why can't we all go together?" I asked. Where was France? Why don't we all go to Lwow to be with my beloved grandparents? "I don't know anyone in France," I cried. "That's the way it has to be," *Mutti* replied.

I tried to find out where France was located. Asking, I learned that France bordered with Italy. From conversations my parents had with friends, I heard that France was still a safe refuge, but the French denied visas to Jews. Somehow I had overcome my earlier feelings of being dislodged and had settled down in our new home. Now I was being uprooted again.

When in November we prepared to leave, friends and acquaintances filled the living room for days as they came to wish us well and kiss us goodbye. We left Milan with all of our belongings minus my trolley car and the Indian outfit I had made in the Swiss camp. My heart was shattered. In Vienna I had been forced to abandon my brand new sleigh, my beloved Teddy, and my irreplaceable silver watch. But at the moment when Rina held me close to her, my greatest ache was having to leave her. Without the slightest notion about where Paris was in relation to Milan, I promised her I would be back to visit.

"I'll get a bicycle and come back," I assured her.

As I descended the stairs, tears running down my face, Rina threw me kisses with her fingers. She was standing on the landing where I had first seen her holding the little gray cat. Unlike the welcoming smiles of that earlier day, she was sobbing and, what little makeup she had put on that morning, was now smudged and flowing with the tears down her pretty face.

A taxi was ready at the front door. "To the terminal," Papa said in respectable Italian and the driver took us to the station where we had arrived eight months before. The train was already waiting on the track. The porter placed our luggage on the racks inside the compartment while, on the platform, my parents held each other in an extended embrace. *Mutti* looked anxious to board but Papa kept holding on. Then came my turn. My father lifted me up in his arms and, just before, he squeezed me tight. I looked into his eyes. They were swollen and red. This was the first time I had seen my father cry.

"Don't cry," I said. "We'll be back together soon."

"Sure, sure." There was an odd sound to his voice.

He kissed me again and, as the conductor's whistle announced our imminent departure, he picked me up, set me on the train, and pushed me inside. Tears were now streaming openly down his face. What a sad picture of a proud man. Even in his double-breasted suit, with his hair neat and his tie in place, he did not exude the dapper look I knew so well. Slowly he pushed the heavy metal door shut—but not before an admonition in a quavering voice: "I want you to listen to your mother."

Back in our compartment, I found my parents speaking through the open window. With a loud whistle and a sudden jerk, the train started to roll. My parents grasped each other's hands. Papa walked alongside the window until the train's speed forced him to let go. Mother, her eyes swollen, pulled back from the window. Quickly I took her place to watch my father's image get smaller and smaller and disappear as the train followed a curve. The tiny people I had seen from the hill in Lwow came to mind, and I finally began to understand what my father had tried to explain on that distant day.

"Mamma, now I know what an optical illusion is."

The ride to Ventimiglia, the Italian town bordering France, took all morning. I sat in silence for most of the trip. So much crossed my mind. I thought of Rina, the dead cat, my trolley car, *Omama*, Millie. But what gnawed most at me was my papa. The sad picture of him standing on the platform had seized my mind and refused to let go. Would I ever see him again? He had seen me leave before—the times I went on vacation with Mother, with Millie, the time I left alone to go to Switzerland—yet never had I seen him so distraught. Did he know something I didn't?

"Do you want something to eat?" *Mutti* asked.

"No, thanks."

"You haven't said a word. Is something the matter?"

"Just thinking."

"About what, *Hasele?*"

"Nothing. The trolley car, Millie, Rina, Papa. Why couldn't Papa come with us?"

"He just couldn't at this time, *Schatzele.*"

When other refugees had come to visit my parents in Milan, they spoke of horror stories of how people, trying to escape the Nazis, had risked their lives crossing illegally into Switzerland or France.

"The Alps are an excellent camouflage," someone had said. "For the young who are capable of scaling the high passes, there is little risk, but for the older and physically weak, life often ends in a long fall down the snowy slopes and an agonizing death."

"And I understand there is no assurance," my father had said. "We don't know that, even if one is successful in crossing the border, France or Switzerland would be willing to offer asylum."

Someone warned that families traveling together were a sure target to be intercepted at the border.

Although an indomitable woman, my mother was not ready to cross any mountain peaks and said so. "I would rather rely upon my own ability. Scaling mountains with a small child is not for me. My husband will be able to join us later."

When the conductor announced we were reaching Ventimiglia, my mother used the toilet to make a quick change from the winter clothes she had been wearing to a flowery summer dress and a white straw hat. She looked radiant without any traces of the tears she had shed earlier that morning.

We left the train and were walking from the small railroad station when, baffled that we had left our luggage on the train, I asked, "What about the suitcases?"

"Somebody will take care of them," *Mutti* said. "We are going to take a long walk now and I want you to act as though you are here to see the sights."

That is how, after stepping off the train in Ventimiglia, we found ourselves facing the breathtakingly beautiful stretch between the Italian border town and Menton, its French counterpart.

Bending at the knees, Mother stooped and brought her pretty face down to mine. With one hand she gave my clothes a maternal yank. She always did it whether they needed it or not. Then, with her moistened fingertips, she smoothed out my hair.

Clutching the fresh bouquet Papa had bought for her in Milan and, holding hands with me, *Mutti* and I advanced toward the French border along the wall overlooking the blue waters of the Italian Riviera. The road wandered along the spectacular azure Mediterranean. High above the horizon, the sun produced an uninterrupted shimmering streak upon the nearly quiet waters. My mother seemed as enthralled by nature's splendor as I was, and we paused to bathe in the surrounding beauty, forgetting for a short, solitary moment all that had happened to us in the previous eight months and the unknown dangers facing us.

As we continued our walk, we passed the Italian customs agents without a hitch and approached the French control point. Mother let go of my hand, walked up to the little shed, and spoke with a border guard. Because she spoke in Italian and used much gesticulation, I was able to somehow follow what she was trying to convey to the bewildered official. We were going to meet some friends for lunch and would return before evening. That's what Mother tried to tell him with many smiles. Finally the man—whether he understood or was confused or was charmed—relented and allowed us to cross the barrier and walk onto French soil. We strolled a bit farther until we were out of view of the border guard.

Mutti mumbled, "I hope he doesn't change his mind," which caused us to hasten our pace with every step.

Mother's nervousness, transmitted through our clasped hands, made me sweat like I had never sweated before. The walk to the Menton railroad station was only a few minutes long, yet I imagined police dogs chasing after us and soldiers dragging us into some dungeons.

As though just waiting for us, a train for Paris was on the tracks ready to depart. We boarded and, though we departed a few minutes later, I did not stop trembling until we picked up full speed.

5

Paris

We arrived in the City of Lights the morning after we had left Milan.

It was 1938, and Europe was still at peace. Mother handed the taxi driver some written instructions and he dropped us off at a small second-class hotel.

Our baggage was already in the room, neatly lined up. "How did our suitcases get here?" I asked.

"Someone I know arranged it."

Mutti took just enough time to remove her hat before using the toilet down the hall. When she returned, she busied herself emptying the suitcases. Some garments went into the armoire and others in the small four-drawer chest. I stayed out of her way. Curious to see the new city, I reasoned that my presence served no purpose since I had no talent for unpacking. The thing to do was to get out and take a walk. By then, having traveled alone from Milan to Basel, I considered myself a world traveler.

"I want to go out, *Mutti*," I said, my hand already on the doorknob.

"I'm busy now."

"I'll go by myself."

"Don't you want something to eat? You haven't eaten since last night," she replied.

"No, *Mutti*."

"How will you find your way back?"

"I will, I promise."

"I want you back no later than four. It gets dark early."

I promised that, too. Then my devilish mind questioned whether *Mutti* was letting me go because she trusted my ability to retrace my steps or really was trying to get rid of me. I was almost out the door when Mother called me back. "Where do you think you are going without a kiss?" As she kissed me, she placed something in my pocket. "If you get lost, show this paper to a policeman. It has the name of the hotel." I knew it all along. She didn't want to get rid of me.

As I left the hotel, I took notice of a large statue of a medieval soldier in full armor astride a horse. Assured that the landmark would help me recognize the street later. I went forth to explore this new city.

Fascinated by each street and every square, I kept walking, trying to maintain my sense of direction so I could keep my promise. I started on the return trip by three o'clock. Much to my relief, fifteen minutes later, high on his horse, I saw my medieval friend. I had kept my promise and was back before dark.

In Paris, Mother contacted the Bretschneiders, a couple whose daughter often had come to our hotel in Vienna to give *Mutti* a manicure. What a surprise, when the young woman came to call, to see a familiar face so far away from home.

Mother also met her old friend Clara. She had lived in our hotel at the same time we did. I loved the plump woman who often poked fun at herself. I referred to her as "Aunt Clara" and *Mutti* referred to her as a comic character. The two spent much time together, laughing and carrying on. Clara was constantly on some diet that did not last and always using exercise machines designed to create minor miracles when she needed major ones.

"Remember when you didn't want to eat your dinner at home?" *Mutti* asked me. "You only wanted to eat with Aunt Clara. Remember? You always said that you liked her cooking better than mine. Well, I used to send your dinner to her apartment. Clara has never cooked a meal in her life."

After a short pause, I broke out in a big laugh at this revelation.

As much as I'd always enjoyed Clara, I loved her father. I used to call him "Papi" and considered him the grandfather missing from my life in Vienna. Whenever he visited Clara, he told spooky stories that kept me awake at night but made me ask for more. Papi also had given me my first piggyback ride."

"How is Papi?" I asked.

"He died just before I left Vienna," Clara replied. "I'm glad for him. He didn't have to witness all that went on."

I was grieved, yet too reserved to show my emotions. "I'll cry when I get back to our room," I said. But I never did.

We remained in Paris a little longer than two months. I had learned my way back to the hotel and was allowed to be on my own. I discovered the electric map in the Metro stations where, at least once a day, I felt the need to test the tracking system. I descended below the Paris streets to reach the magic machines. Not tall enough, I had to stand on my toes to see the row of tiny lights showing the location of the next train. I marveled at the mysterious mechanics that could create such a miracle of information.

But Paris did not hold the same interest as Milan. The small hotel room made it impossible to get involved in any kind of woodworking and, though Mother introduced me to some of the city museums, nothing compared to building things with my own hands. More than anything, I missed my papa and our life in Milan with Rina.

6

Nice

In February 1939, we packed our belongings and, without my knowing why, boarded the train to Nice. Nestled between the blue Mediterranean and splendid rolling hills, Nice was known as the gem of the French Riviera. We traveled by night and arrived in the early morning. Although still tired, we were cheered up by the tall, swaying palm trees lining the streets and by the red, blue, purple, and orange flowers adorning the sidewalk gardens outside the small rail station.

Much to my delight, we had arrived in the middle of carnival time, and I soon learned little else in the world could compare to the joyfulness of carnival in Nice. The festive mood permeated every street, every building, every corner of this small city. Large black cone-shaped loudspeakers blasted music from every tree strong enough to support one.

As in Milan and Paris, Mother had the address of a place where we were going to stay. She hailed a taxi from the terminal and gave the driver the magic piece of paper.

The single room, one of several in a large apartment, was sparsely furnished with some rundown items: one large bed, a cot, an armoire, a dressing table, and a solitary chair. The rent included kitchen privileges, meaning we could use the stove, provided it did not interfere with the landlady's or the other tenants' needs. There, on the kitchen table, we ate our meals under the curious eyes of the other tenants, who looked at us as though we were some exotic animals.

In Milan, where for the first time, Mother had to share a kitchen with someone else, Rina had been eager to please. "I hope this woman will be as pleasant as Signora Gigli in Milano," *Mutti* confided. But Monique, our new landlady, did not even closely compare to Rina Gigli. After two days of failed attempts and frustrated by not being able to use the stove when she wanted it, my clever mother, who needed a kitchen just as a priest needs a church, found a solution. "I'm going to ask her to eat with us."

Mutti left the room with me right behind and found the landlady in the kitchen. "*Voulez-vous manger avec nous?*" she asked.

The woman seemed uncertain but replied, "*Certainement. Merci. Merci.*"

Monique was seduced by my mother's cooking a few times each week and the kitchen became ours.

Not much past thirty, Monique was lanky and a bit tall for a woman. Used to my mother's elegance, I found Monique's dresses to be drab. One dress looked like the other: long, below her knees; half-sleeves; a slight opening at the neck, dark, old-fashioned, and ugly. Without socks, the open sandals showed her dirty toes. Her short haircut made her plain and vaguely masculine facial features even more unattractive. There was no resemblance to my Rina, for whom I still pined and whom, in my naïve mind, I still hoped to visit on the bicycle I did not yet own.

During our seven-month stay, Monique never gained my affection, although in her own awkward way she did try. Like the day, for example she led me by the hand into another tenant's room to show me a photograph of the man's partially nude girlfriend.

"Pretty, no?" she said. "See this here?" she pointed to what the woman's raised skirt displayed.

I felt repulsed. Why would I want to look at a woman's private parts? With an impish look on her face, Monique replaced the photo in the book, then placed her index finger on her lips. "Don't tell anyone. I don't want him to know I saw it." Her voice betrayed the pleasure she derived from showing me the photo, a pleasure I certainly did not share.

Not knowing quite what to say, I said nothing and hastily backed out of the room.

We had been in Nice less than one week when *Mutti* announced, "We're going to see the town." The day was bright and sunny, not different from the other days we had so far enjoyed. When we walked out of our building in the late morning, my mother, shielding her eyes from the sun with one hand, collided with a woman coming from the opposite direction.

Mutti removed the hand from her eyes. "*Pardon.*" she said.

She looked at the person she had bumped. There was a long silence. "Bertl?" she asked.

"Lotte?"

The two friends, realizing who the other was, let out loud shrieks. Their screams made me jump and prompted a pair of men to come rushing to their aid. The women stayed in a long, warm embrace while I stood still on the hot sidewalk until I could feel the bottoms of my feet burn through the thin soles of my shoes.

"When did you get here?" *Mutti* asked in German.

"I don't remember. When did you get here?"

My mother had a puzzled look on her face. "You don't remember? Bertl, you haven't changed at all. Let me look at you. How long has it been since I've seen you?"

"Let me see. . . ."

"Oh, I remember," said *Mutti*. "Where is your family?"

"I don't know where anyone is."

Mother placed her arm around Bertl and asked, "Where are you staying?" But before Bertl could give an answer, Mother said, "Move in with us."

Bertl did so two days later, and the three of us shared the same room: I slept in a cot against the wall. Mother and Bertl doubled up in the large bed. I had hoped the newfound friend would give my mother less time to watch over me. Instead, now I found myself with two mothers—worse, two typical Jewish mothers. This was more than any child needed to add happy confusion to his life.

Plump and barely a hairline taller than *Mutti*, Bertl resembled her in many ways. However, Bertl was not as pretty; while my mother had a petite and straight nose, Bertl's was hooked. Bertl did have a good sense of humor and a sharp mind, and she shared with my mother a strength of character that made both women survivors. The friends' similarities and compatibility made our lives quite harmonious in spite of the cramped quarters. Only their smoking I found intolerable. For hours, the two would sit in their robes in that small room, chatting and puffing on those thin, white paper tubes, creating enough smoke to force me to run out.

"Where are you going?"

"*Mutti*, I'm getting nauseous from the smell."

"Oh, my poor *Hasele?* Come here. Give me a kiss, then you can go."

"I want a kiss, too," announced Bertl.

Ugh! That stench of tobacco on their breaths.

"You don't have to hold your nose," said *Mutti*, as she gave me a slight, playful swat on my behind.

Bertl brought humor back into our lives. *Mutti* had not laughed as hard and as often since we had left Vienna. Laughter proved good medicine for her, often restoring the cheerful mood I so well remembered. Because Bertl was also an excellent cook, my two mothers took turns preparing Viennese specialties.

"Who is cooking today?" I asked.

"Who do you want to cook?" my mother replied.

"I don't care, you both make good *Wiener Schnitzel.*"

Bertl gave this very lucky boy the same warmth and motherly affection my *Mutti* did. On occasion Bertl even took my side by getting my mother to change her mind about one thing or another, like the day I asked for some pocket money.

"You don't need money," my mother said.

"I'll give him some money," said Bertl. "The poor child. Erich, get me my purse."

"You're trouble, Bertie. If I tell him something, please don't interfere. Stop spoiling my child."

"You mean our child."

Mother seemed obsessed with my schooling. Within days of our arrival in Nice, she enrolled me in public school. Again I was forced, like other children, to rise early and do homework.

"I want you to learn to speak French," *Mutti* said.

French? Why did I have to go to school? This made absolutely no sense to me. What was wrong with the way I was living? But I had learned that I rarely came out ahead when I argued with Mother.

My having acquired a good command of Italian made French easier to learn. Only a few weeks after setting foot on French soil, I began to converse in this beautiful language.

Eric at age eight with dog in Nice, France, 1939.

As on previous occasions and, true to my character, however, I was unable to control my impulses in class. Caught for the third time talking to the boy next to me, I explained to the teacher that I was just practicing my new language. The teacher was not in the least impressed by my reasonable explanation. Instead he ordered me to hold out my hand, which he struck with a wooden rod.

Mother saw my swollen fingers. "What is this?" she asked.

On my way home I had thought up a story but in the end came to the conclusion that the truth was the best policy. I did not want to risk the even more severe punishment my mother would mete out had she caught me lying.

"I don't know what I'm going to do with you. Will you ever behave?" Mother's voice was shrill.

I stood silent. What could I possibly say? It was difficult for me to follow rules. Not to speak during class was absolute torture.

"Stay home for two days, then I'll decide what to do with you."

Mutti refused to regress and allow someone else to use the ruler on her son. So she sent a letter to the school telling them her son would not be coming back. After only a few weeks, my scholastic days were cut short. My *Mutti* could be so wonderful at times!

For the next three months I enjoyed the freedom to do as I pleased. The weather in Nice invited people to sun themselves beginning in early spring and bare-breasted young women lying on the pebble beach started to attract my attention. My instincts to look at beautiful female curves gave me a naughty feeling.

"You're getting too tanned," *Mutti* warned. "You can't stay out all day in the sun. It's not healthy for you. Why not spend more time with us?"

"You and Bertl only talk and smoke. I get so bored."

Bertl had entered the room and overheard part of the conversation. "Well, tonight I'll take you out to a fine restaurant."

Since leaving Milan, my mother and I had been to only cheap neighborhood eating places. That night we did dine out and what a treat it turned out to be. Soon after we ordered our food, but without anyone asking for it, the waiter wheeled over a small cart with a large variety of hors d'oeuvres. I could not believe what was on that cart: Russian salad, red beets, small beans, cucumbers, smoked fish, hard-boiled eggs, olives, and more fish.

"Bertl, how many things do you think there are?" I asked.

"Go ahead, count them."

I did and counted forty. Wow!

"You can eat as much as you want," she said.

"Are you sure?" my mother asked.

"Oh yes. It's all included in the price of the meal."

I must have tried a bit from every dish when Mother asked, "Will you be able to eat dinner?"

"Oh, sure!" I said. But when the main course, a veal cutlet, was served, I could eat less than half. But I did force down my chocolate dessert.

The Promenade des Anglais, adorned by a long line of palm trees and, beautified with colorful flowers, ran alongside the beaches for the full length of the city. From here, built on pylons and jetting out into the water, was the municipal casino. Nice's major gambling center also had a large theater where a variety of vaudeville shows were performed. Free passes to these shows were easily available from retail stores and professional offices. A doctor's office, where these passes lay on the reception room table, became my source.

The casino was five blocks from our house. The first time I used one of the passes, I ran all the way home after the show. I had barely opened the door when I blurted, "*Mutti*! Guess what I did today?"

"Calm down, *Schatzele*," *Mutti* said from our room. "Look how red you are. Sit. Do you want some water?"

I was breathless. "No, just guess what I did."

"You got married."

"No, seriously."

"I don't know. Tell me."

"I went to the casino and saw the greatest show in the world."

"That's nice. How did you get in?"

"A friend told me about this office where they have free passes. They wouldn't let me into the rooms where they gamble but only into the theater. They had a magician, a comic, some acrobats and lots of dancers."

"What else did they have?" *Mutti* asked. "It's written all over your face."

I had a real problem getting it out. I had never seen so many bare-breasted women. "The dancers wore nothing on top."

"Why are you blushing, *Hasele*? I'm the only one here."

From that day on, instead of walking the promenade or roasting my skin at the beach, I spent many afternoons at a vaudeville show.

Since coming to Nice, I had envied people sitting at the open-air cafés. Oh, how I wanted to do that! One morning I asked *Mutti* to give me the half franc needed for a continental breakfast. "It would be such a treat," I said.

In spite of money being in short supply, she handed me the coin. "Go, have breakfast out."

Fresh rolls, a croissant, butter, jams, coffee, and a small pitcher of hot milk. What a breakfast! Relaxing in the fresh air under an immense open umbrella and, having an elegant server wait on me, made me feel so grown up. With great care, I sliced the roll and spread butter and jam on each side, restored the two halves and, with a slight squeeze, sunk my teeth in it. Oh, how *merveilleux!* I devoured both rolls, the croissant, with the rest of the butter, jam, and the full pot of French coffee. Then, with a touch of flair, I asked for *l'addition* and handed the man the fifty *centimes*.

The beach was a short walk from the café. My shorts and shirt removed, I enjoyed the balmy air in the bikini trunks I wore underneath. Only the sandals stayed on my feet, for I had not yet adapted to walking on the stony beach.

Rarely did I find other children on the beach. The tourist season had not started and school was still in session. For almost two months, until the end of June, I spent those magnificent spring days surrounded by hundreds of strangers but feeling so alone.

At one o'clock, I often went to the casino for a show I had seen before. I seldom ate lunch on those days, satiating my hunger with the few candies the artists threw from the stage at the end of each performance. Although there was always a great lunch waiting for me, I rarely was willing to give up my liberty in exchange for food.

On those few days when the casino featured totally nude dancers, they refused me admission, so I would walk up the hill overlooking the port. The harbor, narrow and short, was large enough to hold only a few small craft. There I saw three British submarines, my first encounter with military hardware.

During the turmoil of the previous fourteen months, I had not been to a synagogue once. Although we were able to bring very few personal items when we escaped from Vienna, my mother had taken along the old family prayer book. Throughout our nomadic days, she handled that book with great care.

Both my parents had been raised in Orthodox families where the dietary kosher laws had been strictly observed. In Vienna, my *Omama* came to visit every week but seldom on a Friday or Saturday, for she would not travel on the Sabbath. She always visited us after supper and never shared a meal with us. "Our home is not kosher enough for *Omama*," *Mutti* explained. Nor did my grandfather in Poland allow anyone to turn the lights on or off on the holy day. Lights were always turned on before sundown Friday and left burning until past sundown on Saturday.

My own religious upbringing had been less strict, although, beginning when I was only five, I had to put up with a tutor who came weekly to give me religious instruction. Like most Jewish families who had come from eastern Europe to settle in Vienna, my parents chose a more secular lifestyle. Yet, throughout our roaming, my mother rarely failed to light the Sabbath candles, say her prayers for the High Holidays, or fast on the Day of Atonement. In later years, unable to find out the exact date for Rosh Hashanah, *Mutti* would make up her own.

"How can you just pick a date? Yom Kippur is designated by God," I said.

"God will forgive me," she replied.

On our first Friday night in Nice, Mother had just lit the customary Sabbath candles when Monique appeared in the doorway.
Three times ritually, my mother swept her hands over the tiny flames,
then covered her eyes.

The woman was horrified, her face ashen. "What are you doing?"
she asked, her voice growing louder with each word. "Are you some
kind of witch? Are you bringing the evil spirits into my house?"

Mother approached the hysterical woman and tried to place an
arm around her shoulder. "*Ma chère* . . ."

Monique rotated herself away. "No, no. Don't you touch me!" she
shrieked.

In a conciliatory tone, struggling with her poor French, *Mutti* reassured the frightened woman she had nothing to fear. It was all part of our
religion. If Mother had not been as convincing, surely we could have
found ourselves out in the street without a place to sleep for the night.

I assumed that my mother, mindful of her experience in the Gigli
home, did not want to discuss our Jewishness with Monique, nor did
the woman ever ask about our religion.

When Bertl came to stay with us, *Mutti* told her about the incident. Bertl thought it hilarious and wanted to perform some invented
ceremony just to inflame the landlady. *Mutti* couldn't control her own
laughter.

"You're crazy," she said.

"Let's have some fun," Bertl suggested.

"Sure and then find ourselves on the street with a nine-year-old."

The subtropical weather in Nice was a glorious experience for a kid
who grew up in Vienna, with its gray winters of snow, rain, and cold
weather. Sunny day followed sunny day with hardly a rainy one in
between. Even a day with a dark cloud in the sky was a rarity. In Nice,
flowers were everywhere, from the well-maintained public gardens to the

many street vendors: azaleas, gardenias, geraniums, gladiolas, carnations, bougainvilleas, but mostly roses of every conceivable color even dark blue.

"Are they real?" I asked the woman at the street stand.

"Of course they're real. All flowers in Nice are real," she replied.

Winter and spring passed unnoticed and summer slid in unannounced. Not counting the weeks I spent in school, my life was quite enjoyable. But I knew a good thing couldn't last forever and something had to happen to disturb my carefree life. My fear turned to reality when, by the end of June, Mother shipped me off to a farm to spend the summer away from the lure of the city streets. Why did she waste her energies trying to deprive me of the things I enjoyed most? Was this what a parent was supposed to do?

"Why can't you leave me alone?" I asked. "You always have to find something, a school, a camp. When I have children, I will never do this to them." I thought of my father. "I bet you Papa would not send me there."

"He would," replied *Mutti*. "You will like this. It's a nice farm, nice people and lots of animals. You liked the camp in Basel, didn't you?"

"Sure, but I like it here now. Do I have to go?"

Mother wiped the dampness from my eyes and gave me a hug. "I make these sacrifices because I love you. It is not cheap to send you to a farm, but I'm not happy to see you walk around by yourself or go to the casino. You'll see. You'll like it. And Bertl and I will come to visit you every Sunday."

Partially convinced, I gave in.

The owners of the farm, the Barons, a simple and friendly couple, made me feel at home from the moment I arrived. Their weathered skin, wrinkled by too much sun, made it impossible to guess their ages and so, whether judging from their appearance or from their energy, one could easily err by twenty years or more. Every summer they boarded three or four youngsters. From the way they treated us, I think they did this as much out of a desire to expose a few city children to country life as for the extra income.

My mother introduced her gloomy child using my French name. "This is Henri. He is very unhappy because he didn't want to come. I've told him how much children like it here and I know he will like it also."

The woman walked up to me, crouched down to my height, and placed my hand in hers. She pulled me closer and with a gentle hug drove away my bad mood.

Every day we were kept busy, very busy, but I never felt they were taking advantage of us. Our days started at six with a big country breakfast of farm bread, fresh butter, jam, honey, eggs, and milk. Then off to take care of the goats, chickens, and cows. I milked and fed the animals and soon they recognized me whenever I entered the barn. There was also time for games and an afternoon nap followed by snacks of freshly picked fruit or a piece of candy and a fresh baguette.

"Here, look how I do it," said one of the children. With one finger, he burrowed a hole in the crunchy bread and filled it with a chunk of chocolate.

"Like this?" I asked.

"Yes. Now push the chocolate inside."

I did, then took my first bite of the combination. Heaven. I rolled my eyes and rubbed my belly. "This is the best. *Merci, merci!* I'll never forget you for this."

Dinner was a celebration of sorts as we sat around the table and told stories. Some of us reported what had happened that day, but mostly we listened to Monsieur Baron as he recounted the events of his life. He told us how one winter, all alone and without a gun, he chased away a pack of wolves that was attacking the chickens. When he returned to check on his animals, they flocked all around him in gratitude for having saved them. "You should have seen those chickens. If they could have talked, they would have said, *"Merci! Merci, mon ami."*

I was never quite sure his stories actually had happened, for they were so unbelievable, yet each evening we all looked forward to the great tales of Monsieur Baron.

By the end of the first week I was in love with my life in the country. To be around farm animals or to fetch freshly laid eggs from under the hens was an exciting experience. Even the distinctive odor of cow manure was no longer unpleasant to this nine-year-old city boy.

One morning I walked into the large kitchen carrying a small pail partly filled with milk. "Look! I milked the goat all by myself."

"*C'est formidable!*" said Madam Baron. "Please, Henri, take it back to Monsieur Baron before it spills."

I didn't mind having to carry the heavy pail out again, so proud was I of my accomplishment.

My mother never missed the weekend visit, sometimes bringing Bertl with her. While I loved both women, being with my friends or doing some of the daily chores had become far more interesting. My life on the farm suited me just fine, and I was ready to stay forever.

"Come here, you miserable kid!" *Mutti* said. She had a broad smile on her face. "I come all the way here and you would rather be with some cow?"

I ran to her and flung myself into her waiting arms. Being hugged by my mother was always a special treat. She kissed me, straightened my clothes, then, gently shoved me on. "Go, go. Have a good time." She stayed to share the midday meal, watched me play, then caught the train back to Nice.

Summer was not yet over when my mother came to take me home.

"No one else is leaving. Why can't I stay longer?" I pleaded.

"You didn't want to come in the first place. Now you don't want to leave. I'm sorry, *Hasele.*"

Reluctantly, I packed my suitcase, took leave of my hosts, and said goodbye to my summer pals.

7

San Remo

At the end of July 1939, people spoke of war. However, the threat of hostilities was just that, a threat. Except for us, danger seemed to be wherever we went and my mother, in her infinite wisdom, felt that France was no longer safe for a Jewish woman alone with a child. My father's letters kept urging us to go back to Italy. So, after an emotional goodbye with Bertl and with Mother's many acquaintances—even Monique shed some tears—we crossed Menton and Ventimiglia, retracing our steps of the year before. But this time we did not walk. Mother had some kind of official paper that she presented to the border guard who had come aboard the train, allowing us to continue without a problem.

"What did you show the man?" I asked.

"Must you always know everything? I showed him the permit to allow us back into Italy."

I was in awe of my mother. How could she always get the right papers?

After a two-hour train ride from Nice, we arrived at the small railroad station of San Remo. A few people stepped off the train to walk on the narrow platform, made narrower by the enormous bundles of colorful carnations stacked on every available space.

An elderly couple, recommended by a mutual acquaintance in Nice, rented us a furnished room in their third-floor apartment with a balcony overlooking the main street.

Guerino Grimaldi, our new landlord, was born to Italian parents but raised in France. Our room was adequate. The furniture was old and in poor condition, but the balcony added a pleasant dimension.

Signor Grimaldi poked his beret-covered head through the door minutes after our arrival. "If you need anything, just let me know."

I formed an immediate bond with him. Short of stature, not much taller than I, Guerino was a quiet man in contrast to the woman he had married forty years earlier. His voice was calm and soft, hers raspy and loud. I often watched him stand in silence, patiently listening to his wife's bickering and letting her vent her frustrations. He never contradicted her. Instead, he would remove his stained beret, hold it with one hand, and roll it over the fingers of the other, then with a tug of both hands pull it back over his bald head and respond with a gentle, "Ah ha."

Guerino took care of all the household chores. He did the shopping, cleaning, and cooking.

Because of her negative outlook on life, his wife was incapable of restraining her constant nagging and complaining. "The radio doesn't play the same music as they did years ago," she would say. "That was so nice. Even the butcher doesn't sell the same meat." A complaint she repeated often in my presence. "You never have time for me," was an obvious reference to the time her husband was devoting to me.

Then, having finished one of her tirades, she would storm out of the room.

"She can't help herself," her husband said. "Her mother was like that and she has been this way all her life."

Guerino did spend much time with me. I was the child he never had. He taught me checkers, then chess, at which I became pretty proficient. Guerino also owned a large, magnificent telescope. He had it in his bedroom, mounted on a tripod sitting by the open balcony door. Each time I passed his bedroom, I stopped to admire that instrument and yearned that he would someday allow me to look through it. One day, having gathered enough courage, I finally asked him.

"Come in," he said. "Isn't it beautiful? It is my most precious possession. Here, step up and look through it."

I was so excited, I could hardly speak. With his help, I stepped on the footstool and placed my eye on the scope. He helped me adjust the focus. "Look through and tell me when it gets really sharp."

I spied on people walking in the distance and watched a man eat peanuts in front of the railroad station, several blocks away.

"Signor Guerino, look here!" I exclaimed. "I can see every peanut the man is eating. He's standing so far away."

I stood back as he placed his eye where mine had been and adjusted the focus a bit.

"Oh, yes. Isn't this some instrument?" he asked.

Mother walked by the open door. "Signor Grimaldi, I want to thank you for all the time you're spending with my son."

"Don't even mention it. He's such a pleasure, so well brought up."

Mother beamed, "Why not speak French with Signor Grimaldi?"

Guerino was pleased with the suggestion and at the prospect of practicing his mother tongue. "*Très bien. Nous parlerons français,*" he said.

"No, Mamma. *Non voglio.* None of the boys I know in the park speak French!" I didn't want to be different. Speaking a foreign language became a dead issue.

Across the street from us I befriended the lady who worked at the corner news stand. She noticed that I liked reading the comic magazine and one day suggested I take some home.

"Bring them back in new condition," she said.

Mother stopped by one morning to thank the lady.

"Oh, it is a pleasure. Your son is such a delight," the woman said.

Soon after arriving in San Remo, we received a letter from Papa. Germany had annexed Austria, occupied Czechoslovakia, and was threatening the rest of eastern Europe, while my father's two brothers had joined him in Poland. His unmarried brother Norman had been ordered to leave Italy, where he had lived for many years, while Oswald, married and residing in London, elected to be with his brothers rather than follow his wife to Canada.

"*Takke meshuge!*" Mother commented in Yiddish about the three brothers' insanity. "Everyone is running away and they go to Poland." Although she was talking to me, I did not understand what was going on.

The Lifschütz family in Poland, May 1939. The author's grandmother (in black dress) is seated in the front row; Aunt Sallie is the third from the left in the rear.

At that same time, in June 1939, a young American woman, Sally Ratner, was visiting Poland for a family reunion, when she met my uncle Norman. They fell in love and were married. Papa wrote us that Norman's new wife would be coming to visit us on her way back to the United States.

Aunt Sally, a petite and pretty redhead, arrived in August. Uncle Norman had stayed behind in Poland until his new wife could obtain the necessary visa for him to join her in America.

I was very excited to speak with someone who, only two days before, had been with my father and his whole family. The image of Papa, the dapper, elegant man, commingled in my head with the sorrowful picture of him standing on the platform in Milan the day of our departure for France.

Mother and Sally conversed in Yiddish, their only common language, while I used German, careful to be understood.

"Tell me about my papa, please," I said.

"He is fine and he misses you very much."

"How does he look? Did he tell you when he is coming here?"

"He looks wonderful," Sally replied. "He talked about 'my *Erichl*' all the time.

"Did he say when he was coming?" I repeated.

"Only that he would be with you soon."

"And how is my *Opapa*?"

"He means his grandfather," my mother clarified.

"They are all fine and everyone sends you their love."

"Did Mischa say anything about our American visa?" Mother asked.

"He hopes it will come through soon."

"I think America is not too anxious to let in more Jews," *Mutti* remarked.

"Oh, no. That is not true," Sally said. "I cannot believe my country will not come to the aid of people in need. America is the most generous country in the world. We have always been open to people in trouble."

"Then why is it taking so long to get a visa? Don't they know what's happening to the Jews in Europe? Nobody wants us. Not Germany, not Austria, not Italy nor France. Not even Switzerland." Mother was crying and her voice had become louder.

"You know, bureaucracy takes its good old time," said Sally.

"Meanwhile our family is separated and we are living like gypsies."

"I wish I could help." Then turning to me, Sally said, "I have something for you from your father."

"What is it?"

She opened one of her large suitcases and handed me a small package.

"A camera, *Mutti*, a camera!" I was so excited I thought I would burst.

"Your father gave me instructions on how to operate it, but I cannot remember anything."

It was a Kodak Retina. "This is more than I ever dreamed. It has all these buttons and numbers. Oh, *Mutti*, Papa remembered he had promised it to me."

The next day, Aunt Sally took me to a camera shop to purchase a roll of film, there the man showed me how to use the camera. His complicated instructions were of limited use, because as soon as we left the store, I forgot most of what the man had shown me. My Papa would have made the learning process much easier.

Sally spent three days with us, then sailed for New York from Genoa. It was August 1939, and San Remo was still tranquil. This was the heavenly spot that had so enraptured Alfred Nobel and the parents of the Queen of Italy to make them choose it as their final resting place.

On September 1, the news was everywhere: Germany had invaded Poland, marking the beginning of the Second World War. Soon after, France and Great Britain declared war on Germany, and in June 1940, eager to cement his relationship with his ally, Mussolini entered the conflict on Hitler's side.

"Why are you gluing all this paper on the windows?" I asked Signor Grimaldi.

"The narrow strips will stop the glass from shattering," he said. "The large sheets will not allow the light to shine outside."

I couldn't understand why we needed all that. So what if the light shined outside?

Because streetlights were no longer lit at night, many of the sidewalks' edges were painted with a special paint.

"What's that for?" I asked.

"This phosphorescent paint shines at night."

I didn't understand but asked no more of the busy man.

At the corner newsstand, my lady friend allowed me to look at the artists' drawings in *La Domenica del Corriere* that depicted the events of the war, making it possible to follow what was happening in faraway Poland. I would then run home and tell *Mutti* all I had seen.

"There is a picture showing all those German planes dropping hundreds of bombs and the buildings burning."

The invasion of Poland terrified us. I wanted to know what was happening to my father, to my grandparents and to all the aunts, uncles, and cousins living there.

A few short weeks later, our fears became more intense when we learned that Poland had surrendered and Germany now occupied the entire country. My mother tried to obtain news about our family in Lwow, but because San Remo did not have foreign consulates, she learned nothing.

Soon after the start of hostilities, the German army had selected the Italian Riviera as a rest-and-recreation area for their soldiers, transforming this peaceful resort town into an armed arena.

One evening, with my mother's permission to keep me out past my bedtime, the Grimaldis took me with them to visit some friends. The grown-up talk was boring, but I was happy to be out past my usual time. We had just said good night to our hosts and were walking home when we heard an ear-piercing sound, a whistle coming from up high and approaching with great speed.

"What is it?" I gasped.

Before anyone realized what was happening, we saw a big flash in the garden that surrounded the Municipal Casino. Then we heard the boom.

"Get down!" Guerino screamed. Too late.

The air pressure created by the explosion knocked Guerino against the short retaining wall that separated the garden from the outside pavement. Being a bit shorter than the wall, I was shielded by it. Guerino's forehead was bruised and bleeding profusely and his wife, although unharmed, went into hysterics at the sight of his blood dripping on the pavement.

"*Madonna mia! Madonna mia!*" she screamed. "They're going to kill us."

"Calm yourself," Guerino admonished her.

"Look at you. You're bleeding to death. Help, anyone! Help!" she yelled.

"Be still. I'm not hurt and I'm not bleeding to death."

I wanted to know what had happened, but no one knew for certain. "I think we are in the middle of an air raid," Guerino said.

It was an air raid, San Remo's first, a terrifying experience, one we would relive many times again.

Two more bombs exploded at a distance and then total silence. Frightened, I clutched Guerino's hand. The silence was absolute, hairraising. We let some minutes go by before we stood up from our crouched position.

"Let's go," Guerino suggested.

Nothing was moving and not a single light was shining as we made our way home. All electric power had been cut. As in a spooky fairy tale, only the outlines of the buildings were visible in the moonlit night.

Back in the apartment, Mother, a lit candle in hand, came to the stairwell when she heard our voices. "Oh, Enrico, I've been worried to death. Where were you?"

"I saw the bombs explode!" I shouted. "We were on the street right where they fell. It was so exciting."

"You thought it was an adventure while I worried my head off." She gripped me in a tense bear hug, which seemed to bring her some relief. So concerned was Mother about me that she had not noticed Guerino's bleeding forehead. Once she did, she rushed to wash the man's face and bandage the superficial wound.

The next morning, news that we had been in the midst of the bombardment spread quickly. Every tenant in the building came by to ask what had happened.

"Did you see the explosion?"

"Did you see the bombs?"

"How about the planes? How many were there? Could you see them?"

Mamma entered the room. "Please, please. Can't you see Signor Grimaldi is still in shock? Give him a few days to recover, please."

Later that day, we learned why they had attacked this peaceful resort town. No, it had not been a mistake. A French plane had targeted the Municipal Casino, where a group of German officials was being entertained, but the small bombs, which were dropped manually by someone in the plane, had totally missed their target.

Air raids became the order of the night. They came with such frequency that, after a few days, Mother laid out my clothes at the foot of the bed so I could dress in darkness the moment the sirens blared. No matter what time the sirens sounded, my mother was always ready first, waiting for me at the door. She must have taken to sleeping in her clothes. How else could she have dressed so rapidly?

In silence and in haste, we descended the three flights to the basement. All the tenants assembled there. A solitary light bulb at the end of a dust-encrusted electric cord floated from the high ceiling. Swaying and twisting ever so slowly, it cast a spooky glow on that damp, bleak place. I fantasized that the lonely light was dancing from the joy of seeing so many people and at last felt no longer lonesome.

While we waited in the cellar, my mother would tell me family stories of her growing-up years. She told me how, after graduating from high school, she worked in a bank. "I had to help *Omama*. My father had died when I was still an infant. I had two sisters and one brother. We all had to help." I loved when she shared those experiences with me.

Some of our neighbors sat on blankets, some had brought chairs, while others sat on the bare concrete floor. Mother and I had wrapped ourselves in an old military blanket that her sister, my Aunt Stefi, had sent with the Turkish student. I snuggled close to Mother and held her hand.

Most people sat still in the cold dungeon. Only a few small children ran around. With each blast of a bomb exploding nearby our blanket quivered while Mother and I trembled. Yet of all the people there, I was the only one who had actually seen real bombs fall. The explosions and the terrifying flashes were still very vivid in my mind.

Several women, rosary in hand, recited their prayers out loud. Whenever a bomb fell close enough to make the building shake and the electricity failed, throwing us into total darkness, the scene became a bedlam. The men invoked the name of the Lord, the Holy Mary, and every saint. I never knew so many saints existed. Because the men yelled, the would wailed and the children screamed. The noise in the basement was louder than that created by the bombing outside. I curled up to my mother for protection. As frightening as those nightly episodes were, my fears would evaporate as soon as the "all-clear" siren sounded; thoughts of games and beaches would soon replace the angst in my head.

For weeks, small planes deprived us of a full night's sleep. Once, when the all-clear sounded a few minutes after the initial alarm, it was rumored that the siren had been sounded to allow Mussolini to go through town unnoticed.

The French battleground was about thirty-five miles from us. Day and night, the gruesome images of war were with us in the constant flow of ambulances rushing through the narrow streets to one of the two local hospitals. Small, canvas-covered *camionette,* built to carry only four stretchers, came from the front with eight or ten wounded soldiers at a time. The sight of heads hidden behind bloody bandages and limbs partially detached from the bodies by the furor of war terrified yet fascinated me. I remembered the war stories Papa had told me that night on the train as we fled Vienna. Now those remote images had turned into powerful and horrible realities.

Much changed in San Remo in a short time and there was little left to remind us of what, only a few weeks before, had been a peaceful and idyllic place.

Homeowners and storekeepers were busy lining their windows with newspaper and long strips of tape and all cars had their headlights masked by heavy, dark paper so that only a thin beam of light could shine through.

In San Remo, most of the pretty villas, draped by luscious flowers and tropical trees, were surrounded by decorative wrought iron fences.

I enjoyed running a piece of rolled-up cardboard or a scrap of wood across those vertical bars to create the sound of a drum roll. To my dismay, within days after the war broke out, I saw men with acetylene torches cut down these elaborate metal enclosures.

"What are you doing?" I asked.

"Mussolini needs the metal to make guns," they explained.

Because air raids always happened during the night, the only victim was our sleep. But as soon as we left the shelter, Mamma would insist on my going back to bed. "You have to get some sleep, *Schatzele*," she'd say.

For a kid of nine, these nightly raids had become more of an adventure than the danger the adults claimed them to be.

In spite of the racial laws in effect since 1938, local authorities seldom took steps to enforce them. True, aliens were not granted work permits, nor were Jewish children allowed to attend public schools, but other than these restrictions, Italy was still a safe haven for those attempting to escape the German jaws.

San Remo, like Nice, enjoyed delightfully balmy weather year round, and almost every day I went to the beach to swim in the placid blue Mediterranean Sea. Unlike Nice, San Remo had fine, silky sand beaches. Barefoot, I would walk on the sand, feeling its softness caress my feet as the sun bronzed my body.

On those days when I didn't go swimming, I went to the city park. Many local boys gathered there and in a very short time I made a number of friends. We would shoot soccer cards against the wall or race small metal cars weighted down with putty, or run all over town, up and down the stairs of four- and five-story buildings, playing cops and robbers. My favorite of all the games was shooting paper cones through metal or bamboo tubes. I became proficient at it and could soon hit a target from quite a distance. Playing with my friends in the park took a back seat the day the circus set up its tent in town. Upon hearing the circus needed people to work, I eagerly volunteered my services. I was given the job of making sure no one went through the gate without a ticket, and I took my responsibility very seriously. Roaming between the seats, watching for people who had failed to pay the admission price, made me feel official and important.

Determined to do a good job, I usually showed up at my post at least one hour before show time. One day, while making my early rounds, it happened. "Tickets please," I asked.

The authority in my voice had no impact on these two transgressors. The two men smiled and patted me on the head but kept climbing up the stands.

"Tickets, please!" I shouted.

Again they ignored me. My heart was racing. I dashed down the stands, jumping from bench to bench to report the two intruders. No one was around. The tent would not open for another hour. In the distance I saw a clown practicing his juggling. I ran up to him and grabbed him by the arm.

He freed himself from my grasp with a sudden jerk. "Eh, what do you want?" he grunted.

"You've got to come and arrest these two guys. They came in without a ticket."

As I ran up the wooden stairs with the clown in tow, I saw them. They were still there, sitting in the last row.

I pointed my finger, an unnecessary gesture, since the two men were the only people there. "There they are!" I shouted.

I had visions of the clown dragging these criminals down in chains, then calling the police to take them to jail. The next day's headline would read: "Enrico, San Remo's hero." How proud my mother would be. I was even willing to share the spotlight with the clown, who smiled and bowed to the two men, then turned to me with scorn on his painted face.

"These gentlemen are the owners of the circus," he barked, then whacked me across the back of my head with his large rubber hand. More than my head, the blow stung my ego. Nevertheless, the clown did keep my misapprehension to himself, thus saving my nonpaying job.

Working with the circus, I got to see the performance every day. I liked the clowns but, most of all, I loved the wild animals. Bears, lions, elephants. Each time I saw the lions perform, I had a vision of owning a cute cub and raising it in our small apartment. I told Mamma how great it would be to bring home a little lion cub.

"A *meshugene*. A lion he wants to bring home. He can't kill me by himself, so he looks for help."

The circus, together with its sideshows, remained in town for a month. I enjoyed the camaraderie with many members of the troupe and stayed on the job for the duration. The following year, when I reapplied, they were happy to hire me again. No one asked me if I was Jewish. Little did I know they had problems finding dependable boys who were willing to work for nothing.

8

Mother Goes to the Hospital

Despite our own hard times, Mother always found someone who was worse off. Soon after we settled in San Remo, she had met two German refugees, an older man and his daughter, and immediately invited them to share every Sabbath dinner with us. "He lost his wife recently and I found out when they escaped, they left with nothing," Mutti explained. "The man is half blind and cannot work. I don't know how they manage."

One Wednesday morning I was awakened by my mother lying next to me moaning in terrible pain. She looked dreadful and scared me out of my mind. "What's the matter?" I asked.

She made an attempt to answer but, no intelligible sound came from her lips. Bent over from cramps, she waived me out of the room with one hand. In my pajamas I ran to Guerino and breathlessly told him about Mamma. In his slippers he rushed to the nearest phone down the street at the butcher shop. He returned, running up the steps panting and puffing. "The ambulance will be here soon."

Together with *Mutti* I rode in an old, open-air ambulance holding her hand in mine. When we reached the hospital, the two attendants rapidly carried the canvas stretcher inside. One of the men stopped me at the door. "Wait here."

Through tear-blurred eyes, I watched as my mother's sheet-covered body, her face pale and her eyes unfocused, was carried down the corridor. I thought for sure my heart would stop ticking.

A nun, wearing a white habit and apron, arrived to escort me down a long corridor that reeked of medicine. With her hand on my back, she eased me into a small hall. "Wait here," she said. "Your mother has to be examined."

I waited for what felt like hours. While sitting alone in that quiet room, terrible thoughts ran through my mind. I was still a child, I had been forced to move three times. My papa was who-knows-where, all my possessions were left behind, and now I was about to lose my *Mutti*.

I was half asleep in the chair when a nun came for me. "Your mother has to remain here. She has had a gall bladder attack and must rest. Perhaps by tomorrow she will be able to go back home. I think you had better go now."

"Is she going to die?"

"No, no!" The nun reassured me with a big smile.

"Can I see her?"

"I'm afraid not."

That meant I wouldn't kiss my mother good night. "Can I at least stay here for the night?" I asked.

"No, little boy, there is no room here."

Reluctantly, I turned away from the good sister, who seemed heartless to me. As I walked out of that gloomy place, the tears I had tried so hard to contain now freely streamed down my face. As the fresh air hit my nostrils, unconsciously, I set my worries aside and hopped down the hill toward home. All around me were large fields overflowing with brightly colored carnations. Halfway down, I stopped for a moment to take in the view and allow the flowers' fragrance to fill my senses while the afternoon sun bathed my face.

Once home, my grim thoughts about Mamma came back to haunt me. What were they doing to her in the hospital? Would they feed her? I should never have left her there alone. Then I realized I too, would be alone that night.

Guerino prepared my dinner, challenged me to a few games of checkers, then helped me get ready for bed.

"You are a real friend," I said and kissed my friend good night.

Early the next morning, after a glass of milk and a slice of bread and butter not to be compared to the breakfasts my mother prepared for me, I retraced my steps up the steep incline to the hospital. Inside the clinic I spotted a clerk in the hallway.

"Do you know where I can find Signora Lifschütz?" I asked.

"Sorry. You'll have to ask a nurse."

I walked the full length of the white antiseptic corridor before I saw a nurse coming my way. "She is in room two-oh-one," she replied.

The room, also white and austere, was crowded with four white metal beds where only two should have been. A hand lifted from one. It was *Mutti*'s hand. She had seen me and was slowly waving me over. She looked so weak and pale and I could see she was still in great pain. I gave her a long hug and kiss. I still feared I would lose her.

"Why are you sucking on ice cubes?" I asked.

"They do not allow me to eat anything," she whispered.

With no chair in the room, I sat on the bed and reached for her hand. With her smile, she let me know my being there was of great comfort to her. *Mutti* motioned for me to come closer to her face. She had trouble talking. In a weak tone she reminded me of the German couple who would be coming to dinner the next day. She wanted me to contact them.

"Do they have a telephone?" I asked.

"No. You have to go to their house. Tell them what has happened." She halted. Her head sank deeper into the pillow. She looked so exhausted. My poor *Mutti*! "As soon as I get better, they will come to dinner again. They'll understand."

I sat up. "No," I said, "I'll make dinner. I can do it. Just give me some recipes."

A big smile lit up her chestnut eyes and spread over her pretty face. "You can't do that."

But she was much too weak to argue and argue I did.

Resigned, she said, "Get a pencil and paper." After some hesitation she gave me the recipes, more important, she showed how much confidence she had in me.

"Give me my handbag," she said, then asked for her coin purse. "Here is some money to buy the groceries." She stopped for a moment. "I'm sure Signor Grimaldi will go with you."

As I was leaving, she whispered a last warning. "Be careful not to burn the onions. They should be yellow."

The next morning, after my short visit with *Mutti*, Guerino and I went shopping. "What are you making?" he asked.

"German potato soup, *Wiener Schnitzel*, green salad, and fruit for dessert."

"You want me to help you?" he offered.

"Oh, no! I want to do it myself."

Fixing that meal marked the start of my fascination with cooking, and on that afternoon I did not visit my mother. Judging from the guests' comments, the Friday dinner was a great success and, filled with pride, I rushed to the hospital the next morning.

"Everything was delicious. Herr Gustaff and his daughter couldn't believe that I had cooked it by myself."

"I knew you could do it. Never doubted it," *Mutti* said.

Though she looked healthier, I was certain my mother had lost part of her mind. Normally, she would have said, "You couldn't do that." Oh, sure, no one was finer than her *Erichl* when she spoke to an outsider, but to me she withheld those sentiments. With all the love she showed me, she rarely expressed her confidence to me or complimented me directly.

When *Mutti* returned home a few days later, she was still weak and incapable of doing much. Taking care of her made me feel so grown up.

In the narrow alley across from our building was a small, dingy looking eating place where, for the modest price of fifty *centesimi,* the cost of a trolley ride, they served a brimming dish of boiled tripe. The semi-dark tavern, with a few old tables and old wobbly chairs, served nothing but tripe and was primarily a poor man's eatery. The patrons had to bring their own bread and wine if they wanted a full meal. Guerino took me along one day and offered me a taste of what looked like worms floating in a soupy tomato sauce. At the sight, I immediately lost my appetite.

"Come on, try one bite," he coaxed me.

"I think I'll just sit here."

I watched my friend as he ate the repugnant dish with such gusto. "Is this ever good," he murmured.

Guerino had reached his last few spoonfuls. The aroma of the tomato sauce, the grin of satisfaction on his face and my hunger pangs tempered my revulsion and gave me the courage I had lacked minutes earlier. "All right, I'll try one bite. A small bite, with only one worm."

He handed me the overflowing spoon. With eyes shut tight, I shoved it in my mouth. Ugh! I didn't know what to expect. Now, moving around in my mouth, that stuff didn't taste too bad. Without thinking, I bit into the tripe and after that, I knew little else in the world could taste as good.

"Well?" he asked.

"Not bad. Not bad at all. In fact, delicious," I had to admit.

When I told *Mutti* about my new discovery, she crinkled her nose and grimaced in utter disgust. "How can you eat such *chaserai* and rave about it? I make such delicious meals but you prefer garbage."

From that day on and whenever *Mutti* wanted to give me a special treat, she either prepared a *Wiener Schnitzel* or gave me the coins to buy a plate of tripe.

On June 21, 1940, France surrendered. Store owners all over town placed radios in their windows and outside of their shops. News bulletins blared, from time to time interrupted by a Fascist hymn. Victorious Mussolini signed an armistice with France and the whole country was exuberant.

Much to my bewilderment, when Mother heard the news, she began jumping up and down in the street. What was going on? She could not have wanted Mussolini and Hitler to win.

"How can you be glad that France lost?" I asked. "This means the Nazis will win the war."

"Maybe it will bring this horrible bloodshed to an end. Or maybe I'm just losing my mind and don't know what to hope for anymore. I just want this war to end. Maybe that maniac will allow our families to get back together and go back home. Maybe."

Even though I was a kid and understood little of what was going on in Europe, Mother's logic made no sense. I couldn't recall hearing that the war had ended, only that, based on what the Fascist radio told us, Italy had defeated France.

The celebrations continued for days. Men and boys wearing the customary black shirts and caps with the long dangling tassel, marched through town singing Fascist hymns.

Mother's initial elation turned to anguish. Unable to bear what was going on, she stayed home for days. "I can't stand going in the street. *Schatzele*, please do the shopping for *Mutti*. Here is the list. You can find everything at the vegetable stand." She handed me the piece of paper and some money. Holding my hand and caressing my cheek with her other hand, she added, "Erich, don't tell anyone what I said the other day," she whispered.

"What did you say?"

"That I was glad the war might be ending soon. I don't know what came over me."

Our quarters at the Grimaldis' were cramped. Though I had just turned ten, I still had to sleep in the same bed with my mother. Mother too, was unhappy about that as well as having to share the kitchen with the ever-complaining landlady. Conveniently, we had received a new sum of money from the parents of the Turkish student who was living at our hotel in Vienna. Now we could afford better housing.

After France's surrender, Mamma needed "a moral boost," she said. And so much to my distress, she started to look for another place for us to live.

"I found a beautiful full-sized apartment up on the hill," she whispered to me. "Not just a furnished room like we have here."

The thought of moving away from Guerino dampened my spirits. I wanted to remain with him. I would never find a better friend.

"You can come and visit. It's not that far," *Mutti* said.

Guerino tried to make light of it. "You'll find a nice girl and you'll get married."

My mood soon changed when I saw our new place. For the first time since we had left Vienna, we would have an entire apartment: living room, two bedrooms, kitchen, and bath. At last, nothing to share with anyone else! I would again have my very own room. Since we had only our clothes and a few accumulated books, the physical move was uncomplicated. Not so the emotional one.

Mrs. Grimaldi looked pleased to see us leave. Not Guerino. His deep-set gray eyes were moist. "Take good care of your mother and don't forget to come see me sometime."

"I will. I swear I will come to see you often. I still have to beat you at chess."

We never saw each other again. I met Mrs. Grimaldi on the street. She told me that Guerino had died a few weeks after we moved. I promised myself then I would never again swear to anything in my life.

9

Our New Home on the Hill

The small apartment house, standing alone halfway up the hill, offered an extraordinary view of the valley below. Looking out from our second floor balcony, I held my breath. A gentle breeze stroked my face as my eyes embraced the town below and the blue waters of the Mediterranean. Straight down I could see the two small gulfs forming part of the coastline, the fishing port to the right and the sandy beaches to the left. Turning left a bit to the north I could see the delicate rolling hills that became the majestic Alps, while to the right lay the fields of flowers gracefully undulating on smaller hills followed by streams that ran down to the beaches. This wonder prompted the local people to call San Remo the pearl of the Italian Riviera and had inspired Goethe to pose the question: *"Kennst du das Land woh die Zitronen bluehn?"* Across the street, a bit down in a valley, separated by a narrow creek and surrounded by several large fig trees, was the church of San Romolo. Farther down lay large fields of white, pink, red, and yellow carnations in bloom, one of nature's great works of art.

That first evening, before darkness set in, I stepped out on the balcony again to watch as scores of fishermen rowed out in their small boats. Bright-burning acetylene lanterns hung from the bows, while the sea reflected their glimmering rays.

"Are you going to stay there all night?" my mother asked.

"*Mutti*, you have to come and see." She joined me and we both admired what man and nature had laid out for us to enjoy.

Our little villa, as I referred to it, was neither ours nor a villa but a multifamily, three-story building. To the left, the road running in front of our home led to the main golf course and up the mountains; to the right, it snaked down the hill, past villas wrapped in lush tropical greens. At every straightaway the road intersected a cobblestone footpath, until both the road and the path merged and like two rivers flowing down the mountains, spilled into the market square of the town below.

The footpath, an endless sequence of wide cobbled steps smoothed from years of wear, was only a few paces from our villa. Every day I walked that path and soon learned to match my gait to the width of the steps so I could run rather than walk down. The same didn't work for the uphill climb, forcing me to do it at a much slower pace and with greater effort. But whether going up or down, the balmy weather, nature's gift to the region, made the hike a pleasure.

Many months had passed since Aunt Sally came to visit and brought the last news from my father.

"Can't you write to Papa?" I asked *Mutti*.

"Where do you want me to write to him?"

"To *Opapa*'s home," I said.

"Sure."

I didn't quite understand what that meant but did not persist.

Before summer neared its end, as I had learned to expect, Mother searched and found ways to have her little *Erichl* go to school.

Undaunted by the racial laws and ignoring my Jewish heritage, she enrolled me in a Catholic school where, in their zeal to keep sexes segregated, the nuns allowed boys to attend up to the third grade only. Though past my tenth birthday and old enough to be in the fourth grade, I was obliged to attend third grade.

Each morning, after the good breakfast my mother always prepared, I hopped down the uneven cobblestoned path to join the nun who waited at the corner of Via Roma, just one block from the market square. With each hand hidden in the opposite sleeve, this middle-aged, quiet servant of the Lord guided us down the long street. One by one the pupils joined the line until we reached the school, located about one mile away. The walk covered almost the entire length of the town and was an enjoyable way to start the day for it gave me a chance to talk to my heart's delight. And talk I had to or I would have exploded during classes. Though older than the other kids by at least one year, I got along well with my fellow schoolmates.

What disturbed me most about the school were the many crucifixes hanging from every wall. Had I not known better, if I considered misbehaving the message would have been, "This is what can happen to you."

The teachers, all nuns dressed in long, dark brown habits covered by a large white apron and wearing a matching head gear fashioned into a long cylinder, spoke in a soft whisper. They gave me the definite impression that this was the school I had always dreamed of. Here, the devil in me would be free to roam, my vivid imagination my only limit! On my second day I faced a rude awakening and grasped how appearances can be deceiving.

My teacher caught me talking during a lecture. "You will remain after class," the nun said softly. She had a kind smile on her partially visible face.

I had a good knowledge of punishments, having withstood my share of them, but staying after classes was new to me? "What will I do and how long will I have to stay?" I asked.

"We'll let you know." I was sure the nun had curtsied to me.

The smile on the nun's face was always there, almost as though it had been painted on. Otherwise, why would anyone smile when they were punishing a child? If I was being detained just for talking, what would have happened if I had pulled one of my really bad shticks?

By six in the evening, five hours after the last class had let out, a nun poked her head through the door. "You may go home now." The smile was still there.

I gathered my books and in the fragrant evening air, climbed the stony path on my way home. Having to stay after classes didn't bother me one bit, but I did worry about having to face my mother. With each step, I thought of a million excuses of why I was so late. Sooner or later she would find out the truth and so, once again to save my skin, I refrained from lying. Luck was on my side that night. Mother was already dressed and set to go out and, rather than dispense one of her more drastic disciplines, she simply sent me to bed earlier than usual on a very empty stomach.

I had tasted my mother's wrath a few times before. Once a year, almost like clockwork, after accumulating my transgressions and drawing a grand total, Mother would mete out her single punishment. As the fateful hour was approaching, she would utter in a wry tone, "I can see we are getting close to that time of year."

When I did something to break the thin thread of her patience, Mother used whatever tool was within her reach: a belt, the rug beater, even a broom were perfect to mete out her punishment. Mother was determined and efficient. First she locked the door and placed the key in her pocket, then she chased me through the house or under the bed. She would not give up until she had accomplished what she had set out to do.

The discipline I suffered in school didn't make me any less mischievous, only more cautious and restrained in the classroom. My newly found restraint might also have been inspired by a divine looking ten-year-old fourth grader, named Anthemis. I had noticed her as we were leaving school and remained captivated by her Shirley Temple look: long, silky blond curls falling about her lovely round face, dimples in her smooth cheeks, and large, deep, penetrating eyes. We were studying poetry at the time. I wished I could have written a poem describing how this angel looked to me.

For days I waited outside the school, hoping to attract her attention or perhaps earn a simple smile. When one day she stopped to talk to me, my tongue froze and the words I had prepared so carefully and for so long vanished, sending my first love affair into a fatal spin and leaving me with a tightening in my chest whenever our paths crossed.

Being in third grade gave me a distinct advantage. Homework was easier than if I had been placed in the grade where I belonged. Most days my assignments were finished soon after lunch, leaving me the afternoon to get into whatever mischief I could find.

Sugar, coal, sulphur, and potassium nitrate, someone told me, made a powerful explosive. Sugar and coal we had in the house, the other two ingredients I had to buy in a pharmacy. I went to a pharmacy.

"Potassium nitrate and sulphur," the pharmacist repeated. From his looks I knew he had guessed my sinister intentions and, judging my age to be less than that of reason, he sent me scrambling. "I know what you're up to, you little scoundrel. You're lucky I am here alone. Otherwise, I would grab you by the ear and drag you to the police." His shouting followed me the full length of the store.

I was out of sight before the echo of "police" could bounce off the wall. Being picked up by the police and thrown in jail would really kill my mother—unless she killed me first.

Buying the items from two pharmacies averted a repeat of my first experience. Next, I set out to find some fuse and a casing. With tension making my chest feel as though it were cast in cement, I entered a store that sold material for miners. When the clerk wanted to know what I was going to do with the fuse, I decided to make a fast retreat and slid out of the store.

Not one to easily be defeated, I found a good soul on the street who took my money and offered to buy the fuse for me. For casings I found spent shotgun shells in a nearby shooting range, then went to our cellar to prepare my creation. I pulled out the hidden shoebox containing the ingredients. First I smashed the coal between some old newspaper; the resulting fine powder floated in the air, coating everything in sight. With my hand I tried to clean the oily patina, but it adhered with even greater tenacity. Not wanting to be delayed by some dirt, I resumed the more important task of measuring the components.

I mixed the ingredients in a brown paper bag, a rare commodity in those days when groceries were wrapped in newspaper or placed in your own net shopping bag. Beads of sweat started running down my face. Could this explode in my hands? Gingerly, I set the bag on the concrete floor and took refuge in a corner.

When nothing happened, I packed one of the cardboard shells, placed a length of fuse inside the powder, and tied the end with a thin chord. Again, rivulets of sweat ran down my forehead, something was being pumped furiously into my blood, and my breathing had reached an unmanageable rate. I hesitated, trying to regain control.

Grateful that I did not run into Mother, I gathered the supplies, placed them back into the shoebox and put them all in a secret place. Box of matches in hand, I ran to the field where I had collected the used shells. With my bare hands I dug a hole and moving as carefully as a mother holding her newborn baby, I slid the bomb into it, gave it a little love pat, and packed dirt and stones all around.

In slow motion, my shaky finger pushed open the small matchbox

and reached for one of the skinny waxed sticks. From my toes to my head
I trembled. My whole shirt was drenched in cold sweat. Suddenly my
breathing, so fast moments before, stopped dead. Kneeling at the edge of
the hole, I lit the match. By now I was wound up like a compressed
spring. The small flickering flame that I held in my fingers searched for
the fuse, but my jittering hand needed my other hand to hold it steady.
Success! Caught by surprise and shocked by the flame's sudden swish, I
lost my balance and fell backward, the burning match still between my
fingers. Desperate to put distance between the bomb and myself, I rolled
over on my belly and furiously crawled on all fours. I had never been so
clumsy. My clothes stuck to my clammy skin and my body felt paralyzed.

Rolling onto my back, I waited. Nothing happened. I waited some
more. Why did that bomb not explode? I even considered digging the
bomb out of the hole, but visions of it exploding in my hands, blowing
off my fingers, and blinding me in both eyes flashed through my mind.

I reached for a branch laying close by and used it to pry out the
bomb. After just a little digging, the loaded cartridge, with several of the
stones, shot out of the ground and up into the air. Startled, I collapsed.
Panting, I stared at my creation lying two body-lengths from me.
Nothing moved, neither I nor it. With stupidity granted only to a ten-
year-old, I reached for it and with force clasped the bomb between my
trembling hands, hoping that by holding it firmly, it would not explode.

With the help of my faithful penknife, I slit open the fuse and
found that the thin filament, meant to carry the flame to the powder,
had broken. In the cellar, I replaced the fuse and rushed back to the
field and the waiting hole.

My clothes were still damp, but no new sweat was running down
my back. I felt like a seasoned professional. With a steady hand, I
packed the bomb back in the ground and lit the fuse. This time one
hand was sufficient to hold the match. Now I felt only curiosity.

I walked backward while watching the smoke from the tiny flame disappear. Little drums beat in my chest . . . but not for long. The blast outperformed my greatest expectation. The stones I had so carefully packed flew high, very high, as my body hit the ground in a rigid state.

When the shock wore off, I was happy to still be alive. What an accomplishment! The kind of news one shared with his friends, his neighbors, his mother. Oh, no. Not my mother. Lotte Szyfra Lifschütz would never understand and could do me more damage than any exploding bomb.

One day I was carrying a few of my bombs when two German sailors crossed my path. I approached them in German. "Would you help me explode these bombs?" I asked.

They looked surprised. After a short glance at each other, with animation they responded, "*Natürlich.*"

I handed each one a bomb and used their cigarettes to light the fuse. The three of us hurled the flaming devices across the stream. Waiting for the explosions, I tried to guess what my mother's reaction would be if she saw me exploding bombs with German sailors. I must have had a worried look because one of the sailors placed his arm on my shoulder.

"*Dass kann dir nicht weh tun,*" he said, trying to reassure me that the bomb wouldn't hurt.

For me, France's surrender brought an end to the war. Air raids halted and ambulances stopped bringing wounded from the front that no longer was. Few people owned a radio and, at ten, I wasn't much interested in the events that engulfed the remote parts of Europe. My life in San Remo had normalized, with school in the mornings and the afternoons left to spend with my friends or practice billiards.

Thanks to my mother's passion for bridge, I learned to play billiards. The billiard tables were off to one corner in the same room where the ladies played bridge. Mother wasn't happy about my hanging around at the *caffè* but said it was better than my roaming the streets. Many afternoons, when she joined her regular game at the small coffeehouse across from the city gardens, I tagged along, for had I gone there alone, the owner would have kicked me out because of my age. But when the unfriendly proprietor wasn't there, I often could find someone to sharpen my skills with or practice by myself.

School ended. The war, despite France's surrender and Mother's fleeting hope of a quick end, raged on. From what little I overheard, France's early capitulation did nothing to improve the fate of European Jews.

The news from *Omama* and Aunt Stefi had stopped. The Turkish student, who provided us with information on our relatives, wrote that he had lost contact with them and did not know what had happened to them. Nor had we heard anything from Papa since the German invasion of Poland. But Mother, always protective, tried to keep these painful facts from me.

"How come Papa doesn't write any more?" I asked.

"I guess the mail is bad because of the fighting. Soon we'll hear from him. You'll see."

That autumn Mother did not re-enroll me in school, for the nuns' sex-segregation rules prohibited boys from advancing past the third grade, which I had already attended. Instead, much to my surprise, since hoping for a bicycle in those days was tantamount to wishing for an airplane, my *mammina* bought me a bicycle as a belated birthday gift.

The day the three of us, Mother, the bike, and I, walked out of the shop. I wrapped myself about her neck. "Oh, *Mutti*, I can't believe it. I will be the best son any mother has ever had."

"You already are. I want you to promise me that you will be extra careful when you ride in the street. Promise?"

"I promise."

"I also want you to promise me that you will not lend the bike to anyone or leave it alone in the street. Remember what happened in

Vienna?" She was reminding me of the time I had lent my brand new scooter to a total stranger. It had never come back.

"I remember. How could I ever forget? I only had it for a day."

I had never ridden a bicycle and now I owned one. Shiny black, the bike was the envy of any boy who knew me and big enough to last me for the next two, three, or even four years. But for now, not yet tall enough, I could not sit on the saddle and pedal at the same time. Yet nothing could stop me from riding it, not my lack of balance nor the many falls that created a number of minor scratches on my bike and major ones on my knees.

The previous year, a rich friend from school had invited me to go to a soccer game. I was thrilled to get a free ticket, but because I didn't have the money for the car fare, I had to run alongside the trolley car with my friend riding in it.

Another day, when Prince Humbert of Savoy, the son of the reigning king of Italy, came on an official visit, my bike afforded me the thrill of riding alongside his motorcade. I was riding so close to his open convertible that I felt I was part of the royal family.

I even dreamed of one day riding my bicycle the full length of the Riviera, but the time I tried to pedal toward Genova, I discovered that my legs didn't yet have the strength my mind had given them credit for. I also remembered my promise to Rina, but riding to Milan after my failed trip to Genova was completely out of the question.

Since none of the boys I knew owned a bicycle, I had no one to ride with for fun and so used the bike for transportation only. San Remo enjoyed a rich variety of seafood, which the sparkling Mediterranean yielded generously. At a street-stand near the port, I had often seen people ever so gently hold a raw oyster between two fingers, drench it with lemon juice, and slurp it down with obvious pleasure. As I saw those raw, rubbery, slushy things disappear down the people's throat, I felt the chill follow the same path down my own spine. One afternoon, with a friend, I stopped at an oyster cart. "Let's have some," my friend said.

"You're crazy," I answered.

My friend seemed challenged by my refusal and would not stop pushing me. Finally I succumbed and, with eyes closed and two fingers pinching my nose shut, he saw me swallow my first oyster. I was glad the thing was drenched in lemon juice to disguise whatever flavor the sea may have given it. I waited for my body's reaction. But to my great shock, I enjoyed the spineless glob slithering down my throat.

"That wasn't bad!" I said. Then I searched my pockets for more change to buy one more.

Our time in San Remo was a happy period in my life when I enjoyed an almost normal childhood. We had stopped wandering, and I began forgetting the upheavals of the previous three years. The town was small and in a short time, I had gotten to know every corner of it. Even when not going to school, I filled my days with a variety of activities.

This peaceful life came to an unforeseen and sudden halt the day, when coming home for my midday meal, I found our apartment in disarray. "What's going on?" I asked.

"We must pack fast. We are leaving in two days." Mother's face showed the stress I heard in her voice.

I was baffled and convinced Mother had decided to disrupt my life one more time. "Where are you taking me this time?"

"I don't know."

"Why don't you know? How will we get there?"

"They will let us know when we are ready to leave."

"Who are they?"

"The police."

Police! I felt my knees buckle. "We haven't done anything," I said.

Then it flashed through my mind. Oh, my God! They found the

bombs. Did Mother know? What would the police do to us? What would *Mutti* do to me? All day I pondered whether to confess and throw myself at her mercy or force my tongue to remain idle. I left my meal on its plate, for I had lost my appetite. Nor did I sleep for two nights. I couldn't help feeling that my own stupidity was going to punish us more than Hitler ever could.

Mutti asked me to gather my belongings so she could decide what I could or could not take. What to do with the bombs? I certainly was not about to tell my mother or take them with me. What other choices were left? Could they explode by themselves? I didn't know. After much inner delibera- tion, I decided to leave my arsenal where it was, hoping someone would find it before it, together with our beautiful little villa, created a fireworks display.

Mother told me about the notice she had received to go see the police commissioner. "For almost two years this man has let us remain here, ignoring German orders. I hope nothing happens to him. He was funny. He said something like by sending us away, Mussolini would no longer be threatened by criminals like us."

Too tormented by once again having to pack and leave, I paid little attention to what my mother had said.

A plain-clothes detective came on the day we were to leave to help place our luggage and my bicycle in a taxi and accompany us to the train station. Much to my relief, no one said a word about the bombs. As the cab negotiated the sharp curves of the serpentine descent, fresh emotions of sadness overcame me at the thought of leaving this delightful town and yet another home.

"Where are we going?" Mother asked.

"To a town in the province of Avellino," the man replied.

"And where is that?"

"South of Naples. Nice country, *Signora*. My family comes from around there."

It was June 1941.

10

Internment

For the fourth time in little more than three years, I was being forced to go where I did not want to go. Although this time I did not cry, not sure whether I had matured or just become hardened by experience, I'm unsure, the move raised similar emotions. I started to love San Remo. In school and in the park I had made many friends and even gained some status and now was being taken again to some unknown place where I didn't know anybody and I would have to start all over again. When was all this going to stop?

Looking at the bright Italian countryside slip by and watching passengers getting on and off the train at the numerous stops helped lessen the anxiety during the hot afternoon hours. But all that night, sitting in a third-class compartment, on a hard, dirty wooden bench, made sleep impossible.

Mutti offered me her lap. "*Erichl*, put your head here."

"No. I'll be fine."

The detective stayed in the corridor, smoking near the open window till the morning light. He did his job. He had prevented our escape off the fast-moving train.

After long stops in Rome and Naples, we arrived at noon in Avellino, some twenty miles south of Naples. A porter took our luggage off the train, placed everything, including my precious bicycle, on a large cart and wheeled it into the street.

"Oh, I'm so relieved this detective is taking care of everything," Mother said.

Our escort hailed the lone taxi sitting outside the terminal. The cabby, holding the door open and, using one hand on the steering wheel, pushed the vehicle the short distance to where we were standing. As the car rolled up, he hopped inside with only half his body to pump the brake pedal. After a short ceremonious greeting directed to my mother, he loaded our belongings, some on the roof and the rest inside the cab, leaving less than enough room for the three of us.

My two-wheeler was still leaning against the terminal while we were ready to leave. I was frantic. "What about my bike?"

"It must come later, there is no room on the taxi," the policeman said.

I was not willing to leave my bike there. "I'll stay here with it."

My mother talked to the detective. There was no other solution. He would arrange for the bike to follow the next day. It would be safe. He would make certain of that.

The taxi was not just old, it was ancient, its parts held together by rusty wires and frayed cords. The driver's door stayed shut thanks to his elbow holding it so. I noticed the many cracks in the age-worn canvas top and was thankful it was a sunny day.

The journey to Ospedaletto d'Alpinolo, less than five miles up a graded, dusty, and unpaved mountain road, took more than two hours.

The clunker's slow speed contributed to the delay. but the main causes were three breakdowns and the countless times the engine just quit, unable to take the uphill strain. Getting it restarted was not a simple task, since the electric starter did not seem to have a part of the original design. Instead, dangling from the front of the engine was a partially rusted metal crank that required all the strength the small cabby could muster to give it a half turn. Starting the engine also required an additional person to stop the car from rolling down the hill, for the hand brake had long become a useless metal grip which the driver made no attempt to engage.

While pressing one foot on the brake pedal, the driver fished out a block of wood from under his seat. With deference, he said to the detective, "*Commissario* can you put this under the back wheel? I don't want our lovely lady to end up back in Avellino." He snickered as he tipped his beret to my mother. It was like a scene from a movie.

Our escort took the wood and wedged it under one of the rear wheels. "I'm only a detective, not a police chief," he said.

Each breakdown brought out a series of invectives from the driver, most of them directed at Italy's head of state. "*Quel benedetto Mussolini!*" He removed his cap and used his arm to wipe the sweat off his forehead.

What for us was an annoying experience seemed to be an everyday occurrence for this driver. By then I was too tired to care. It was boiling hot at midday on that dusty road, but I was sure Mother's perspiration was due less to the heat than to her restraint from making comments.

"Close your eyes, *Hasele*, and try to get some rest." She placed her arm on my shoulders and caressed my hair. I could feel her heavy breathing.

The poor quality of wartime gasoline caused carburetors to clog up with regular frequency and, while the driver may have been annoyed, Mother was incensed, especially when, after asking how far our destination was, she was told we could have walked the distance in less time than it took to drive. "I'd just as soon start walking," Mother said.

"*Signora*, we'll get there soon. Don't worry. You're much too pretty to worry." The driver spoke in dialect.

Tired, dirty, and hungry, we arrived at our destination, hoping our ordeal had finally come to an end.

The detective had told us he was going to spend time with his family. Now, his assignment almost completed, he looked eager to leave. With the taxi driver, he lifted our trunk and suitcases off the cab and set everything on the street at the entrance of the *carabinieri* headquarters. "I have to make sure I place you in the good hands of the local police officer, Signora."

At the sound of the car stopping, a *carabiniere* stepped through the heavy wooden doors. He looked as though shaken from a deep sleep and not yet awake. Our detective approached him, and after exchanging more gestures than words and handing over our documents, he wished us luck, made a respectful bow and left us standing, a bit baffled, on the narrow road.

People's heads peeked out windows and doors. Our arrival must have been a newsworthy event for this small village. A group of boys of various ages, dressed in rags and without shoes, had followed the broken-down taxi from the moment it entered town. Curious, they now stood near us. More than anything, their filth caught my attention. The dirt that had accumulated on these boys was greater than I had ever seen on anyone before. So encrusted with it were their bare feet that their skin had the appearance of hardened leather.

"*Mutti*, did you see the feet on those boys?" I asked in German.

"It's disgusting. Keep an eye on them while our things are in the street."

The *carabiniere*, entrusted with his new charges, was wide awake now. He invited us to come through the small inner door, cut out from the heavy wooden portal, then motioned to two boys in the group. "Take the luggage and bring it inside. Now!" he commanded.

"I'll wait till everything is inside," my mother said.

"*Signora*, trust me. I will take care of it. Eh! Let's go, fellows. Hurry!"

Instead, Mother waited until everything was securely inside. I looked at her watch; it was 2:30. We had not slept the night before and the two-hour taxi ride had left us exhausted.

We followed the policeman through a dirt courtyard and into a small office that was badly in need of paint.

"*Signor maresciallo, sono arrivati i nuovi internati!*" The man announced the arrival of the new internees to his superior, who was stretched out on a wooden armchair, wearing regulation dark trousers with red stripes down each side, a gray shirt with visible sweat stains under his armpits, a loosened black tie, and suspenders. The officer must have been sleeping, judging from how slowly he responded to the news.

During a few minutes of silence, I glanced around the room. A jacket and cap hung from a nail on the wall not far from the pictures of Mussolini in full uniform, King Victor Emanuel, and the queen. A variety of round water stains made the dark wooden desk look out of place in a police station. A coffee shop would have been a more appropriate place for it.

The man, rubbing his eyes and yawning, lifted himself from his stretched position. Extending his hand to Mother, he introduced himself. "Maresciallo Marchetti. At your service." He had placed more emphasis on his rank of *maresciallo* than on his own name.

"Please sit down." He pointed to the lonely chair facing his desk. Before my mother could do so, he pulled out a handkerchief from his trousers and hastened around the desk to wipe the dust off the chair. The once-white handkerchief appeared to have seen much more use than washes, for the white appeared only in isolated spots.

Reading from the documents the *carabiniere* had handed him, the *maresciallo* moved calmly back to his desk and flopped into the dilapidated swivel chair. Only for a short moment, when attempting to read our name, did his body show the mind's concentration by stiffening upright. "Welcome to Ospedaletto d'Alpinolo, Signora . . . Lifaschutz,"

"The name is 'Lifschütz,'" my mother corrected him politely.

"So sorry, Signora . . . Lif-sch-utz. If you ever need anything, I want you to know we are here at your service."

"Thank you. That is very reassuring." My mother said.

The *maresciallo* settled back and read from some worn sheets he had pulled from his desk drawer. These were the rules.

"I am embarrassed to have to read this to you. But orders are orders," he said, I'm sure you understand. "You are not allowed to leave the hamlet's limits unless you ask for a permit. You must be in your home by twenty-two hours. We overlook it sometimes. You understand, *Signora*?" I thought I caught a wink in his eye.

"Do you think I could talk to you about these rules at some other time?" my mother asked. "We have not slept all night and we would like to find a place to stay."

The man showed a genuine sympathy about our plight. Apologetically, he said, "Of course, of course."

He opened the top drawer of his desk, replaced the sheets he was holding, then pulled out another slip of paper and handed it to Mother.

"What is this?" Mamma asked.

"A list of the families who have rooms to rent."

My mother scanned the paper more than once. "I don't see addresses."

"You won't need addresses, not in Ospedaletto. Just ask anyone and they'll direct you. I'll show you how to get to your first place."

With some effort, for his girth was somewhat in the way, the man lifted himself from the chair and, bowing in respect, pointed his arm toward the door. He followed us out then, hurrying around Mother to walk ahead through the courtyard. *"Signora, posso?"* His hand extended, he helped my mother step over the high metal threshold and through the smaller door in the portico.

"Signora, watch out for the boys," the *maresciallo* warned. "They may follow you. They may want to carry your luggage. You leave it here for now; once you find a place to stay, have a couple of boys pick them up." Then, standing in the middle of the narrow road with his legs planted wide apart, he pointed us in the direction of the first house on the list.

In spite of the elevation and the time of year—it was only June and Ospedaletto was 2,200 feet above sea level—the summer heat was brutal: 35 degrees centigrade (95 degrees Fahrenheit) and salty sweat streamed down our faces. The dust combined to the steep incline of the gravel road and the oppressive heat made each step a strain.

At the first stop, an old woman dressed in black with a head scarf of the same fabric responded to our knock. She wore no shoes and her feet resembled the dirty feet I had seen on the boys outside the police station.

"The *maresciallo* told us you have a room for rent," said Mother.

"Oh yes, yes. Come in. I have a beautiful, redecorated large room. Just beautiful." She spoke in heavy dialect, difficult for me to understand.

As we entered, I passed by the old woman. What a smell! Behind her back, I pinched my nose and Mother almost cracked up. The woman, unaware of what I had done, ever so slightly pinched her own cheek with two fingers and gave them a partial twist.

"Forgive me, *Signora.* What did that mean?" Mother asked.

"What?"

"What you did with your fingers on the cheek." Mamma imitated the woman's gesture.

"Oh, that! It means *bono o bellissimo*."

We walked through the kitchen into the short hallway and to an open door. "Here, just look at this." She pointed to the room with the pride normally reserved for priceless family heirlooms.

I looked. None of her adjectives applied to that room, not unless 'beautiful' referred to artwork created by the watermarks on the ceiling and "redecorated" alluded to the scores of cobwebs adorning each corner of the four walls.

Mother smiled at the old woman. "Oh, yes. This is a beautiful room."

I couldn't believe she said that. That was a beautiful room? Was my mother losing her mind?

"I've had some important guests stay with me."

"Oh, I can see why," Mamma said. "We will be back."

"You won't find anything this nice in Ospedaletto," the woman called out as we were leaving.

Once out of the house, I asked, "Did you really think that was a beautiful room?"

"*Eyn stick dreck,*" Mother said.

"*Mutti*, you just called her a piece of dirt."

"I had to tell her something."

I felt so relieved hearing those words. *Mutti* had not lost her mind.

My mother showed the list to a woman sitting in front of her house. "Do you know where this lady lives?"

"Just up the street, the third house from the barber shop."

Here also, an old woman, dressed in black and barefoot, showed us a room. "Oh, yes. *Il Signor maresciallo* knows I have the best room in town. I have a beautiful, large room that was just redecorated." The room was clean. But as to beautiful, one needed a fertile imagination and as to redecorated, that must have happened many years before, maybe even before my mother was born. It began to look as if only old women dressed in black, barefoot and using the same adjectives, had rooms for rent in this village.

"Where is the bathroom?"

The woman hesitated. She looked puzzled by the request. "Oh, the toilet," she corrected. She walked down the corridor, stopped, and turned her shrunken, stooped body. Her head was twisted as it peeked from under an arm. "Come with me." Through the air, she formed a large semicircle with her hand.

At the far end of the dark hallway, overhanging the side of the building, was the toilet. The woman removed a piece of wood to allow the door to swing open by obeying the laws of gravity. I was behind my mother when the putrid smell escaped from an open hole in the cubicle's floor and made a violent collision with my nose. Mother took two steps backward, placed one hand over her nose and, depending which part of her face you saw, displayed a frown or a smile.

Then, with a grunt, she asked, "How much are you asking for the room?"

"Forty lire. And this is a real steal. Nobody will rent you a room for so little."

Mother had already retraced some of her steps in the hallway, trying to distance herself from the horrible smell. "Oh, I know. You don't have to tell me. Everything is so expensive nowadays. I must decide and will let you know."

"Maybe I can give you a small reduction," the woman said.

Mamma pulled me by the hand and, rushing to escape the woman's body odor, we slipped outside. The old woman followed us and, just like the first woman, she called out in a mixture of local dialect and Italian, with a threatening ring, "You will find nothing like this in Ospedaletto!"

"I surely hope so," Mother whispered.

"You're talking under your mustache," I said.

Mutti got a kick whenever I referred to the delicate, blond fuzz visible above her lip. She gave me a love tap on the head and we both enjoyed a short laugh.

"I'm sure. The room is very beautiful," she lied. "We will be back when we decide."

Then, turning to me, she said in German, "I thought the stench was going to kill me."

Having always lived in cities, moving to a small village had been an intriguing thought. But I was getting more discouraged by the minute. "I don't want to stay here. I want to go back to San Remo."

"We can't go back, *Hasele*. We have to stay here. I don't like it either. Every one of these places stinks."

I was about to ask why we had been sent here when Mother's words flashed through my head. "Because we're Jewish. Just because we're Jewish."

We spent almost two hours covering the rental list. This had to be a conspiracy, I thought. From one house to the next, nothing changed. Every room had the same austere look, a wash basin on its own stand, a big crucifix over the bed's headboard, and an outhouse hanging from the side of the building. None of the houses had running water although, thank heaven, they did have electricity.

After our third stop, the prospect of finding a room we would have the courage to rent had greatly dimmed. "Even in my own backward little *shtetl*, Nadworna, we didn't live like this," Mother said. "Our servants had better rooms."

We asked a woman on the road if she knew of some place in town with running water. There was only one house that had running water and she directed us to the Dello Russo residence.

We retraced our steps and, despite the steep incline, quickened our pace. A house with running water! We were anxious to test our luck and see if the people would rent us a room. By now our nostrils were stuffy with the fine dust that our steps raised. We trudged by the police station and reached the top of the narrow road. There, to the left, we saw what we guessed to be the house. The freestanding three-story stone building, encircled by an elaborate wrought iron fence, faced the village's large piazza and the municipal garden. Its appearance was palatial compared to the houses we had seen so far.

At the rich-looking massive portal, I lifted the heavy metal knocker and let it drop against its plate. It made a hollow sound as if only emptiness lay behind. Soon I heard the rusty sound of a key turning in the lock and the squeaking of the oil-hungry hinges. A young, barefoot girl pulled open the heavy door and greeted us. The entrance opened into a long stone archway, then into a courtyard. Mother asked to see the lady of the house.

"*Venite*," the girl said, inviting us to enter. "*Un minuto, Signora*," she added before leaving us standing.

In one glance, Mother took in the whole floor. "This is nice!" she whispered to me. "Oh, Erich, I hope they will rent us a room."

A woman in an untidy house dress and with disheveled hair came down the stairway to greet us. Wearing house slippers that only partially concealed her dirty feet, she looked better than the women we had seen earlier. She did not wear black and that was a pleasant change. With her outstretched hand that had accumulated dirt under her fingernails, she welcomed us in good Italian.

"*S'accomodi, Signora*," she said, using the popular expression for "make yourself comfortable." Then she shook hands with us both.

A broad smile on her face, she made a useless gesture at fixing her unkempt hair. Then, running her hands down her skirt to try to either smooth out the wrinkles or wipe away the grease spots, she added,

"Please forgive the way I look. I didn't expect company. How can I help you?"

"We just arrived this afternoon and I have come to see if you would rent us a room. I understand you have running water. Is that true?"

"Oh sure, sure. We do have running water and a vacant room. We have never rented it, but I can show it to you."

We climbed two flights of the circular marble staircase. The gold leaf-decorated plaster on the domelike ceiling lent, in spite of the many cobwebs, an air of elegance. Through the open doors I could see the large, well furnished rooms. "Could we see the bathroom?" Mamma asked.

"*Il bagno?*" The woman repeated, as though puzzled by the request.

At least she did not call it a toilet, which was a good sign

"Of course, but don't you want to see the room?" I realized my mother had already decided she did not need to see the actual room. This was a royal palace compared to anything else we had seen in the village. "I'm sure it will be just fine. Your home is so elegant. We had an elegant home once. It just seems so long ago."

At the top of the stairway the woman led us down a long, well-lit hallway, where at the far end she opened a door. "Here you are, *Signora.*"

Mamma's face brightened. For the first time in more than twenty-four hours, she was looking at a modern bathroom. Bidet, wash basin, toilet, and bathtub. They were all there. Even I rejoiced at that sight.

But what was that black stuff filling the tub to the rim? Coal! Optimism turned to incredulity. "What is coal doing in the tub?" Mother asked.

"Oh, nobody takes a bath. Too expensive, you know. All that water and you have to pay to heat it. So it's a good place to store the coal." The woman had a strange glee on her face, perhaps expecting Mother to recognize her cleverness for having put dead space to a practical use.

As we walked down the stairs, *Mutti* was silent. I could tell how disillusioned she was. At the foyer my mother thanked the lady and shook hands with her.

"I would certainly love to rent from you, Signora Dello Russo. How much are you asking for one room?"

"I will have to speak to my husband and will let you know," the woman said.

It was getting late and we did not have a place to rest. As we left the large house and walked into the square, we saw the sun about to set behind the mountain. The time was a little after five and soon it would be dark.

"I didn't expect we would have such a problem," *Mutti* said.

A man directed us to the next address on the list. The house was just up the street from the ex-mayor's home, but our steps lacked the optimistic bounce they had had when walking toward the house with running water.

We approached a small white building and found a clean home and an amiable landlady happy to show us around. The room she had to rent was spotless, perhaps even redecorated and nicer than anything we had seen so far. The furniture was plain but in good condition. We were tired, so Mother did not ask to to see the toilet.

"I like you, Signora Antonietta. How much are you asking for the room?"

"Fifty lire. If that is too much, I may take five lire less."

Mamma looked overjoyed and, without hesitation, made her decision. "That's just fine. I believe we'll be happy here." She looked at me. "We'll take it, Enrico."

11

Getting Settled

Antonietta Matarazzo looked older than her thirty-two years. Perhaps it was the old-fashioned country hairdo—gathered in a tight tress and rolled into a bun—or the dark-colored, plain dress that added years to the women of this village. She wore wooden *zoccoli*, reminiscent of the Dutch shoes. *Zoccoli* served well inside the house and out, summer or winter yet never wore out, for the wooden soles were thick enough to last a lifetime.

"Where is your luggage?" asked Antonietta.

"It is at the *caserma dei carabinieri*," Mother replied.

Antonietta walked to the front door. "*Che vulite?*" she asked the two boys standing outside, who had followed us since we left the police station. While shaking her outstretched fingers in admonishment, she ordered the youths to get our suitcases. "And hurry up!"

It took the boys two trips. The last suitcase secured in our room, Antonietta gave them a few lire. "It's better I take care of them," she explained. "These thieves will steal the eyes from your head."

Before the day was over and, in spite of her lack of sleep, Mamma had found a place for most of our belongings. The suitcases, only partially emptied, I shoved under the high brass bed. The dresser Mother decorated with a crocheted doily from our home in Vienna. A small vase arranged with wild flowers, courtesy of Antonietta, added a smile to the room. Only the large cross, prominently hanging over the bed, did not belong in our bedroom. For Mamma this created a big dilemma.

"I don't know what to do with this? I don't want to sleep under it."

"I'll sleep over it, if that will make you happier," I offered.

"Oh, stop it," *Mutti* said smiling. "I'm serious. I'm afraid to take it down. It might offend Signora Antonietta."

Exhausted, we let practicality win over conviction and left the crucifix in its place. Earlier than usual and without eating, I fell into a deep sleep.

When I awoke the next morning, Mother, as was her custom, was already up and out of the room. The sun struggled through the narrow slits of the French shutters. The thin rays formed a geometric pattern on the wall, giving the room the look of a still-life painting. It felt good lingering in bed after a good night's rest.

From the corner of my eye, I caught a glimpse of something moving on the wall not far from my head. With a jump I sat up. A dark brown animal, the length of a cigarette pack and with an erect tail that doubled its total size, was crawling on the white wall. Scared by the sinister-looking creature, I let out a shriek.

Mother came running. "What is it?"

I pointed at the threatening form on the wall, making sure my finger remained at a safe distance. "Look!"

From her gaze, it didn't take me long to realize she was not going to be of any help. I couldn't tell who was more afraid, me or *Mutti*. Taking away my only protection, Mother yanked the covers off and jumped back. "Get out of bed."

Attracted by the commotion, Antonietta peered into the room. "Anything wrong?" she asked.

"What is that thing?" Mamma asked.

"Oh, that? It's nothing. It's just a small scorpion."

"A small scorpion?" I repeated. "What does a large one look like?"

"Well, they get to be two or three times that size, sometimes larger."

The sight that terrorized both my mother and me did not bother our landlady at all.

"Do they bite?" Mamma asked.

"They don't exactly bite," Antonietta replied. "They sting with their tail. People have been known to die of the poison." All the while our landlady kept her eyes fixed on the scorpion. Then, with one of her wooden shoes in hand, she hobbled up to the head of the bed and delivered a mortal blow to the pest, which curled on itself as it fell to the tiled floor behind the brass headboard.

As though other options were available to me, I announced, "I'm not sleeping here again."

Antonietta left the room and quickly returned with broom in hand to sweep the dead body from under the bed.

Ospedaletto d'Alpinolo was infested with many insects, spiders, and other more or less repulsive inhabitants. These creatures were part of everyday life and townspeople accepted them. Flies and fleas were harmless though annoying and we soon resigned ourselves to their presence. But mice, lice, scorpions, and cockroaches we just couldn't handle.

"How are we going to live with these horrible beasts, Mamma?" I asked.

"*Non so, ma ci dovremo adattare.*" Mother usually spoke to me in German, for she didn't want me to forget my mother tongue but, when I started the conversation in Italian, she generally continued in the same language.

"I'd like to see you get used to mice," I said. Mamma was terrified of rodents and, no matter how small, the mere appearance of a mouse turned her into an Olympic high jumper.

In so many ways, Ospedaletto represented a step back in time. Life in this isolated village was not set in 1941, but rather the way it must have been at the end of the previous century in other parts of Italy. Superstition ruled people's lives. Except for the ex-mayor's home, no other home had running water. Just the simple act of washing our faces took us back to the past. And although electricity was in almost every home, electric outlets were a rarity.

After my dramatic encounter with the scorpion, I was faced with a new dilemma: I had to relearn how to wash myself. Antonietta had filled a carafe with fresh, cool mountain water and placed it alongside a ceramic basin sitting on its own stand. I poured some water into the bowl and stood there baffled as to what to do next. Should I wash my hands, then use the dirty water to wash my face, or should I do it the other way around without knowing if my hands were clean enough for that task? For no rational reason, I decided to wash my face first.

I found Mamma in the kitchen. She was elated. Antonietta had invited her to use the clean and well-equipped kitchen. It was good to enjoy Mother's breakfast, after which I ventured out.

The air was crisp from the night's coolness but fast warming in the bright sun. The day would soon become another scorcher. I stood at the door, wondering for a moment which direction to take. Then down the two house steps I jumped, turned left, and walked about one hundred yards to the town's square.

Italian villages and towns, just like cities, all have a central piazza and a separate municipal garden where a monument to fallen soldiers or a statue of Garibaldi or of one of the kings of the house of Savoy stands. In Ospedaletto the piazza and the garden were one and the same and no statue had ever been erected. Except for a few wooden benches, a *boccie* field, a sculpted stone water fountain, and several large trees, the park was bare.

The clear stream of uninterrupted flow from the mountain, spurting from the fountain's single lion head, sent out a tempting invitation. The water was ice cold, sparkling clear, reflecting the purity of the surrounding nature. Holding my fingers under the fast-moving stream I tasted the droplets. Hastily, I cupped my hands to drink the water and the more I drank, the more I craved it. My thirst refused to be satisfied. To bring my mouth near the gush of the precious gift, I clambered up and half-sat on the edge of the narrow stone that was the fountain's cradle. Only the arrival of a young woman, who had come to fill a large vessel, made me jump off to make room for her.

The fountain in the main square, Ospedaletto.

She rested a large copper cauldron on the metal grate. This was heavy, judging from the thud it created. The fast rushing water quickly filled the container. While the vessel was filling, I watched the girl twist a large rag around one hand to form a ring, then position it on her head. She was small and surely not more than three or four years older than I. How was she going to carry that heavy container? To my great surprise she slid the filled vessel onto one hand, tipped it to spill off the surplus water and, with a twist of her body, lifted and positioned the container on the curled rag she had placed on her head. Her legs spaced apart to gain balance, she grasped the vessel's handles and stabilized it. Then, with her back erect and a distinct rhythm, she waddled down the dirt road, letting her bare feet absorb the full brunt of the pebbly path. Soon the girl was lost in the distance.

More women and girls came to the fountain to fill their containers, but on that morning I never saw a man carry more than a small pail. As soon as the fountain was available, I gulped down a few more sips of the refreshing gift of nature before setting off to explore the village.

I hopped down the steep, dusty, gravel street that cut through the heart of the village. The road was narrow, just wide enough for a horse and buggy or a small passenger car. Every one of my hops raised a puff of dust and shot the sharp feeling of each stone through my leather sandals, adding to my admiration of the skill needed for the girl to balance that heavy load barefooted.

Located at midpoint between Avellino and the monastery of Montevergine, Ospedaletto d'Alpinolo was bordered by dense chestnut forests on two mountainsides. The other fringes overlooked a vast valley embracing the provincial town of Avellino below. A sign, posted on the first house at each end of the village read: "Ospedaletto d'Alpinolo, 725 msm 1825 pop" (725 meters, or 2,200 feet above sea level, with a population of 1,825).

The road formed a twisted shortcut from one end of town to the other. Passing by the *carabinieri* station, I was comforted to recognize a familiar sight. Down the incline I passed the boarded stores and the open barber shop, where a row of colorful strands of wooden beads, extending the width of the entrance, hung from ceiling to floor. I peeked inside.

"*Buongiorno.* What are these things for?" I asked, pointing to the hanging beads.

Their constant swaying helped keep flies out, I was told. Similar beads hung from the *caffè* and other shop doorways.

I was struck by the sameness of the two-story whitewashed houses joined into one continuous chain. Unlike San Remo's, Ospedaletto's houses all looked alike. The only difference was in their outside colors, which ranged from dull white to dirty gray.

My hopping brought me to the small piazza in the village center, where the church stood. There, the road turned ninety degrees to the left before ending at the edge of town.

In less than an hour I had covered the village from one corner to the other. The large bell atop the steeple, reverberating in my ears, signaled 10:00.

Just as the raising of the theater curtain signals for the action to begin, so the clang of the bell awoke a flurry of new activities. A barefooted boy about my age swung open the *caffè* doors, then untied and let drop the multicolored beads. Slipping inside several times, he carried four timeworn tables and several chairs out into the square. Women flung open the shutters of the surrounding homes and using flexible tree branches, they beat the dust out of blankets, pillows, and rugs.

The cobbler, in black pants, white shirt, black open vest, and an apron, brought out his small work stand that held all the nails and tools of his trade.

Curious, I waited to watch the man set up shop. He reappeared again carrying a three legged stool and a pair of unfinished shoes stretched over wooden lasts.

Straddling the stool, the man looked up at me, mumbled a greeting, and commenced his work. Holding one wooden last between his thighs, he placed a handful of small tacks in his mouth and, one by one, fed the tiny nails to his fingers. He stabbed each tack into the leather, while the hammer, in a well coordinated motion, pounced on the nail, hammering it into the awaiting shoe just as the fingers nimbly slipped out of the way.

"My name is Enrico. We've just come to Ospedaletto," I said.

With his mouth full of nails, he could only grunt and shake his head.

When his mouth had released the last nail, I asked, "Do you make many shoes?" I had asked my question just in time, for he was ready with another batch of tacks in his hand.

"Only when someone orders them. Maybe six, sometimes even ten pairs a year. I do mostly repair work. New soles or heels."

I needed to make a real effort to understand the man's dialect. "Are there other cobblers in town?"

"Oh, yea." He began to laugh. "One guy thinks he is a shoemaker." He laughed some more. "Every time he repairs someone's shoes, they come to me to get them fixed right."

Absorbed in the conversation and in watching him work, I didn't realize how much time had elapsed until the church bell rang eleven times.

"*Arrivederci!* I'll see you soon," I said.

I walked by the *caffè*. A priest had just sat at an outside table. "*Vieni qui!*" a voice called, asking me to approach them.

I pointed at myself. "Are you calling me?"

"Yea, yea. Come here. What's your name?" the priest asked.

I walked up to his table. "Enrico. What is your name, Father?"

"Don Pasquale. I'm the monsignor. I've never seen you before. You're new here, aren't you?"

"Yes. My mother and I arrived yesterday. We came from San Remo."

"Where are you staying?"

"At Antonietta's. I don't know her last name. She has two daughters."

"I know who you mean. Matarazzo, eh?" He looked for approval from the men at his table. "Well, welcome to Ospedaletto. I hope you will enjoy your stay with us and I expect to see you in church for communion."

"I'm sorry, Father, I don't go to church. I'm Jewish."

A surprised look appeared on his wrinkled face. "Oh. I will want to talk to you soon."

I left the priest and continued my one-legged hop down the hill. At the bottom the road formed a T with the road that came from Avellino. There, facing me, was another fountain. Quickly I bounced across the road eager for another taste of that fresh icy gift of nature. A boy more or less my age approached.

"Who are you?" he asked in heavy dialect.

"I'm Enrico. What's your name?"

"Totonno. What are you doing here?"

"Oh, we just moved here. How old are you?"

"Twelve," he said. "And you?"

"Eleven."

The barefoot boy looked ragged, with dirt that clung to his skin like what I had seen on the urchins the day before. Afraid of offending him if I left, I continued to talk. "I'm walking around to get to know Ospedaletto. I've never lived in a small town. I just met Don Pasquale. He's a nice man."

"He's a sonovabitch."

Realizing the priest was a bad conversation topic, I changed the subject. "How many people live here?" I asked.

The boy shrugged and answered with an obscene phrase: "*Che cazzo ne saccio?*"

I was at a loss for words. Rarely had I heard such crude language and certainly not from the mouth of someone my age. His reference to a man's genitalia shocked me. The church bell signaled the half hour and saved me from a difficult moment.

"Oh," I said, as though the bell's toll had meant something. "I must be getting home. *Ciao!*"

I followed the uphill road the taxi had taken the day before. Forming a wide ring around the village and marking its outer border, the carriage road reached the top near the main square. There it leveled off and separated one small section of Ospedaletto from the rest of the hamlet. On the smaller side of the village, just at the foot of the mountain, was the municipal garden and Antonietta's house.

"Well, what did you learn?" *Mutti* asked.

"I saw the shoemaker working in the square. You should see him. He puts all these nails in his mouth so he can have them ready when he needs them. And Mamma, I drank the water from the fountain. This is the best water I have ever had! You must try it. I'll take you there this afternoon. I also met Don Pasquale. He is the monsignor. He told me he wants to see me in church. I told him right away that I was Jewish and he shouldn't wait for me."

"That's fine. I want to hear more later, but now wash your hands. Please speak in German. I don't want you to forget it. Signora Antonietta has invited us to lunch."

The combination of mountain air and the missed meals during the last forty-eight hours had given me a lion's appetite. So I was relieved when I entered the kitchen and a delicious aroma filled my nostrils. On a clean wooden table waited a large bowl of pasta and on the stove was a pot with a cut of beef cooking in the sauce.

Mamma wanted to know more about my exploration. I told her all about the young woman at the fountain, how she had lifted the heavy container onto her head and carried it barefoot on that pebbly road.

"They start when they are little. Girls all have to help at home," our landlady said.

Antonietta and my mother hit it off from the beginning and her two daughters, Raffielina, one year older than I, and Maria, one year younger, became my friends.

The next day we planned to stop at city hall to register. I had passed the municipal building on my discovery tour. A simple structure, not any different from the others around it, the building housed city hall, the Fascist club, and two private offices.

"I'll take you there, *Mutti*," I said, proud to know something my mother did not.

City hall consisted of a single room where portraits of *Il Duce* and the king and queen were prominently displayed on its white walls. Don Pepe DePetris, dressed in a dark suit, white shirt with frayed cuffs, and black tie—the only person there—greeted us with a friendly smile. The room was so hot, I wondered how the man had not already fainted. From his heavily wrinkled face I guessed he was old, much older than my mother. He must have known we were coming, for our papers were laid on his disorganized desk.

"*Buon giorno, Signora* Lif-a-schutz." He too struggled with our name.

Don Pepe was genuinely happy to see us. "I love when you people come here to speak with me. Oh, how I wish to have been born in the big city and gone to the university. Dealing with the ignorance of a small village is so depressing. I will never understand why you people are being sent here. Oh, pardon me. I don't mean any disrespect. On the contrary, I think it is terrible that a fine lady like you, *Signora*, should have to stay here. Most of the people who have been staying here as guests of Signor Mussolini are too educated, too refined for a place like Ospedaletto. I wish I could get out of here, but for me it's too late. I'm almost seventy-four years old. Where could I possibly go?"

Mother seemed to be in a hurry, for she had been looking at her watch and giving hints that she wanted to leave, but the talkative man did not seem to notice.

"I'm supposed to make certain you follow all the rules set down by those imbeciles in Rome. They also want me to read all the mail you fine people receive every day. Can you imagine? I should read the mail of so many people? Only idiots can think up such foolish regulations."

It was obvious that he relished poking fun at the Fascist government. I refrained from smiling.

"I am curious," Mamma said. "How many *internati* are here in Ospedaletto?"

"About seventy," he responded. "All wonderful, cultured, and highly educated people."

The church bells rang for the second time. We had been there close to an hour, and the man would have kept us there longer if Mother, as politely as she knew how, had not interrupted him. "I hope you'll forgive us, Don Pepe, but we have to leave. We have made other plans. Maybe we can get together again soon."

"Of course, of course. I'm so sorry I've kept you here so long. I enjoy talking to educated people like you. I hope we will have other occasions to speak again." He handed Mother the list of dos and don'ts and, from his expression of disdain, even I could tell he was not about to enforce any of them.

"But you will have to report to the *carabinieri* twice daily," he added with a wink. "If it were up to me, believe me, *Signora*. . . ." Holding his open hand level to his mouth, he gave his index finger a symbolic bite and threw the hand in the air. "I have nothing to do with that."

Reading from the sheet she had been given, Mother discovered we would be paid a monthly subsidy.

"Look here," she said. "I will be getting two-hundred-seventy lire a month and you will get fifty lire and they will give us fifty lire for rent as well. I had worried how we would manage."

"You come here the first of the month and I'll have the money waiting," Don Pepe said.

On the walk home from city hall Mamma changed her mind. "We'll start reporting tomorrow," she said.

So on our fourth day, we arrived at the *carabinieri* station by 9:30, where we found several *confinati* already standing in line. We were to report at 10:00, which, as experience would soon prove, had no resemblance to reality.

A lone *carabiniere* stood at the small door. The building was not any different from the other houses in the village: a large portal with a small door cut within it, two windows on each floor, and one balcony jutting out above the entrance.

The woman ahead announced herself to the man at the door, "Runia Kleinerman."

As she turned to leave, she noticed us. "Oh, you must be our latest arrival," she exclaimed, with a distinct Polish accent.

Mother's face broke into a bright smile. She had not spoken Polish since our days in Milan, three years before. "You're Polish?" she asked.

"Yes. You too?"

That's all I could decipher, for the rest of what they said got lost in the ardor and rapidity with which they spoke their native language.

"Who is next?" the *carabiniere* asked. The two women did not realize they had blocked the door.

Runia led my mother to the open gate. "*Prosche*," she said.

"Lifschütz, Lotte, and Enrico," my mother announced, then turned away and followed her newfound friend up the hill. "Is that all?" Mamma asked.

"That's it," Runia replied.

It didn't take long for us to see that the process of reporting to the *carabinieri* was nothing more than a farce.

When we reached the main piazza, three internees were standing at the corner—the *internati's* customary meeting point, I soon learned.

"This is Lotte Lifschütz," Runia announced. "Oh, yes and this is her son . . . what is your name?"

"Enrico."

"And this is Enrico."

We met William Pierce, John Howell, and Paula Alster. Within minutes, other internees arrived and Runia introduced us to everyone. We met her son Giorgio, Agnese Caine, and the Spaechts. What a mixture of nationalities: British, German, Austrian, Polish. The sound of the church bells, less disturbing to my ears at that distance, marked 10:00 and, without a word from anyone, the group began their walk. Only Miss Caine with her handsome brown British setter did not come along.

From here the group would leave for a leisurely walk down the main road. About two hundred yards past the square, this road split, the right fork led up the mountain to Montevergine and the left down to Avellino.

"Up?" John Howell asked.

"Fine," some voices answered.

June was a great time for these strolls, because only during that month did the small wild strawberries ripen beneath the low bushes shaded by the branches of the tall chestnut trees. On those morning walks I learned the true meaning of aroma. Nothing could match the fragrance and taste of the tiny berries we discovered growing in those woods.

I also learned how to find the fruits missed by others. Instead of looking while standing erect, I brought my head close to the ground to seek under their protective leaves for the small aromatic berries that others had missed.

In the beginning I felt out of place in the midst of all those adults. Everyone was wrapped up in some political or philosophical discussion while Mother and her new friend enjoyed loosening their tongues in Polish. Though six years older, Giorgio Kleinerman was the only person even close to my age. I tried a conversation with him.

"Do you collect stamps?" I asked.

"No. Do you?"

"Yes." I tried another tact: "What do you like to read?"

"I like Schopenhauer," Giorgio answered. "I also like Cicero and Plato but haven't been able to find any of their work. What do you read?"

Cicero, Plato, and Shoppe . . . what? I never heard those names but was too proud to say so. I thought hard and fast what to answer. "I read a book on wild animals. It was fascinating."

"Only human thoughts are fascinating," Giorgio said.

Did I detect an air of superiority? Because Giorgio wouldn't come down to my level and in no way could I rise to his, I never got to know him well. But as I became more acquainted with his mother, Runia, I concluded that I liked the pleasant woman from Lodz, who was often willing to include me in her conversations. Not a sharp word ever came from her mouth. What a contrast there was between my mother and Runia. *Mutti* an emotional volcano, temperamental and openly affectionate, Runia sedate, reserved, and even-tempered. Considering our displaced lives, when most of us craved a warm embrace or a friendly kiss, Runia was satisfied with a simple hand shake or a light kiss on the cheek.

Giorgio, too, rejected any form of affection. In my impetuous manner, I tried to put my arms around him one day. He pushed me away. "Please don't do that," he said in a distinct yet slight Polish accent.

Runia wanted us to meet her parents, so one afternoon Mother and I were invited to have tea and cake and make their acquaintance.

"This is Enrico," Runia introduced me. "You may speak to him in German and call him Erich."

I shook hands with both her parents and was struck by how much taller Mrs. Rozental was than her husband. I thought the man should always be taller than the woman.

"Are you studying anything?" the lady asked.

"Not yet. We just arrived here, but I am sure my mother will find something for me."

"Do you like to read?" Mrs. Rozental asked.

"I love books."

"Well, if you wish to borrow any books, feel free."

I was watching Mr. Rozental. He had said nothing and, after our introduction and handshake, he had gone back to the table. Mrs. Rozental must have noticed my stare. "My husband is engrossed in translating books from Italian into Polish. It's good mental exercise."

Even at my age, looking at the large selection of German, Polish, and Italian books on their shelves, I realized this family, from son to mother to grandparents, was an intellectual group.

That afternoon Runia showed us photographs taken in Poland. She also brought out some taken at her husband's funeral. I was surprised to see pictures of that event.

"How did you get out?" Mother asked in Polish. She had spoken slowly enough for me to understand.

Runia's response was more than my limited knowledge of that language could grasp. Later, at home, I asked Mamma what Runia had said.

"She, Giorgio, and her parents were able to escape in 1940, a few months after the German occupation. They were smart. They left, not like your father, who traveled there instead." It bothered me that whenever Mother spoke about my Papa she did it in a negative and bitter tone.

Of all the internees, Runia had the most extensive wardrobe. Her costly clothes—I heard my mother make a remark to that effect—were more matronly than stylish. Her severe hairstyle and lack of makeup also added years and gave her a professorial appearance.

Sleep in Ospedaletto was placid. The nights were cool and peaceful and each morning when we walked down our narrow road that lead to the main piazza, the still cool, clear air caressed our senses. A right turn took us past the corner where the two roads crossed and to the *carabinieri* station for our first reporting of the day.

Usually by the time we reached the meeting spot, people had begun to show up. But no matter what time we arrived, William Pierce was always the first one there. His wrinkled face, large bulbous nose, raspy voice, and abrasive demeanor made liking this man somewhat difficult—at least on our first meeting. But our restricted living environment brought us in close and regular contact with our fellow internees and as I got to know William Pierce better, I realized why it was so difficult to like him. He was, without doubt, an unlikable character! He had found himself interned in Ospedaletto because of his British name, he still used William rather than the Italian Guglielmo. Yet his ardor for the Fascist government and unwavering faith in Mussolini made his presence in our midst a unique source of controversy, debate, and scornful jokes.

Someone else who always arrived early at the assembly site was John Howell. English by birth, John had lived in Italy most of his life. Here he had married, raised his family, and managed his glove manufacturing business. In spite of his thirty or more years away from England, John was still the perfect model of the English gentleman. Just short of six feet, straight-backed, slender, a meticulous dresser, with long fingers and well-manicured nails, he carried himself with unmistakably upper-class elegance. His hair, too, parted on one side, had a distinctive British look and was a radical departure from the Italian men's custom of greasing their hair and combing it straight back. Even his flawless Italian sounded distinguished. John never raised his voice no matter how heated the conversation. Not even during an emotional game of *boccie*, when everyone became excited over their own good throw or the opponent's bad one, did John lose his composure. Every time a player landed a perfect hit and the rest of us either cheered or cursed, John would calmly say, "That was a fine throw. Well done!"

One morning Mother and I arrived earlier than usual. Only William Pierce, wearing his customary gray pants, gray vest, and black wool jacket, was there. After the conventional polite handshake, something one did with all members of the group whether you liked them or not, Signor Pierce tried to start a debate with my mother.

"Have you been following the news? I believe the war will be over in less than a year. What's your opinion?" he asked.

My mother, evidently reluctant to reply, busied herself running her moistened fingers through my hair and removing some imaginary dirt from my clothes.

"Don't you think so?" he asked again.

"Well, that would be fantastic, but I doubt that Hitler and Mussolini will be willing to surrender so soon." I knew my mother well. This man had picked the wrong adversary.

He grimaced, then laughed. "Surrender? I don't think you understand. How can you possibly think that our Duce is going to surrender? Mussolini would never have declared war unless he was
convinced of the righteousness of our cause. He won every war in
Africa and he will win this one, too. Mussolini is the greatest leader
Italy has had since the Roman Empire."

"Tell me, Mister Pierce, what is this righteousness you're talking
about?"

He looked baffled by the question and groped for an answer.
"Well, both Germany and Italy need more territory for their people."

"So it is your opinion, then, that any country with too many
people has the right to invade its neighbors. And when Mussolini
invaded Ethiopia he did it so that millions of Italians could move to
Africa? Is that what you are saying?"

"Certainly not. But in Germany's case this is justified since they
are looking to regain only the territory they had before the Great War."

I knew my mother's sense of sarcasm and saw it coming. But she
also loved an audience and was willing to wait before holding this man
up to ridicule. One by one, the internees came and stood silently, not
wanting to interrupt the spirited debate.

Mother, with careful design, dragged out each word. "Oh, I see.
Austria had been part of Germany before 1918. I almost forgot. Poland
was also part of the German empire. You remember, Signor Pierce, the
German empire, don't you?"

A perplexed look invaded the man's eyes. "What German empire?"

"Yes. What German empire?" Mamma mimicked.

"*Boh*?" the man grumped.

"The empire with all these territories you speak about. And of
course Russia was also a German province."

"You don't have to take everything literally," the man stammered.

"If I don't take it literally, how should I take it?"

Runia, though composed, was thrilled. She turned to the others. "Well, Signor Pierce. You have met your match. Let's give Lotte a hand."

Everyone joined in a subdued applause. I stared at Pierce. Nothing fazed this man, neither the argument nor the applause. Was he that dumb? With fingers in his two vest pockets, he fidgeted with his watch in one and the gold chain in the other. The church bell struck ten. William Pierce pulled out his watch and pushed the button to open the lid. Tilting his head toward the shoulder, he crinkled his face. The group commenced its march while he placed the watch back into his vest, then trailed behind looking preoccupied as though trying to gather his disoriented thoughts.

Runia took my mother by the arm. "Maybe he'll stay by himself."

The elder Spaecht came up to me and grabbed me by my arm. "Your mother is something. I enjoyed how she put this guy in his place. Were you born in Poland, too?"

"No, I was born in Vienna."

"We are also from Vienna." He looked pleased to have found a compatriot. "When did you leave?"

"In 1938, just a few days after the Germans came."

Mr. Spaecht, whose wife and daughter we had already met, walked in silence for a few steps. His dark, much-wrinkled skin, slightly stooped posture, and receding hairline made him look more like the grandfather than the father of his twenty-year-old daughter, Suzie. I calculated that Suzie must have been born when both parents were already quite mature.

One afternoon, my mother, chatting with Runia and her parents, commented on the Spaechts' conversion to Catholicism. "Many Jews were afraid to be persecuted, but they didn't run to be converted," she said. "So look what happened even after they got *geschmat*. They ran away to Italy just like we did and ended up here with us." Mother sounded angry.

My mother had a deep-rooted awareness of her Jewishness while the Spaechts had shed theirs without really embracing any other faith. "*Zey zindt keyn fleysh un keyn fish*," *Mutti* said, neither meat nor fish.

It never ceased to amaze me how easily my mother made friends. Though she only finished high school, she could hold her own in any conversation. She spoke seven languages, five fluently, and her unique sense of humor was a magnet that attracted the other internees. Of the many friendships she struck up, her most intimate friends became the Howells, Runia, and Clara Gattegno. Mother also grew fond of Paula Alster and became her protector.

Paula was a pathetic human being. Born into an affluent Polish family, she attended school in her native Poland, then was sent to Austria and Italy to study there. Yet, in her late twenties, she was incapable of completing a sentence in any one of the three languages. Her excuse for not speaking Polish was that she had left the country at an early age. German she forgot because she had moved to Italy, and her poor Italian was due to her short residence of only ten years.

She was a "good soul," as my mother often said, but a "stupid good soul," as someone corrected her. On a few occasions when someone made a derogatory remark about Paula, Mother came to her defense. "Say what you wish. If somebody needs anything, Paula is always ready to help." And because my mother felt compassion for the simple woman, we were often subjected to Paula's company. She ate with us several times each week, not as an invited guest but as one who managed to conveniently show up at the right time. Referring to Paula's frailty, Mother wondered whether the woman ever cooked a meal for herself or ate only when invited to someone's home.

Once she showed up at dinnertime for her customary unannounced visit and Mother asked her to stay.

"I didn't come to stay for dinner," Paula said meekly.

"That's all right. I never mind if you stay for dinner."

Paula was ecstatic as she tasted the small dumplings in the chicken soup. "*Dass ist incredibile*," she said, in a sentence that was half German and half Italian. Then, pointing to the small flecks of dough floating in the soup, she asked, "*Wie heist das?*"

"*Auflauf.*" *Mutti* said.

"You have to tell me how to make those little . . . what do you call them?"

"*Auflauf.*"

"*Auflauf. Auflauf,*" she repeated.

Two days later at our morning reunion, a visibly excited Paula proudly announced that she had made chicken soup with "*Einlauf.*" There was a sudden explosion of loud laughter from those who understood German and knew that *Einlauf* meant "enema."

In a period of our lives when there was little to laugh about, Paula Alster provided us with some hearty laughs.

On another occasion, Paula asked Mother for the recipe of a cake she had tasted at our home. A simple recipe: pound cake with jam filling. The next day Paula came running to report that the cake was not a success. Yes, she did follow the recipe, step by step. Yes, she put it in the right pan. Yes, she put it in the oven for 35 minutes. No, it was terrible.

"What was wrong with it?" my mother asked.

"It was just like when I put it in the pan, soft and running."

Mother fell silent. All at once I saw an illuminating ray on her face. "Did you heat the oven?"

Paula looked as though coming out of a fog. "Heat the oven? You didn't write that on the recipe."

Mutti hugged the woman. "It's my fault. I should have told you about the oven."

Paula's physical appearance matched the lack of her intellectual grasp. Much too thin for her five-foot three-inch frame, day after day she wore the same black dress with the missing belt. Her long, free-flowing and disheveled hair and her lipstick, partly applied to the lips and partly not, gave her a pitiful appearance.

Paula loved to stand in a manner that gave the impression that nature had handed her two left feet. She had the uncanny ability to cross her legs above the knees and under cover of her dress, place the right foot where her left should have been and vice versa. The first time I saw this strange sight, I stared at her feet, certain she had placed the right shoe on the left foot. Only when she walked away from her spot, after having disentangled her skinny legs, did I realize Paula did have one right and one left foot. But true to my teaching, I made no comment. *Mutti* invested much time and effort in teaching me to be sensitive. For her the most important quality in a human being was character.

"Learn to be a *Mensch,*" she would say.

On Sunday, Antonietta and her daughters dressed for church. The girls' hair, combed with motherly care into chignons, looked lovely. Antonietta's hair, freed from her daily kerchief, was combed back, tied into a tight, shiny bun, and covered by a short, black veil. Her home-made dress fit well over her proportionately plump frame and the *zoccoli* had been replaced by a pair of old-fashioned, nice looking, lace-up, high-heeled shoes.

"Are you going to church?" Antonietta asked.

"No, we are not Catholic," Mamma replied.

"Oh, what are you?"

"We are Jewish."

There could not have been a greater expression of shock on the poor woman's face had Satan appeared to her in person. She made the sign of the cross and invoked the name of the Holy Mary.

I could tell Mother was refraining from breaking out into laughter. "Is something wrong with what I said?" she asked.

"Oh no, no, no, no. I just have never seen a Jew. All I learned in catechism class is that Jews were responsible for killing our Lord." As these words escaped from her mouth, her expression changed. I could tell she was troubled by what she had said. "Where will you be praying?" she asked.

My mother was touched by the woman's concern. "We'll pray right here. God is everywhere. We don't have to go to church."

Antonietta embraced my mother for a long moment and left.

The landlady's ignorance of our religion was typical of the townspeople who, because of their prejudices, regarded us as foreigners intruding into their lives. A few of the villagers did befriend some internees, but most kept their distance.

For a few short instants, church bells broke the serenity of the morning. I ventured out to look at the brilliant sky and watched the undisturbed butterflies and the birds flitting among the tall trees. What a glorious day! Not a soul anywhere. The workers at the lumbermill had extinguished the fires of the large boilers and the strident noise of the saws had ceased as if everyone had heard the godly message and wished to preserve nature's tranquility. This serenity was a new experience for a boy who had come from the city. Wandering through the deserted hamlet, passing shops boarded up by dark green wooden shutters, I had the uneasy sensation of being the only living soul in a long-dead village. The sudden apprehension hastened my pace and down I rushed the steep-sloping road that lead to the church.

12

Religion in Our Lives

The three-hundred-year-old village church stood in the center of Ospedaletto d'Alpinolo. Perched at the top of a slight elevation above the town square, it faced the caffè where Don Pasquale spent most of his leisure hours playing scopa or briscola, two classic Italian card games. The steeple, midway between the town's highest and lowest point, towered over the houses as a constant reminder to the townspeople of the Divine omnipresence.

Just as I approached it, the bell struck twice to mark the half hour. It was 11:30 and the church's massive wooden doors swung inward to allow a stream of happy-looking people to emerge. As was the custom in Italy, the crowd was mostly men and children, as the women had attended an earlier mass and now were home preparing the traditional Sunday meal. The people descended the incline leaning back to slow the involuntary speed the steep slope added to their steps. Men wore their Sunday's best: a black suit—some with matching tie, others without one—a white shirt and a black hat or cap. No one in the crowd looked familiar until I saw Antonietta, Raffielina, and Maria.

"Going home?" I asked.

"Sure. Coming with us?"

I joined them up the shortcut, a narrow and cobbled alleyway with wide steps reminiscent of the footpath in San Remo. The four of us cut through the center of the village and, after crossing the main road, we found ourselves a few paces from home, where Mother had prepared a Viennese dinner for our landlady and her girls. For the three of them this proved to be a new experience, for they had never had a meal without pasta. As usual, Mother's culinary talents won them over.

As we sat around the kitchen table, I remarked, "It looked so deserted this morning when I went through town, I was really glad to see all the people come out of church." Then I asked: "How come everyone was so full of smiles?"

"They think by confessing they have been pardoned for all their sins, including the ones they contrived while being in church," the older daughter answered.

Her mother reprimanded her. "That's not nice."

"It may not be nice but it's true," Raffielina said.

One midweek morning, while no one was in sight, I ventured inside the dark church. Laid out in the form of a cross, its walls were mostly barren and reflected the village's poverty. Each step echoed in the large, hollow chamber, adding to its feeling of emptiness. Adorning the otherwise austere altar was a large portrait of the Madonna and child. As I admired the painting, a sparkle caught my eye. Moving closer, I saw the glitter emanating from the Madonna's necklace. At that instant, Don Pasquale emerged from the sacristy.

"Hello, Father."

"Hello. What is your name?"

"Enrico."

"Oh, yes. You are the Jewish boy. I remember."

"Father, is the jewelry on that painting real?" I asked.

"It sure is. The Madonna deserves real jewelry."

I stood in awe. Real jewelry on a painting? That was new to me. Walking through the church I had noticed something else that was new to me: silver miniatures of human limbs decorating the walls.

"What are all those legs and arms hanging from the walls?" I asked.

Don Pasquale placed his arm around my shoulder and, with an encouraging smile, said, "Come, I'll show you."

He guided me to one of the walls covered from end to end with hundreds of silver replicas. "These are gifts from people who received a miracle from the Holy Mother." Pointing to a miniature leg, he said, "For instance, this man was born with a crippled leg. When he was miraculously cured, he ordered this amulet and dedicated it to our Queen of the Church."

"What do the silver eyes mean?" I asked.

"Those are from blind people who regained their vision. We prayed directly to the Holy Virgin and she performed the miracles."

To regain one's sight or be able to walk again? This was more than just a miracle! Not being Catholic, I had not been taught to believe in such miracles. Nonetheless, I was intrigued and, excited by what the priest had told me, back home I related Don Pasquale's stories to my mother. I made sure not to sound too impressed for fear of upsetting her.

"*Mammina*, you have to come and see these things. They are beautiful. And that necklace I would love to give you one like that."

She let out a deep sigh and shut her eyes. "Maybe when you get bigger, you'll be able to buy me jewels. As for miracles? Oy! What nonsense. You know we don't believe in miraculous healings."

On our third Sunday in Ospedaletto d'Alpinolo, Mother had been invited to play bridge at the Howells'. I had not been invited to play, but not wanting to stay by myself, I went along anyhow. Their son Jimmy, whom I had met during one of our morning strolls, was home and I jumped at the opportunity to get to know him better. Towering a full head above me, he had a long, somewhat lazy gait and hair parted to one side, like his father's, which gave him a British appearance. His fingernails were so well shaped and groomed I was prompted to ask him if he had given himself a manicure.

"Not at all." He seemed irritated by my question.

"Do you have any games we can play?" I asked.

"Not really. I may play bridge."

"Why don't you try a game of checkers or chess?" his father asked.

"I don't feel like it."

John Howell said something to Jimmy in English; then he and his son left the room. When Jimmy returned, he looked resigned and annoyed. "Do you know how to play chess?" he asked. His tone gave the unmistakable impression that he hoped I did not.

"Sure, I know how."

From the stoic look on his face I could tell he wasn't thrilled to waste his time with a boy two years his junior. After I checkmated him three times in a row, grudging admiration showed in his eyes, and eventually we became the best of friends.

Late that afternoon, on our way home, Mother and I made our required second stop at the police station to report that we had not yet escaped. Through the small window, cut out from the heavy portal, peered the caretaker's eyes, nose, and mouth and with a vaguely disgruntled "*Bene, bene*," she acknowledged our presence.

"This is the biggest farce I have ever seen," *Mutti* said. "She is the cleaning woman and I'm sure she keeps no records. That's typical."

"Typical of what?" I asked.

"Government."

Some days at the morning gathering, someone I had not met before would pop up. New people were a source of great excitement and interest. For my mother and the other adults it was an opportunity to exchange old experiences from their homeland, depending on where the internee came from. For me it was a chance, slight as it might be, to encounter someone who would enjoy my company.

Agnese Caine, a British subject, was interned with us in spite of having lived in Italy all her life. Unassuming and somewhat reserved, she seldom walked with the group because of her swollen legs but often came with her dog just to say hello. She had a pleasant personality, a cheerful smile and, I soon realized, a large heart. Though I never got to know her well, I spent some afternoons with Agnese and, after learning how she devoted her time and energies, realized why we saw so little of her.

Though internees, deprived of their liberty, often regarded Ospedaletto as forgotten by man, the village was remembered by the thousands of swallows that returned every year. And the birds brought a spirit of freedom to us who had lost our own. Local urchins, not burdened by school or obligations, amused themselves by destroying the nests birds built in the trees, dragging out the newborns, then leaving the helpless little birds to die. Miss Caine told me that once she had seen a baby swallow die on the pavement in front of her window and from that day on had assumed the role of savior for the poor feathered creatures.

She converted her one-room apartment into a hospital crammed with the tools she needed to fulfill her mission. In this time of austerity, when so little was available, her clinic was well supplied. She told me how she had pleaded for donations from the pharmacist and the two local doctors and managed to fill a box with cotton and obtain salves to prevent infections and eye droppers to feed the little nestlings.

One afternoon while visiting, I asked her, "Did you ever study to do this kind of work?"

She had not but, because of her good work, many of the wounded birds were rehabilitated and, as she said, "saved from having to go to animal heaven before their time."

I drew inspiration from this kind woman by watching how she dedicated herself to her small friends. "Will you help me, please?" she asked once. "Hold this little fellow on your lap. He still needs to be fed with the eye dropper. He is less than a week old."

Tiny and not yet fully feathered, the fluffy bundle trembled through the thick wrappings. Miss Caine filled an eye dropper with a liquid paste of flour and water and reached for the little bird in my hands. "Thank you. I'll take him now."

With great concentration, she allowed only one small drop at a time to fall into the open and eager beak. "In a week or so this fellow will be able to eat worms and flies."

Her words shook me out of my spellbound state. Flies were a common occurrence in everyone's home and I was certain she had no problem finding a sufficient supply of them.

"Where are you going to find worms?" I asked.

"Oh, you and other friends will help me find them."

"Me?" I asked. How disgusting. But who could have resisted her captivating smile? The following week, when she asked me to find her some worms, I hesitated but only a bit.

When Miss Caine came to the internees' meeting corner, she often related her bird episodes. Just as these same people shared her sadness when she reported that one did not survive despite her loving care, so did the *confinati* rejoice when a bird regained its freedom.

During one of my visits, on a day when spring had melted winter's snows and the rich scent of wild flowers and pine trees filled the air, I shared an almost magical experience. A swallow appeared and landed on her window sill. Pecking on the glass, the bird attracted our attention. Miss Caine's eyes widened in disbelief and her voice choked with emotion. "I recognize him. I cared for him last year. Oh, my God, I don't believe it!" She looked as though she was going to faint. She opened the window and the small migrant, without fear, flew straight onto her shoulder. She reached for the bird, cupped it into her hands and with motherly tenderness brought it, unresisting to her lips for a kiss. For a few more moments she held the little bird, then placed it on her shoulder, from where, after a few chirps, it took off to fly out the open window. I will never forget the glow on the woman's face or the gleam that seemed to radiate from the bird.

"Does this happen often?" I asked.

"No. This is the first time." She was still trembling with joy. Weeks later, I asked her if the bird had ever come back. It had not.

One of the internees, Isidor Grüner, kept mostly to himself. I saw him when we first joined the morning walk. He was a frail man and few knew anything about him. The times I saw him during our stroll, he chose not to join the group at the corner but caught up to us along on the road. He never smiled nor spoke to anyone. He simply followed in silence, seemingly content to be near the group. I would have liked to speak to him but was too shy to do so.

We had been in Ospedaletto less than a month when Mr. Grüner brought tragedy into our midst: We had to cope with his suicide.

"To think we've run from the Nazis," Mother remarked. "Yet even in this remote place, the evil of Nazism can reach out and take its toll."

Mr. Grüner was deprived of the *Kaddish*, the traditional Hebrew prayer for the dead, because in keeping with Jewish religious laws, none could be recited for someone who had taken his own life. Signor

Wovsi, a senior internee, was considered an authority on Jewish matters. A meeting was held to seek a way to allow a proper Jewish burial, instead, in an ironic twist, the man had to be buried in the only available resting grounds: the Catholic cemetery.

Within the first few weeks I realized that religion played a major role in the villagers' life and not just on Sundays when most everyone attended mass. Going to church may not always have been a sign of religious conviction, for it was a way to avoid being criticized by the village busybodies, plus it gave young men a chance to make eye contact with the available young women.

Holidays—and there were many—presented an opportunity to participate in the religious cortége. They also provided the townspeople a form of escape from their daily doldrums. On those days, the more faithful gathered in church to watch the wooden statue of the Holy Mary being draped in a red mantel with a white fur collar, before being placed on a wooden platform. The crowd waited for the Virgin outside the entrance at the top of the small hill above the central piazza. From there the procession made its start and the heavy platform holding the holy statue was paraded through the village, carried by ten or more devotees. Always at its head was Don Pasquale, two altar boys, the mayor, a clarinet player, a trombonist, a horn player, and a drummer. The handful of instrumentalists, in their funereal black suits, hats and ties, seemed more intent on demonstrating how loud they could sound rather than on how well they could play. But their inability to play the right notes at the right time and their lack of musical talent added a measure of humor to the otherwise solemn event.

The column followed the circuitous narrow road through the village. Up the hill to the municipal gardens, right for a few hundred yards to the last house, then back and down the main road until it met up with the narrower way leading back to the church. The cortége passed by every house as though having the obligation not to leave out any of the inhabitants. As it wound itself through town to the irregular beat of the cacophonous sound, more and more people attached themselves to its tail. Children followed, hopping to the erratic rhythm. For many others, a procession was an excuse for a walk, for leaving one's chores for later, or for exchanging gossip with people other than their immediate neighbors.

As much as I wanted to join the march, I chose to keep my distance and never once joined in a procession.

For the first time in three years, Mother had no need to guess the dates of our High Holidays. That year, thanks to Signor Wovsi, we were able to observe the New Year according to the Jewish calendar. Clutching her worn and precious prayer book, Mother and I, as well as several of our religious brothers joined the Wovsis for services at their apartment.

An Orthodox Jew, Mr. Wovsi conducted all religious services. He had a hard time obtaining the necessary *miny'n*, the minimum of ten men required to perform a religious ceremony. Although more than ten Jewish men were interned in Ospedaletto, not all were observant and willing to attend a religious function. Thus, when there were fewer than the required number, Signor Wovsi would direct his eyes toward the sky and, nodding his head, murmured, "You understand and I hope You will forgive us."

On the day of Rosh Hashanah, not enough men were present to form a *miny'n*, but the service proceeded and we invoked the Lord, asked pardon for any sins committed and wished each other *L'Shana Tova*. Over the period of ten days, Mr. Wovsi conducted an abbreviated service of Rosh Hashanah and Yom Kippur. Missing was the sound of the *shofar*, the blowing of the ram's horn that announced the start of the New Year and the chant of *Kol Nidre* that began the Day of Atonement. But despite these omissions, the simple rituals raised Mother's spirits almost to their old heights.

Throughout the services and during the full day of fasting, my thoughts went to distant Poland. As I heard Mr. Wovsi invoke the prayers, I could see my grandfather conducting services in the Lwow synagogue.

After I had waited for almost a month, word reached us that my bicycle had finally been brought up from Avellino and left at the *carabinieri* station. I ran to pick it up. Out of breath, I let the metal knocker fall against the heavy door. I knocked again for no one responded fast enough.

"Can I get my bicycle?" I asked the *carabiniere*, who finally answered my knock.

He let me in and pointed to my bike against the wall. What grief! My beautiful new bike, which had caused such sacrifice to my sweet *Mutti* and so many scuffed knees to me, had a bent frame. I was devastated. Walking it up the hill, I cried all the way home. We didn't have the money to have it repaired, I knew that. All this time I had been looking forward to taking long trips and exploring the surrounding areas, perhaps even daring to go beyond the limits allowed us. But I could not ride my bike on those rocky roads with a bent frame, for surely it would break altogether.

I returned home in a bad mood, but my mother, as she had done so often before, tried to console me. "One day I will buy you a better one. Anyhow, you're growing up so fast, soon it will be too small for you."

Antonietta's daughters, seeing me in tears, tried to cheer me up. They introduced me to some of their friends in the neighborhood, which helped me to forget the bike, but I was not too happy to play with girls. My friends had always been boys, but Antonietta warned me that most of the village boys were not worth having as friends. So I spent most of my days with girls, learning to play jacks, but when they were busy dressing their dolls, I refused to join them and went home.

During the summer months, the twilight was long and darkness did not descend until 8:00 or later. Ospedaletto only had two solitary streetlights hanging from a thin wire, happily dancing at the slightest breeze. I had orders to go home when it got dark. Walking home with Antonietta's daughters, I saw the air aglow with luminous small flying creatures.

"What are those?" I asked.

"Fireflies," Maria replied.

Without doing it any harm, she caught one and, for the first time in my life, I watched with wonder as the small insect flashed on and off while crawling in the palm of my cupped hand.

One morning as I was leaving the house, I found Antonietta sitting on the front steps searching for something in her daughter's hair. "What are you doing?" I asked.

"Killing lice."

"Lice? What are they?"

Antonietta found one to show me before killing it. As she held it between two fingernails, the pest wiggled its legs in a futile attempt at freeing itself. What a repulsive sight!

I watched her as she used an extra fine comb to capture the tiny bugs, place them on one of her thumbnail and crush them with the other, but once I heard crunch signaling the bug's demolition, I cringed and dashed inside.

A few days later I suffered a worse experience when Mamma found the repugnant critters crawling on my own head. "You must have gotten them from the barber," she said.

My whole body shivered, knowing I had those nauseating insects crawling on my scalp. "If I know where they came from, is that supposed to make me feel better?" I asked. "Are you going to sit on the street crushing them between your fingernails like Signora Antonietta?"

My mother would never do that; instead she ran to the pharmacy where the pharmacist suggested giving my head a good alcohol rub, and for a few days I smelled like a winery.

"*Mammina*, I don't feel well. Can I stay in bed?" I asked.

Since I was never one to spend time in bed, this was an unusual request. Mother felt my forehead with her hand, then did the same with her lips. "You're burning up," she said, then shouted from our room, "Antonietta, do you have a thermometer?"

Antonietta came running. "No, but I can get you one. What's the matter?"

"He has a fever."

A thermometer was fetched from a neighbor up the road. The fever was high. Antonietta sent her girls to call one of the two doctors. Dr. Sellitto, the senior member of the local medical establishment, made the house call. He examined me from head to foot, then, placing his chin in his cupped hand, delivered a precise diagnosis. "It could be a number of things. I need to make some tests." He hesitated. "It could be pneumonia."

He proceeded to give my mother instructions on how to bring down the fever. "I will be back tomorrow. Lots of tea and bouillon. Understand?"

He was very serious when he delivered these measured words. I looked at my mother's face for her reaction. From her expression, I could sense she was anything but thrilled by the diagnosis. She repeated the brilliant conclusion. "It could be pneumonia?" While the doctor was still in the room, I buried my head under the covers to keep from laughing in his face.

With great ceremony, the doctor wrote out a prescription, collected his fee and left. As soon as he was gone, my mother asked

Antonietta, "What kind of doctor is he?" Then to me, newly emerged from under the covers." And what do you think is so funny? I'm worried to death and you think it's a joke."

"I couldn't help myself." I was giggling. "You should have seen your face, Mamma. 'He could have pneumonia!'"

"We have another doctor in town, Doctor DiGrezia." Antonietta seemed to be reluctant to tell us about him.

"Let's get him," Mother urged.

Dr. DiGrezia, some years Dr. Sellitto's junior, arrived less than an hour after the first doctor had left. He entered the room and took one long look at my face. "I need more light, please," he said. "This boy has yellow jaundice. Nothing too serious. Just keep him in bed. I'll give you a prescription and indicate a diet." He sat at the foot of my bed, took out a pad from his wrinkled jacket, and started to write.

The man had not examined me nor checked my pulse or temperature. Mother did not want to offend the young doctor, but I could see she was not satisfied with his diagnosis. With great hesitation and very faintly, she asked, "You don't think it would be a good idea to examine my son, just to be sure?"

"*Mia cara Signora*, I can see from his yellow eyes what he has. But if it makes you feel better. . . . " He placed his ear to listen to my chest, pressed in my stomach, and placed his hand on my forehead. "Same diagnosis, *Signora*. Yellow jaundice."

This time it was Antonietta waiting for the man to leave before expressing her skepticism. "I don't trust him!"

"Why not?" Mother asked.

"Nobody trusts him. He doesn't believe in remedies we've been using for years. Like, he thinks that leeches are an old wives' tale. Can you imagine? Leeches were used by my grandparents."

"What are leeches?" Mother asked.

"You don't know leeches?"

"Never had the pleasure."

"They can save your life." Antonietta left the room and soon returned holding a jar filled with water in which colored, slimy creatures stuck to the glass. "Here. These are leeches." They reminded me of the oysters I ate for the first time in San Remo.

"What do you do with them? Eat them?" I asked.

Antonietta broke into loud laughter. "Of course not. You put them on your body and they suck out the evil blood."

During our short stay in Ospedaletto, we had already heard of the evil eye; now we were being introduced to evil blood. What strange traditions.

As with all news, my sickness soon became common knowledge among the internees. Some came to call to keep my mother company, pop their heads in my room, and comfort me with a book or two. I stayed in bed only a few days, for the jaundice was soon under control—without the help of the leeches.

"*Got sei dank,*" my mother said, thanking the Lord. "We didn't have to use those . . . whatever you call them."

"How do I iron something?" Mother asked Antonietta.

"I'll give you the irons. Come in the kitchen."

We followed and watched Antonietta as she fished out two heavy metal objects resembling nothing I had ever seen before.

"What do you do with these?" my mother asked.

"You put them on the stove and let them heat."

"That means I have to start a fire."

"Not really. You iron after you've cooked your meal."

Mother and I were slowly learning how backward life was in Ospedaletto d'Alpinolo. During our first days, my mother asked Antonietta if gas for cooking was available in the village.

With disbelief, Antonietta repeated: "Cooking with gas? Never heard of such a thing." Only wood, she said, could be used for that purpose.

Anything you wanted to warm required fire. The various items needed to start this luxury were all in short supply: the paper, the wood to get it going, and the critical matches. And if starting it was a task, keeping it lit was even more so, for it was essential to fan it every so often to keep the flame alive and turn the burning wood into embers. Every kitchen had a straw fan for this purpose, and Mamma soon learned to count on me to do the fanning.

The standard kitchen appliance, the cast iron stove, consisted of a large oven with a front door and a top with three or four round openings, each opening holding a number of concentric iron collars. These collars, which could be made to fit the pot size, served to control the heat, thus providing us with the most modern convenience Ospedaletto had to offer.

"Antonietta, I want to try some ironing."

As always, our landlady was accommodating and hurriedly provided Mother two of those metal contraptions. "You know what to do?" she asked.

"I think so."

The stove was still hot and Mother placed the irons on top of two semi-open holes. "Antonietta, how do you know when these things are hot?" Mamma asked.

"You spit on it."

"You spit on it?" Mamma repeated in a murmur. I don't think my mother had ever spat on anything in all her forty years.

Using the potholder the landlady had provided, Mother went to pick up one of the irons. Evidently it was hotter than she thought for it scorched her hand through the thin holder.

"They're hot all right. I don't have to spit."

I was concerned, but Mother, after placing her hand in some cold water, assured me the hurt had gone away.

"This is like living in the jungle," she murmured. "No one has an electric iron?" she asked Antonietta.

"An electric iron? Never seen one. Are you sure they make such a thing?"

Thanks to Antonietta's patience, we learned to adapt to our new life. We stayed there until the end of summer and, while we were comfortable in that house, my mother missed not having her own kitchen. She had mentioned her need to everyone in our group of internees and someone brought us the news that a new apartment, which included a full kitchen, had become available.

13

Moving to Our Apartment

Before fall set in, we rented an apartment for the same fifty lire. We had grown fond of Antonietta, where our stay had been so pleasant, but the new place offered what *Mutti* prized more than anything else: her very own kitchen.

We moved to the apartment on the top floor of a three-story building. The stone building, situated at the edge of town, occupied the far corner of the main piazza and overlooked the municipal gardens. It faced the carriage road that came from Avellino and led to the nearby town of Summonte. Past the building and along that road lay a large forest, while to the rear of the building there were open fields that rolled softly into the valley.

Antonio and Filomena Guerriero were our new landlords. Antonio was modern by local standards, well-mannered, with a university degree. An ex-mayor of the village, he was now one of its public school teachers. An avowed Fascist and proud to tell us that he was a card-carrying party member, he wore his black shirt uniform at every opportunity.

Building with balconies where Eric and his mother lived, Ospedaletto.

In contrast, Filomena had little formal education, was provincial, and reveled in local gossip. She was a bit taller than Mamma, and her oval face had well-balanced features. Pretty and neat in her appearance, she was always clad entirely in black. Thinking she may have had a death in her family, my mother offered her condolences a few days after we moved in.

Filomena looked baffled. Then, realizing what my mother meant, she responded with a big smile. "Oh, the black dress. I just wear it. You know, with a large family, there is always someone dying."

Besides a kitchen, our new apartment consisted of two large rooms. Each one had its own balcony overlooking the main road—a mixed blessing, we would soon discover, depending on the time of year. In September the air was still warm. Leaving the balcony doors open offered an invitation to all the mosquitoes in the neighborhood. As the weather turned colder, we found the larger doors also had wider gaps around their frames, which let the wind blow more freely through our rooms.

The large kitchen, with its traditional cast-iron stove, was halfway down the corridor. It had a table, four chairs, and half of a wooden barrel to hold our water supply. From the same corridor we accessed our apartment: the living room, where I slept next to Mother's room. At last I had my own room and could sleep without a cross over my bed.

Each floor had a communal toilet or, more precisely, a dark cubicle, hanging from the back of the building, with the poor imitation of a toilet seat over an unobstructed hole that discharged into the ground. Thin, non-uniform wood planks formed the outer walls, which were intended to shield the user from curious eyes and the outside air. But because of poor construction, only privacy was achieved, while the outside air easily flowed inside, creating a problem in every season. During summer, hot air helped ferment the putrefied waste into foul-smelling fumes, in the cold winter, it required exceptional courage to undress. Thus, unless faced with a dire emergency, rather than brave the stench during the warm months, I made use of the surrounding woods, while in winter I learned to rush the process in order to shorten the exposure of my private parts and protect them from freezing. Though we had to share this deplorable toilet with the other five people on our floor, the chances of finding it occupied were almost nil. No one stayed inside the hanging stall any longer than was absolutely essential.

When forced to use the toilet and to protect myself from inhaling the putrid fumes, I had, in short time, learned to be a contortionist. In order to be able to urinate standing erect, I had to twist my upper torso to one side and at the same time struggle to aim my stream into the hole rather than on my feet. But owing to a number of misses, no matter what my needs, I began to sit, letting my buttocks take the brunt of the obnoxious fumes. The outhouse was so archaic that in comparison, our toilet paper, a batch of torn newspaper squares that hung from a nail, represented a step into modern times.

Mother had returned from reporting to the police station when she exclaimed, "Guess what I got us? A chamber pot."

Watching my mother gleefully waving that white enameled metal container in the air made me realize how low we had sunk. Then, in a lighter mood, I suggested that we had reached our zenith and had finally become an integral part of Ospedaletto d'Alpinolo. We owned our very own pot. "You're a genius, *Mammina.* "Are we going to empty it from the balcony?"

"No! Of course not! Don't forget where we come from, because one of these days we're going to leave this place and go to live among civilized people. No, we will not empty it from the window. We'll pour it down the toilet." She really seemed furious at my remark.

"Did you think I meant it?" I asked.

"With you I never know if you're serious or acting stupid." She had calmed down and put her arms around me and together we enjoyed a hearty laugh.

I was never called upon to do the unpleasant task of emptying the pot. As my mother had done throughout my life, she always relieved me of the most unpleasant chores.

Since I was not able to carry forty liters of water on my untrained head, we had to pay a young woman twice and occasionally three times a week to do so. With a copper cauldron brimming with water and precariously balanced on her head, a barefooted thirteen- or fourteen-year-old would climb the two flights to our floor and, carefully turning on the landing, walk into our kitchen. With very little effort, she would hoist that heavy vessel from her head and pour the water into our wooden half-barrel. All this for fifty *centesimi*, a little more than the cost of mailing a letter. The strength of these young women never ceased to amaze me. Once, when Mother and I tried to move the barrel, we were unable to lift it and could only drag it across the floor.

The water served for drinking, cooking, and washing. Now, for the first time, it would also serve for our weekly bath. For three months, while living at Antonietta's, we'd had to share the kitchen with the landlady and her girls and had not been able to take a bath.

Bathing, even in our own apartment, presented a challenge. The new landlady had provided us with a basin to wash our laundry, which was just large enough to hold an infant. Mother pronounced this to be our new bathtub.

"How am I going to take a bath in this?" I asked.

"What we'll do is take two half baths."

Never really doubting my mother's wisdom, I asked what she meant by a half bath.

She explained her novel solution: "First we'll wash the top half of the body, then the bottom half. Clever, no?"

But bathing in two stages had a few drawbacks. Since we did not have a sufficiently large pot, we had to heat one pot of water at the time.

"By the time we take the first half-bath and heat up the rest of the water, our bodies will get dirty again," I said. Mamma's laugh told me she took my logic in good humor.

The floor below ours was the landlord's residence, except for one small room, which was rented to a family of seven: Vincenzo, his wife Annunziata, and their five children.

Small of stature, plump, and loud, Annunziata was a woman of limited skills and even less education. Her major functions were to cook pasta and bear children. Her hair, not washed in years and snarled from months of begging for a comb, created the perfect habitat for lice. Her splotched dress, one of three I saw her wear during our twenty-five months stay, displayed samples of tomato sauces weeks or perhaps months old.

Vincenzo was lanky and prone to outbursts of temper. The twenty-first born in his family, he carried on him the dirt he had accumulated during the thirty-two years since his birth. He led a simple life. Six days a week, he sat cross-legged on the side of the dusty road that skirted the village and led to Montevergine, crushing rocks into small pebbles. He would place a rock on a large flat stone resting on his lap and smash it with a stone in his hand.

One day I found him there, alone on the mountain road. Staring at the holes left by three or four of his missing teeth, I asked, "What are these stones used for?"

He shrugged his shoulders. "Bah! I'm glad I'm working." He said more but I had trouble understanding his heavy dialect.

Vincenzo's main meal consisted of a loaf of bread and a tomato. Some days, though, he could afford only half a loaf. For Vincenzo, each work day started at sunrise and ended at sunset. As he did not own a watch, he relied on the sun to tell time, thus working more hours in summer and fewer in winter.

It was easy to tell when Vincenzo came home at the end of the day, for his homecoming was marked by either an argument with his wife or the beating of one of his children. Judging from my own upbringing, I accepted that the children needed a heavy hand, but this man would slap the children even before knowing if punishment was warranted.

Like most women in the village, Annunziata had been busy producing children and had given birth every eleven months. Only the two older boys were more than two years apart, for three children born in between had died in infancy.

During our first three months in Ospedaletto, I thought I had seen as much filth as any person could ever accumulate, but Vincenzo's children seemed to be competing to see who could win first prize. Perhaps it was their way to make up for their lack of clothing, hoping the grime would cover those parts of their small bodies where clothes should have been. None of the children had shoes, not even the simple *zoccoli,* and the bottoms of their feet, from the youngest to the oldest, had toughened into a hardened leathery condition that made them insensitive. Once the oldest boy removed a tack imbedded in his calloused foot. The nail had left a small, bloodless hole and I could tell the boy didn't feel pain.

While the older children ran around all day, the eleven-month baby was carried by the mother. One day I watched as Annunziata wrapped the infant using a stained and well-worn strip of cloth around the little girl's buttock. She pulled the bandage so tight that the poor child was unable to bend or move from the waist down. Later that day I told Mamma about it.

"That's barbaric," she commented.

With cold weather approaching, the only difference between summer and winter was marked by how much snot ran from the children's noses and was then smeared across their cheeks each time the mother, in her vain attempt at stopping the constant trickle, wiped her open hand over their faces. I don't think those children ever felt water cleanse their skin, for I could detect the various layers of mucous Annunziata had spread on their cheeks.

Whenever someone called out Vincenzo's name, my ears perked up. "Why do they call him Bicenz?" I asked Filomena, our landlady.

"In dialect a *V* is pronounced like a *B.*"

Later I learned that *bacio,* the word for "kiss," was pronounced "vazo," for *B*'s were pronounced as *V*'s. I concluded that these people were backward.

One day my insatiable curiosity led me inside Vincenzo's family's vacant tiny quarters smaller than either one of our rooms, it housed all seven of them. It was obvious from the number of beds that at least two of the children had to share their parents' bed. That's all I was able to observe, for the foul smell forced me to make a rapid retreat.

I ran upstairs to tell my mother. "Mamma, I was in Annunziata's room. It's terrible how these people live. You wouldn't believe the stench."

"Stay away from there! Do you want lice again?" she asked. Remembering those crawling pests brought on a shiver.

The Dello Russos, our next-door neighbors, were a delightful contrast. The family lived in a four-room apartment. Their two children shared their own room and even Ida, the fourteen-year-old live-in help, had a small cubicle for herself.

Antonio and Dora Dello Russo soon became Mamma's close friends. Alba and Gino, their children, although younger than me, were good companions within the confines of the house.

While my mother was an extraordinary cook and an admired baker, she could create real chaos in the kitchen. Dora, in contrast, was a spotless housekeeper. Every day she was up before the rest of her family, started the fire and prepared breakfast—a bowl of *caffè-latte* with chunks of homemade bread—then got her children ready for school.

During the week, Dora found little or no time for her own grooming. Her attractive dark hair, sprinkled with a bit of gray, was drawn into a bun. Precariously held by a number of poorly placed hair pins, it received Dora's attention only on Sunday before going to mass. Despite her untidy appearance, however, she was clean about her person and meticulous about her home. Each room was tastefully furnished. Crystal and porcelain were displayed in the china cabinet. On a table in the living room, a wedding picture in a silver frame showed her slim attractiveness of eight years earlier, contrasting with her present chunkiness at twenty-eight.

Antonio Dello Russo *il commerciante*—so known to distinguish him from the other Dello Russo, the ex-mayor with the coal-filled bathtub—was a good provider, a caring husband and a doting father. Freshly shaven each morning, he looked neat in his black suit, white shirt, and black tie. Dora made sure his clothes were clean and pressed, even washing his suit from time to time.

The Dello Russos were steps ahead of most townspeople and led, much to Mother's relief, a more modern and hygienic lifestyle.

Sunday was a special day in Italy, and even more so in this small mountain village. It was when families sat together at the table to enjoy their best meal of the week, a feast prepared with particular care by the women of the house. Even Annunziata boiled a hefty dish of pasta and once in a while added a tiny cut of meat hardly big enough to feed half her lot.

In the Dello Russo home, however, Sunday was marked by more than just food. Hand-embroidered table linens were placed on the dining room table, graced by crystal glassware, porcelain dishes, and silverware—all part of Dora's considerable dowry. Served with the meal was local wine and freshly home-baked bread, a luxury in those days when so many grocery items were strictly rationed. But Dora used her bread coupons to buy flour that, combined with whatever Antonio was able to buy on the black market, enabled her to bake enough bread even to be generous with us.

Early each Sunday morning, Dora brushed her shiny hair, slipped into a clean black dress and left home before eight to attend the early mass. Ida, the young live-in maid, got the children ready so Antonio could take them to church later. Each Sunday, while the family was at church, Dora prepared different kinds of pastas, meats, and desserts. In awe, I watched how fast she used a sharp knife to create even-sized fettuccine or a fork to score small bits of dough to create fresh gnocchi.

"Can I help?" I asked.

"Sure, pull up a chair and I'll teach you how to make gnocchi."

I sat next to Dora, trying to duplicate whatever she was doing. Often my mistakes had to be scrapped and reworked into dough, creating much frustration for me but not for Dora, who never seemed to mind. Only after several weeks, having mastered the technique, could I be of help to her.

Every Sunday morning the scent of tomato sauce filled her kitchen and seeped into the hallway. Dora started cooking before leaving for church, because, as she once said, "A good sauce needs to simmer for at least six hours." Basically the sauce was always the same, plain or with a small meat roast, but I never tired of that exquisite bouquet of fresh tomatoes, oregano, garlic, and basil. One of my great treats was whenever Dora invited me to share the Sunday meal with her family.

"Dora, I will not let you invite us to dinner. You cannot afford the extra flour," Mamma protested.

"Don't worry. I have plenty. Even if I didn't have enough, we would be happy to share it with you." Dora's invitations came from the heart, and I was allowed, from time to time, to accept, although my mother declined more often than not.

The weather in late September was still summery, so at night we left our balcony doors wide open to the crisp mountain air. I had always loved the mountains that, along with the local water, were two of the few joys of Ospedaletto.

We had been in our new apartment just a few days when, in the middle of the night, we were shaken from our sleep by hundreds of feet grinding the gravel road. Shattering the night's silence, the sound had a spookiness to it. I jumped out of bed, as much curious as scared and, without knocking rushed into Mother's room to find her sitting in bed. Together, barefoot and holding hands, we moved to the balcony to see what had awakened us. We leaned far back against the wall to make us less visible and peered down the moonlit road. An uninterrupted column of people was snaking along the main road and breaking their silence with occasional chants.

The pilgrimage season to the monastery of Montevergine had begun. The pilgrims walked for days, some from as far away as fifty or more miles, with only a few loaves of bread and perhaps some tomatoes to appease their hunger. Men walked barefoot and carried their shoes over one shoulder, while a large napkin, its four corners knotted together so as to hold their provisions, hung from a tree branch resting on the other shoulder. The women, close behind, some with *zoccoli* but most barefoot, skillfully balanced a suitcase or a heavy vine basket on their heads. We watched whole families, from infants in their parents' arms to old men and women walking with the aid of handmade canes, go by our balconies.

They were going to Montevergine to pray and from Ospedaletto, they had to tackle the steep stony path up the mountain. After their long and exhausting walk to the top, as their final task the faithful would ascend the twenty-three steps leading up to the sanctuary on their knees. Day and night for six weeks, the columns of devotees passed under our balconies.

I soon memorized their dissonant chants as they passed through the village.

"*Simmu arrivate ad Ospidaletto e a Maronna cce Stan rimpetto.*"

"*Simmu arrivate a Summonte e a Maronna cce Stan in fronte.*"

During that period, dozens of wooden stands, would be erected and lined up along the pilgrims' path. I had seen some of the preparations but had not realized what an important event this was for the town. The stands displayed strings of dried chestnuts and smoked hazelnuts as well as the popular homemade honey nougat. The merchants sold this local specialty either in pre-wrapped pieces of various sizes or in bulk. Bulk nougat was priced less by the pound than the packaged goods because the weight of the chunks could be deftly manipulated to make them appear to weigh more than their actual weight.

"Don't put your lousy finger there," a woman shouted. She had caught the man using his small finger to give the scale that extra downward push. Having seen that so often during my short stay, I assumed no one considered it a crime. "You're just outsmarting the customer," someone told me.

Many of the townspeople earned a portion of their annual income during this short period of six or seven weeks. Whole families were engrossed in the enterprise. They worked in shifts, manning the stands day and night. Grandparents, women nursing babies, fathers, and children of various degrees of dirtiness, clothing colors, and ages, all took turns selling their wares and guarding their stands around the clock. The season was short and they needed to take advantage of every minute. At night the stands, each lit by one acetylene lamp, presented an eerie scene in the looming shadows.

During pilgrimage season, Ospedaletto d'Alpinolo bustled with people, lending this otherwise dormant village an uncharacteristic liveliness. Only the twice-a-year concert by a roving band of musicians similarly energized the townspeople and shook them out of their lethargy.

A few steps from our building flowed a narrow and shallow rivulet where local women gathered to wash their clothes. Looking down from the small bridge, I realized the gossip as much as doing the wash was what brought these women together. Their skirts raised above their knees—the only time in Ospedaletto when one could see a woman's bare leg above the ankle—they stood in the cold mountain water. Some used soap and a corrugated metal washboard; others, holding the garment at one end, would swing it hard against a protruding rock to beat the dirt out of it and save the precious rationed soap. When all the gossip was exhausted, the women intoned local songs, which must have been passed down for generations.

But Ospedaletto d'Alpinolo was also a very industrious village. Chestnuts and hazelnuts were its natural resources and nougat was produced with pride.

One morning, walking through town, I watched a young man banging and turning a large wooden spoon in a copper cauldron hanging over a wood fire. The spoon was the size of the oars the fishermen used in San Remo and the kettle was at least twice as large as the water-filled ones the local women carried on their heads. Forcefully he pushed the spoon down, then half a turn around the kettle in a constant one, two, three rotation. From time to time he switched hands and continued his hypnotic labor without missing a beat. I asked the man how long he had to do this. Without stopping his constant rhythmic pound-and-mix movement, he replied that he needed to stir the mixture of honey and hundreds of egg whites for eight hours and keep the fire going before adding the roasted hazelnuts and create a superior nougat.

Days later I again stopped by that shop to watch the young man. I might have liked to try my hand at it, but realized the mere size of that ladle made it too heavy for my small frame. At the end of the day, the man stopped and reached for a towel to dry his face and body. After resting for a few minutes, together with abothe man they poured the thick paste onto a marble slab. Slowly it spread to the edges, but the men were quick to stop the run with a large wooden paddle.

The young man came to me. "When it cools I'll give you a taste. But it will take another hour."

By asking many questions, I soon grasped a geographical picture of where Ospedaletto d'Alpinolo was located. Over the mountain that hugged the village and less than twenty-five miles to the north lay Naples. To the west, down the valley and almost equidistant, was Salerno, while to the east, following the main road from Avellino and continuing past our building, was the city of Benevento.

In Ospedaletto chickens and pigs lived in people's courtyards and sometime inside their homes.

Summer was coming to an end but the days were still hot. Laboring up the hill coming back from city hall, I was startled by a high-pitched squeal. I stalled my steps just as a large fat pig, chased by a wild mob, came charging from a small opening between buildings and almost crashed into me. Men and boys of all ages were falling over each other, their screams and laughter competing with the hunted animal's oinks. Every time one of the chasers grabbed the tail or leg of the pig, the animal let out a squeal that ran an icy chill through me.

Without leaving my spot, I turned on my heels to watch the numerous chases up and down the road and the fine dust that rose into the air. One of the men always managed to get in front of the animal, forcing it to turn around and run back into the chasing crowd. Inwardly, I cheered for the outnumbered pig. The animal, in spite of its large size, was swift and agile and with sudden stops and turnarounds, it outmaneuvered the frenzied mob until one boy threw himself on the exhausted hog and the others, quick to take advantage of the swine's immobility, grasped its limbs and dragged it back squealing into the house from which it had escaped.

Dozens of onlookers came from around town to witness the animal's slaughter. The spectacle was a break in the monotony of the villagers' everyday lives.

The hog was strong, a good match for the strength of the seven muscular men holding it down over a wooden barrel. While the animal finally yielded to the superior forces and stopped kicking its legs, it continued its endless, soul-piercing, high-pitched screeching. Standing there, inside the house, I was fantasizing an escape plan for the pig, when a man approached the animal and, with one pass of a long sharp knife, slashed its throat. *Swush!* The sound, sent a tremor rushing through my body while the dying pig's grunts slowly decreased into a low murmur.

The small room overflowed with people pushing and shoving in their attempt not to miss any details of the gruesome spectacle. Children created a circus-like atmosphere by jumping up and down, women spoke loudly, some men either helped in the killing or gave the semblance they were and a few older men enjoyed stinky little Tuscan cigars. In this mix of humanity, flies were everywhere, landing on me, on people, and on the bleeding pig.

The chase might have been bedlam but the killing ritual was well orchestrated. Just before the first drop of blood gushed out from the opened throat, someone had squeezed through the crowd and placed a wooden bucket on the floor to collect it. The pig did not take long to die. I hated to watch the animal twitch and, while it was not totally still, it quivered from time to time. I was hoping it could no longer feel pain.

The steaming blood had stopped spurting into the bucket and the man with the knife slit open the animal's underside. From its throat to its tail he cut a straight line. Then, with the help of two others, the butcher parted the two sections and cleaned out everything the animal held within its body. I had never seen intestines, hearts, lungs, or any insides, or blood gushing freely from a living creature and the sight made me nauseous. Only my compulsive curiosity kept me watching, making sure not to miss anything for I wanted to describe it all to Mamma.

These people wasted nothing. I was full of questions and the man standing next to me was very obliging. He explained that every part of the animal was used. The blood served to make sausages and some other gross concoction, its intestines served as casings for sausages, and the thick, fatty skin would be fried.

I stayed longer than half the people there, until the procedure became routine. On the way home, mentally I prepared the details to be shared with my mother, but as soon as she heard the words "pig" and "slaughter" she stopped me, thus foregoing the gory description of the butchering and limiting my explanation for being late.

"What a foul smell. I didn't know whether it came from the pig, the people, or the house. Mamma, you cannot believe the filth. Worse than Annunziata's room."

In the succeeding months, I met many more townsfolk and, in their homes, found similar squalor, where dogs, chickens, fleas, and flies mingled freely with villagers. But most of the people I met were kind and hospitable. I seemed to be a novelty to them: foreign, clean, and well dressed. Often, I felt they kowtowed to me.

14

New Internees Arrive

Seasons changed rapidly in Ospedaletto. As summer gave way to fall, the weather turned dreary and the incessant rain and shorter days dampened our moods. The roads deteriorated to mud and our morning walks became fewer. Thus, when in the early fall of 1941 we greeted two new arrivals, our spirits lifted. These two men were confinati politici, the true enemies of Fascism.

The morning after they arrived in Ospedaletto, Ettore Costa and Pietro Russo joined the group of internees at the customary corner. Pietro smiled often, displaying a slightly chipped tooth that kept attracting my attention. Ettore wore such thick glasses to make his eyes appear enormous. Once the obligatory, somewhat lengthy introductions were out of the way, a barrage of questions hit the newsworthy Italians.

Ettore was the first to respond and the vigor with which he answered each person revealed his vibrant personality.

"Why am I here?" his voice rang out as he answered the question someone put to him. "Well, for one thing I am a professed anti-Fascist. I will write against this miserable dictator as long as I have strength left to hold a pen. After that, I'll ask someone else to write for me."

"Aren't you afraid to speak so loud?" Mamma asked.

"Why? What are they going to do, send me to an internment camp?" His laughter was an obvious sign he enjoyed his own bitter humor.

"Frankly, I'd rather not discuss politics in the street. You never know who is listening," my mother said.

"What about you, Signor Russo?" John Howell asked. "Why did they send you here?"

"I said the wrong things at the wrong time in the wrong place. Frankly, I don't quite remember exactly what I said. It had to do with Mussolini. Anyhow, someone overheard me and reported it to the police and so here I am."

"Were you tried in court?" John Howell asked.

"Are you joking?" Pietro replied. "If someone reports you, that's it. No trial."

Nobody seemed to notice that it was almost 10:30 and the group was still standing at the corner. "If we don't start walking, we might as well stay here," someone said.

"Are you going to join us on our morning stroll?" John asked the new men.

"Nothing else to do," Ettore responded.

As we left the piazza, I attached myself to Pietro Russo. I had endured a disruptive life over the previous three years, no father and few friends my age. But this man's charisma and friendly, sparkling eyes broke down my reluctance to open up to an adult.

"Tell me, how do you spend your days?" he asked me.

"I try to do things. Sometimes I get to play *boccie*. I am also learning bridge, but the adults don't let me play often. Do you play bridge?"

"Yes. I picked it up when I was going to law school in Palermo."

"Is that where you're from?" I asked.

"I'm from Mazara del Vallo, not far from Palermo. Do you know where Palermo is?"

"I've only heard about it."

Patiently he drew me a verbal map of Sicily, Palermo, and Mazara del Vallo. Mother walked up to us and put her arm about me. "Is my son bothering you?"

Pietro grabbed my hand. "Not at all."

"Enrico can be full of questions. But as long as he doesn't bother you, that's fine." Then looking at me, she added, "Why don't you ask Signor Russo to join us for lunch?"

Mother also invited Ettore and on that day we were the first to learn much about these two captivating individuals. I liked both. although my mother had reservations about Signor Costa.

That evening after dinner I asked Mamma, "What don't you like about Signor Costa?"

"He's too brash for my taste. Signor Russo is a real gentleman."

Both Ettore and Pietro became very popular among the *confinati* and remained so.

I formed an immediate attachment to both men, to Ettore Costa for his devilish character and to Pietro Russo for his infectious charm. Before their arrival, the morning walk had been a way to reduce the daily boredom. Now, I couldn't wait to bask in Pietro's warm smile and hear Ettore's satirical political comments.

Autumn brought the chestnut season. The luscious green, dense forests, Ospedaletto's natural blanket, produced a large chestnut harvest. But in spite of the crop's abundance, I could risk my life if I as much as entered the woods during that period. Various families from the village laid claim to sections of the woods and protected their territories with shotguns. But nature, in its generosity, allowed a few chestnuts to fall outside the woods from the heavily laden trees that bordered the roads. Children and adults hastened to compete for the rich fruit, for it provided a delicious meal or a dessert. Although only eleven, I was aware how much my mother struggled to provide food with the little money she received and anytime I could, I was proud to make a minor contribution.

"Before this stinking war, this region was renowned for producing the best chestnuts in the world," one villager told us.

The harvest season lasted about sixty days, but the sweet, tasty nuts were easy to preserve and ours to enjoy for many months. Chestnuts could be prepared in many ways. I preferred to boil them in their shells, drain them, and let them cool. Then, with my teeth clenched around the narrow tip to create a crack, I squeezed the luscious purée into my mouth. What a delicacy! They were also delicious roasted or boiled without the shell. For roasting we placed the slit chestnuts on a rusty roasting pan, or buried them under the ashes of the open fireplace.

Some evenings, for fun, I would intentionally omit slitting a few of the chestnuts, then wait for them to burst, showering glowing coals and ashes all around us. If the explosion had ever started a fire, all of Ospedaletto would have gone up in flames since by the time one of us could run down to the square to awaken the postmaster, to open the office housing the only telephone in the village and call the closest fire truck, five miles away in Avellino. But at that age, such consequences never entered my mind.

In December of 1941, Antonio Dello Russo was inducted into the Italian army and sent to fight in Albania. Dora came to us, wringing her hands over her pregnant belly. "What am I going to do? *Madonna mia*, what am I going to do?"

Mother tried to console the poor woman. "I will be here anytime you need me."

Dora was hysterical, a heavy stream of tears rolling down her round cheeks. "Do you realize I have never lived alone before I married Antonio, I lived with my parents. And now I have two children and one on the way. This criminal Mussolini is going to kill my Totonno."

"No, no. He is not going to get killed. He is too smart for that," Mamma said.

"Do you really think so?"

Mother placed her arms around the woman. "Of course. Meanwhile, if you need anything, I'm right here, next door. Remember that. You and the children come for dinner tonight."

"I can't. I know how many coupons you have. You cannot afford to feed three more mouths."

"You come. No discussion." Mother pointed a scolding finger at her friend.

"I will give you some of my coupons." The two women embraced and kissed, then Dora kissed me, too.

Dinner was a new experience for our neighbors, as they approached each dish guardedly.

Alba was the first to express herself. "This is absolutely delicious, so different from what Mamma makes."

"I'm glad you like it. You'll have to come more often," my mother said.

Over the next twenty or more months, Dora became increasingly more dependent on my mother, strengthening the bond between them. Our door remained always open for Dora and hers for us.

"Dora, is this an iron?" Mother asked. She was intrigued by the contraption in Dora's hand. It was different from those Antonietta had.

"Yes. No need to keep two irons hot on the stove. Just keep hot embers inside this one."

"How do you keep the embers burning?" Mamma asked.

Dora twirled the hot iron through the air. "Like this."

Mother saw sparks flying from the iron's small side holes. She pointed at the glowing ashes falling through the air. "What about these? Don't they burn your clothes?"

"You have to be careful."

Mother laughed. "Just like you."

The first time my mother tried the iron, she used it on a torn rag. "I'm glad I didn't experiment on something good. Look what I did to this *shmatte*." She showed me the rag with several ash marks and one scorched spot. "What has my life come to? I'm learning to use tools your grandmother stopped using years ago. We're going backward."

"Someone is taking my handkerchiefs," Mother complained.

"Don't look at me, Mamma. I wouldn't use those girly things."

"Always joking. I know exactly how many handkerchiefs I have. First, one was missing now three are gone."

"Who do you think is stealing them?"

"In this town, who knows?"

I was helping to search for the hand-embroidered items when Mother let out a shriek. "Oh, good heavens! No!"

"What is it?" I asked after quickly crawling out from under the bed.

Mutti stood totally motionless, staring out the balcony window. Clutching my shoulder, she said, "Look."

There, in a corner of the balcony, neatly wrapped in Mother's missing handkerchiefs, were five newborn mice.

"They're cute," I piped.

"Cute?" Mother screamed and stormed into Dora's apartment. I could hear her from the hallway. "He thinks they're cute. He doesn't care that his mother may have a heart attack."

"What's happened?" Dora asked.

"There are mice in my apartment. Dozens of them. Hundreds! Come, quick."

Dora, armed with a long broom, came marching through the open door. Mother followed at a distance. "Where are they?" Dora asked.

My mother remained outside her room. "Enrico, show Dora where they are."

I was amused by her fear but didn't dare laugh. Frankly, I was not too brave myself. Pointing to the balcony, I said, "There!" Then made a fast retreat and backed out the door.

Dora turned the handle of the balcony's French door. Mother, still in the other room shrieked and fled into the hallway at the squeak of the balcony door being opened. At forty my mother, who had lived through the Great War and had braved crossing into foreign countries and cities, disintegrated at the mere sight of a small, harmless little mouse. As Dora reached for the embroidered linen squares, the larger mouse leaped in the air, making a feeble attempt at protecting her babies. With a push of the broom, Dora shoved it off the balcony, then wrapped the newborns in Mother's fancy possessions and carried them away.

As she passed me by, with the bundle in her hands, I asked, "What are you going to do with them?"

"Drown them."

Dora returned a few minutes later, bringing back Mother's treasured handkerchiefs. "That's great. Your mother was supposed to give me strength and she falls apart at the sight of a few mice."

15

Our First Winter

Winter blew in abruptly, early, and furiously to Ospedaletto in 1941. Living in a dwelling without heat, where the wind was free to invade the corners of every room, we learned new ways to cope with the cold. Because the only source of heat in a home was the stove and sometimes a fireplace, the kitchen was where residents spent most of their waking hours. We were lucky; in our kitchen, we had both a stove and a fireplace.

Though wood was all around us, it was an expensive commodity. The logs we bought to cook for one month cost ten lire, which was one-fifth of my monthly subsidy. The wood needed to keep us warm became my responsibility. Daily I combed the woods for the scraps left behind by some careless woodsman, a task made more difficult by the scores of villagers trying to do the same.

We rarely had enough wood for the fireplace and were thankful that most evenings either Dora or the landlady invited us to be with them. When spending the evening at the landlady's, we had to brave being crowded in with Vincenzo and his family. Although we had learned to accept the dirt we saw on others from a distance, to be close, shoulder to shoulder, was more difficult.

"Maybe if we live here long enough we'll be able to stop taking baths," I said to Mamma. "Then we'll be as filthy as they are and we won't mind it anymore."

With a perfectly straight face, Mother responded, "I'll tell you what. You go and live in the woods, and I'll leave you a food basket at our door."

I was certain she was joking; nonetheless, not willing to chance it, I never mentioned my bright idea again.

Electric power was supposed to be available until 10:00 every evening, but many nights the lights failed long before the designated time. Though most of us kept a scarce candle ready by our side, we rarely used the precious commodity as a guide to our bedrooms. Candles were used for short periods only, while for prolonged times of darkness we improvised. A glass or other container half filled with water, a thin layer of hard-to-find olive oil, and a wick provided a handy lamp. The few who could afford it owned a new type of flashlight with a built-in generator. Never needing batteries, it required only the continuous squeezing of one's hand to keep the wheels turning.

By 10:00 at night, when the electricity was shut off, everyone was ready for bed. Rarely did the evening gathering extend past that hour. Before retiring, we would share the embers from the fireplace to fill our borrowed brazier, making the dash into the icy bed less of a shock.

Braziers came in all sizes and shapes. Artistic copper ones, resting on their own elaborate stands, were displayed as heirlooms. One evening, as we were dividing the glowing coals, Filomena remarked that someone in the village had died in their sleep the night before. "The doc says he died of the brazier's bad fumes."

"What are bad fumes?" Mamma asked.

"Nobody knows," Filomena said.

That was enough information for my mother to buy a hot water bottle, and we never used embers again.

There was something to be said for winter. We could wear the same heavy clothes inside as well as outside, for the temperature didn't vary much between the two zones. During the war, at a time when clothing, just as everything else we needed to survive, was either difficult or impossible to find, I realized that needing only one set of clothes was a blessing of sorts.

One November morning while still in bed, through my sleepy eyes, I saw white flakes flutter by the window. Snow! In my bare feet I jumped onto the freezing tile floor and glued my face to the icy window. Fresh powder had blanketed the ground and decorated the woods during the night. I was spellbound by the majestic picture nature had painted outside. The two imposing mountains facing the village had lost their menacing aspect and now looked like a collection of large, fluffy cotton balls. The snowfall, the first I had seen since leaving Vienna three years earlier, gave me an uncontrollable urge to run out.

"Put your slippers on or you'll catch pneumonia," Mother warned.

"Oh, *Mammina,* I want to go outside. I haven't played in snow for so long." In a whisper I added, "Please."

Because the snow had come unexpectedly, my mother had not yet prepared heavy garments for me. A few days earlier, commenting on the sudden drop in temperature, Dora had said, "Snow never comes this early."

That morning Mother broke just about every one of her rules when she allowed me to skip breakfast, dressed me in the only suitable clothes she could find, and let me go out to play. "Go, go." She prodded me with her hand. "Have a good time. Be careful!" She kissed me as she always did and, eagerly, I dashed down the stairs into the total stillness of the morning.

The crunch of fresh powder under my feet evoked memories of my Vienna. I looked around. No one else in sight. Only I was there to see this magical landscape. But not wearing gloves was hardly appropriate for this weather, nor could my shoes withstand the cold and wetness. Staying outside became painful. Obstinate, I stayed as long as I could tolerate it. Then, still unwilling to face defeat, I stayed a few more minutes. Back in the house, I struggled up the two flights with my half-frozen feet each step was torture. Even my fingertips were blue. But it had been worth it.

My face must have shown the pain. "Come here, *Hasele.*" Mother wrapped me in a blanket, kissed my forehead and held me tight. Oh, how I melted in my mother's arms!

That day Mother went through a still-unopened box of clothes to find a sweater set she had knitted for me in Vienna. "Come here, *Schatzele.* Let me see." She placed the pullover against my back. "I can't believe how much you have grown. This will never fit you. We'll have to make another one. I hope there is enough wool." From the box she pulled out a scarf, a pair of gloves and a hat. She examined the items laid out on the bed. "Oh, yes. There is enough. Let's unravel these and make you a new sweater."

Mother found a beginning thread and as she began to pull, she asked, "Do you want to help me?" Without waiting for my reply, she handed me one end of the heavy wool thread. "Here, hold this and wrap it around your fist." Mamma took my hand, made it into a fist, and placed the yarn firmly under my thumb. "Hold it tight." It felt good to be working with Mother.

The light blue thread rapidly formed a ball around my fist. The wool had a soft, warm feeling. What riches my hand was holding!

Wool was impossible to find. The Italian army needed it for itself. For hours over the next few days, I sat winding the wool around my fist as Mother unraveled it. I remembered how hard she had worked knitting those items, even taking them to the coffeehouse in the afternoons. Now, in a fraction of time and with hardly any effort, she had reduced her creations into a few neat balls of yarn.

Then, armed with much advice and a set of borrowed large needles, my resourceful *Mutti* began to recreate a sweater that would fit me. For days, Mother's knitting was the major topic of conversation amongst the internees, evidence of how any little diversion helped relieve the monotony of waiting for the war to end and our freedom to be restored.

Finally finished, Mother asked me to put on the new sweater. I had trouble standing still. "Slowly," she said, "you're going to tear it."

"It's gorgeous, *Mutti*!" I exclaimed. I've never seen anything so beautiful, *Mutti*! Can I wear it today?"

"Of course. I made it for you." *Mutti's* warm smile expressed her happiness for having pleased me.

"You're the best mother anyone could have."

The cold weather brought our enjoyable morning walks to an abrupt halt and with them, much of our socializing. Now the afternoons were spent with only a handful of friends, either playing bridge or meeting in one home or another to share a cup of tea. Mamma loved to entertain and now, with a living room in our new apartment, she was able to reciprocate. As people tasted her baked goods, especially the apple strudel, she became the "sensational Lotte." When she made a walnut or Dobusch torte, it became the event of the week.

Pietro spent most days with us, whether for bridge or tea. He also shared lunch with us on several occasions, the only person who ever did. Often he surprised Mother with a bottle of olive oil he had received from Sicily or, in warmer weather, a bunch of flowers he had picked himself. Once, as I entered the kitchen, the two abruptly stepped away from one another.

While during the warm weather we had shared whatever news anyone had been able to snatch, now the cold weather forced us to stay inside isolated from our friends. One afternoon, Mamma commented, "Would you believe it? I even miss my arguments with old fellow Pierce."

Local newspapers did not exist, and only once in a long while did a villager bring back a newspaper from Naples. Occasionally, some internee received a daily by mail with news that was more than a week old. Thus, without a radio of our own—*confinati* were not allowed to own one—Mother and even I, though only eleven, felt cut off from the outside world. We had been in Ospedaletto six months and the only news we had access to during that period came from the local folks who listened to the government censored radio and the Fascist propaganda.

Late that December we learned about America's entry into the war. At a time when our lives hinged mostly on hope, knowing America had joined Great Britain to fight Germany provided us the sweetest hope yet. At the time U.S. forces were engaged solely in the Pacific theater and the Italian radio made little mention of that. We longed to know more, but only a few townspeople owned a radio and we doubted any of them would be brave enough to defy the law or even interested in tuning to the short waves to listen to the BBC. In our building, only the landlord owned a radio.

"Can you imagine our landlady listening to the BBC?" Mamma was responding to Ettore Costa's question.

"Ask her," Ettore suggested.

"You're right. I have nothing to lose."

The next morning, while Filomena's husband was at school, Mamma approached her. "Could we listen to the enemy radio? I just want to see how they twist things around."

Much to my mother's surprise, the woman offered no objection. "Do you know how?" Filomena asked.

"No, but we can try."

Passing through the undulating noises of the short-wave stations, made it difficult to differentiate between music and voice. "I think this is it." There was a timbre in my mother's voice that had long been missing.

In perfect Italian, the frequently fading voice was reading the newscast. Mother's nervousness reflected in her short back and forth pacing. "Isn't this exciting, Filomena?" Mamma asked.

"Oh, yes. This is incredible. I'll have to tell Antonio."

"No, no. For heaven's sake, don't tell him! This has to remain a secret just between us."

The newscast over, Mother suggested moving the dial to another spot then placing a finger on her lips, added, "We don't want anyone to know. Remember, just between us."

The next day Filomena came upstairs to our quarters. "Let's go listen to our enemy." The woman was wringing her hands as she spoke. "I'm so nervous."

We walked down with Filomena. By now, my mother knew the spot on the dial and locked onto the station with little effort.

"Allied armies, augmented by a new American armored contingent, have started a counterattack in North Africa," the BBC reported. Seven thousand Italian soldiers and their officers had surrendered. For them, the commentator continued, the war had come to an end. These prisoners were being sent to the United States, where they would spend the remainder of the conflict in safety.

"I wish they would take us prisoner," Mamma said.

Filomena looked puzzled. "Why?"

"Then we could be sent to America."

The official Italian newscasts had never made mention of American soldiers fighting alongside the British or of Italian soldiers being taken prisoner. We always heard of Allied soldiers being taken prisoner. Only retreating armies are taken prisoner and, according to the Italian radio, the German and Italian armies had never retreated.

Another afternoon during their clandestine listening, with ears glued to the receiver, Filomena jumped from the stool. "I heard a different version of the same news on our own station last night," she shrieked. "They told us that the Italian army was victorious. These English people are just lying. Do they think we're so stupid to believe whatever they tell us?"

"Maybe our own radio didn't tell the truth," Mamma said.

Filomena didn't think too long for her answer. "That could be. Maybe Mussolini is filling us with lies?"

Mother had found an unexpected ally. Each day, together the two women absorbed the news like sponges. Then, hurriedly, Mamma disseminated the information throughout our small community of internees. Even I became an assiduous listener, mindful of turning down the volume whenever the BBC's "bum-bum-bum-boooom," the recognizable drumlike beat forming the first notes of Beethoven's *Fifth*, blared over the speaker.

"Do you think Filomena is on our side?" I asked Mamma.

"I don't know which side she is on. I don't think she knows."

During those days, Mother became more tense than usual. "If anyone reports me to the *carabinieri*, they'll shoot me."

I didn't know whether that was true, for I knew Mother could be melodramatic. "Stop scaring me like that," I said.

Thanks to Filomena's betrayal of her husband's cause, my mother was being kept up to date on what was happening in the world and our lives became more meaningful. Although, more often than not depressed by the successes of the German armies, everyone took great solace from the little bits of good news the BBC transmitted. But good news could also be frustrating, for we had to restrain ourselves whenever we heard of a German defeat. Unfriendly ears could easily have concluded that we must have heard it from the BBC.

At the Howells' we followed the battlefields on a map covered with pins. Having to acknowledge that Germany had conquered most of Europe, part of Russia, and North Africa during the winter of 1941–42 was very depressing.

For me the most fascinating aspect of the BBC broadcasts was the coded messages: "The monkey has gone home," or "The sheep has escaped from the barn." Months went by before I found out that these messages were meant for the resistance fighters throughout German-occupied Europe.

"I get ecstatic thinking people are revolting against the Nazis," Mother said. "I pray every day for the war to be over. So much blood is being spilled because of Hitler."

Hope for the future helped us endure our day-to-day hardships of being prisoners and waiting to be free again. Encouraged by some of the news, my thoughts went to how soon we would be reunited with *Omama* and Papa.

Although most internees were Christians, Christmas and New Year passed us by with very few festivities. With German forces victorious on every front, the *confinati* had nothing to celebrate. Even the townspeople had their own share of bad news. Most men of military age had been drafted and sent to the front lines, many to Russia. Three of these had already been listed as missing and the internees, who had lived in Eastern Europe and had firsthand knowledge of the harshness of a Russian winter, expressed their gloomy prediction: "Missing means dead."

"I feel for these families," Mamma said. "They didn't want to be part of this lousy war."

Even I had overheard some townspeople express their opposition to the war. They called it "Germany's war."

The days were shorter. Sunrise was late and by 4:00 in the afternoon, the sun had set behind the mountain, casting a long gray shadow over the village, that matched the shadow of our own mood. *Mutti* and I spent the long, icy evenings huddled around the fireplace in the landlord's kitchen. While our legs were burning from the fire's heat, the rest of our bodies, though wrapped in blankets, felt the chilly drafts whistling through the many breaches in the poorly constructed windows. Sitting near the fire for so many weeks, the women, contrary to the men whose legs were protected by pants, suffered most. And their blotched skin stayed with them year round.

Sitting around the fireplace gave Mother the chance to display her extraordinary ability to have animated discussions with people of all ages. She learned to do small talk. The only educated person in our midst was our landlord, Don Antonio, but Mother rarely got into a serious conversation with this ardent Fascist. Instead, she delighted us with stories about her own youth, from when she first arrived in Vienna during the last war up to the time in March when we were forced to flee. She was a superb *raconteuse*, riveting the rapt attention of everyone around her. During one of those evenings, she told how she went to work in a bank as soon as she had finished school to help her widowed mother. From those chats around the fireplace, I learned much about my own life as a baby, how she had toilet-trained me and how I refused to eat creamed spinach. But I never did find out how my parents met.

"When Enrico was little, he was such a poor eater. I wish he would eat as little now. We could have lots of ration coupons left over." I knew she was joking, for at every meal my mother encouraged me to eat more.

During that first winter, siblings Gusti and Davide Kampler were transferred to Ospedaletto from the separate camps where they had been kept since 1939. Both in their early twenties, with little knowledge of Italian, they had been isolated and alone in the new country. Their story quickly gained them the sympathies of the Wovsis, Runia, Mother, and all the other *confinati*, who took turns at inviting these traumatized young people to their home for a friendly meal.

The young brother and sister had escaped to Italy hoping to get their parents and their other seven brothers and sisters out of Germany. Instead they found themselves imprisoned after a few months and soon taken in chains to two separate camps.

We could feel David's anguish as he related their experience. "I felt like a common criminal. I finally was able to convince the guard that I had done nothing, and he removed the shackles from my feet."

At the same time, we also welcomed in our midst an emaciated and pathetic young man from Argentina and two brothers from Czechoslovakia. The unusually shy man from Buenos Aires seemed satisfied to stand quietly by, unable or unwilling to blend into our group. He spoke little Italian and, since none of us spoke Spanish, conversing with him was impossible. We learned little about him, only that he had been a barber in his country and had landed in Italy—we didn't know why—at which time he lost his personal possessions. He was a pathetic fellow, emaciated and malnourished. Every day he came to our meeting spot wearing the same frayed, stained clothes and shoes, of which only the tops were left without holes. He smiled and shook the hand of anyone who had outstretched theirs, but hardly said anything.

"Is it all right if I go to the fellow from Argentina for my haircut?" I asked. With Mother's blessing, I went to the man's small room in a building across from the main church. Using gestures, since we did not speak the same language, I tried telling him what I wanted. He snipped a little here, a little there. He must have combed my hair more than twenty times. I waited for the trimmer that all barbers use but he never used one. Nor did he use a barber's razor. Instead, he pulled out a safety razor, which probably served to shave him in the morning. The only tools this barber owned were a comb and a pair of scissors. The second ringing of the steeple bells made me realize that for two hours I had squirmed on an uncomfortable wooden chair for a haircut, a task that the local barber, who had a padded chair, did in twenty minutes.

For two months I waited for my hair to fully recover from this man's many blunders. For weeks I was in tears each time I combed my hair, while Mother couldn't stop laughing whenever she looked at the botched job. Needless to say, in spite of my feeling sorry for the poor fellow, never again did I go to the barber from Argentina.

The two brothers from Czechoslovakia, Karel and Willy Weil, were eager to become part of the group and adapted quickly. They were personable young men, medium in height and slim. Willy, a bit heavier than his brother, was more reserved. Elegant in their slightly worn double-breasted suits, meticulously knotted ties, and breast-pocket handkerchiefs, they reminded me of my own father. Their refined demeanor played down the wear their fine clothes had suffered through the two years since leaving their homeland. I never learned why they had been deprived of their freedom since they never admitted to being Jewish.

In December of 1941, Pietro Russo rented the small room on our floor situated halfway between the kitchen and the outhouse hanging at the end of the corridor. Mother, in need of supplementing what money she was getting from the government, offered to cook for him.

"That is great. I could not have asked for anything better," Signor Russo said.

Twice a day Mamma cooked for the three of us, and Pietro became a permanent and loving fixture in our kitchen. I enjoyed the mealtime political and literary conversations and casual Latin lessons Pietro brought to us. Being exposed to this intelligent man gave me the opportunity to start developing a political philosophy and to learn Italian literature and Latin in a pleasantly informal way.

I liked Pietro. In fact, I more than liked him. He was amiable and kind, and he brought poetry and the beauty of the spoken word into our lives. I envied his mastery at reciting Italian poetry from memory and his ability to make the passage fit the moment. The works of the illustrious Dante, Foscolo, Leopardi, Carducci, D'Annunzio, and the not-so-famous were all stored in his fertile mind and, though he had never composed poetry, his delivery of the works of others had the ring of heavenly lyrics to my ears. The pure beauty Pietro Russo possessed in his soul was missing in his physical appearance. Large in body, his hair reduced to a sparse strand on each temple, a round face accommodating a slightly slanted bulbous nose and a short neck, made somewhat shorter by an incipient double chin, all gave him a less-than-handsome appearance. Yet, when he looked at or spoke to you the sincerity in his eyes, the warmth of his voice, transformed him into a remarkably attractive human being.

Dottor Russo, as everyone called him out of respect, for he was not a doctor, had never been outside of Sicily but had skillfully blended the academic culture of a university graduate with the outdated thinking of his native town.

"What did your brothers and sisters study?" I asked.

"Well, I was the only one who went to the university." He explained that local customs called for the youngest in the family to go on to higher learning while his seven brothers and sisters stayed home to care for the family farm and their widowed mother.

I was allowed to spend some nights in Pietro's room and was captivated by him reading to me. Mother seemed pleased to watch our affection for one another grow. "Do you like Pietro?" she asked.

"Oh, yes," I responded with impetuous enthusiasm. "I like him a lot. Why do you ask?"

"Nothing special."

Whenever Mamma said "nothing special" that meant it was something extra special, so I started to look around without knowing what to look for. At times I even eavesdropped, trying to learn what was happening when the two of them were locked behind closed doors. But I learned nothing.

I did notice changes in my mother. She looked happier, eager to do things she had been reluctant to do before. She was more meticulous in her dress, though it was hard to detect since she had always dressed well. She stopped smoking. Old enough to understand about the relationship between a man and woman, I thought of my father and was unwilling to accept that a romance was blossoming right before my eyes.

Pietro did not pretend to be a cook, but on a few occasions, he insisted on introducing us to some native Sicilian dishes, such as lemon or orange soup, roasted sardines, or cooked intestines. I had watched him prepare the soups, ate them, and found them interesting. Now, watching his long, well-manicured fingers rinse the long tubular strands of a chicken's intestines disgusted me. "What are you doing with that?" I asked.

"You'll see. After I wash them, I'll wrap them over parsley and garlic and make a soup. It's delicious. You'll see."

It reminded me of the tripe or oysters of San Remo. I watched Mother, anxious to see if she would try it.

"Mamma, what do you think? Will you eat it?"

"What did you say?" she asked.

"I said, will you eat it?"

Mother ate it and so did I.

"Well, what do you think?" Pietro asked.

"It's very good." I replied.

"I think the cook deserves a kiss," Mamma said.

On her serene and lovely face I saw a glow I had seen only when she looked at me. She exuded a new youthfulness, making her look younger than her forty years.

Pietro did not look as surprised as I was by Mother's remark. "Is it all right with you?" he asked.

What could I say? Embarrassed, I ignored both his remark and her suggestion. Mother leaned over and kissed me, then turned and shared a long kiss with Pietro. They kissed on the mouth and, bashful, I turned my head while all along my eyes kept trying to steal a glance at the two of them.

I had never been close to a man and a woman when they kissed. My parents had never kissed like that in front of me. My thoughts turned into bedlam. What did this mean? Was my mother loving another man? If so, what about my papa?

Mother and Pietro spent much time together, and I found myself going to bed alone while they remained in the kitchen even after the lights went out. As hard as I tried, many times I could not stay awake long enough to hear my mother go to bed.

The weather, especially harsh that year, kept us inside most of those shortened days, and I learned much about this gentle man. Pietro spoke about his family with great warmth. The love this thirty-two-year-old man expressed for his mother and siblings was contagious, and I prayed I would never lose the same feelings for my own parents.

Weather permitting, Mamma and Pietro ventured out some afternoons to play bridge at the Howells'. On the days they did not, they taught me the finer points of the game. I cherished our time together.

"*De gustibus non disputandum est.*" This was Pietro's philosophical comment, prompted by Mother's disapproval of his brown tie and gray suit.

"What does that mean?" I asked.

"It means you cannot argue about taste. It's Latin," Pietro replied.

Another time, when we were talking about our stay in Ospedaletto, he recited a long passage from Dante's *Inferno*, which began: "*Perdete ogni speranza / O voi che entrate. / Queste parole di colore oscure. . . .*"

Afterward, I sat immobile, staring at the man who had uttered those words, reveling in the music he had created. Only when Pietro broke the spell with a smile was I able to speak. "When did you learn all this?"

"When I went to high school."

"And you still remember it?"

"All beautiful things are worth remembering." he said

That evening, as we prepared to retire, my mother dropped a bomb into my lap. "*Enricuccio,* would you like to sleep with Mamma and Pietro tonight?"

I couldn't have been more shocked if the whole ceiling had fallen on me. What did that mean? No other man, except for Papa, had ever slept with us or even in our home. Even in Vienna, I had never slept with my parents. Now Mamma was going to allow Pietro to sleep in the same bed? I had trouble understanding and didn't know what to answer. The more I thought about it, the less I knew what to say. In the end, but after a long pause, guessing there was nothing wrong with all of us sleeping together and that it could even be fun, I replied, "Sure."

"Only on one condition," Mamma added. "This has to stay between us. Do you understand?"

No, I couldn't understand why I had to keep this a secret, but nodded my head in assent.

After that first night, Pietro slept in my mother's bed many times, although I was never asked to sleep with them again.

There was a change in the air. I did not know what was going on, but I knew something was not the same. There was much talk I did not understand. Even Mother's friends spoke in languages I knew but using words I could not grasp. My whole world seemed to have left me behind, somewhat alone and incapable of finding out from anyone what was happening.

Winter's cold lured me into the billiards hall where I was sure I could earn some spending money by capitalizing on what I had learned in San Remo. What an awakening it was when I found out that almost anyone in that hall could separate me easily from what little money I had saved. Only the afternoon lunch break, when the parlor shut down between one and three, slowed down my losing process.

"Why not read a book? Since you've been going to the billiards room, you have done nothing else," Mother exploded.

"I like to play billiards."

Mother was angry. "You'll become a gambler, just like your father." Then, losing control over herself, added, "*Eyn curten spieler!*" making reference to my father's habit of playing cards.

Little did I know about my dad, nor had I ever seen him play cards. I adored my mother. She represented everything to me, yet her remarks about my father enraged me. "He was no gambler!" I shouted.

"Yeah. What would you know? While he gambled our money away, I sat home and worried where the next meal was coming from."

"I don't believe you!" I slammed the door and dashed down the stairs to the floor below.

Mother ran after me and, despite our twenty-nine-year age difference, proved to be fast enough to catch up. She grabbed me by the arm and dragged me back upstairs.

"Don't you ever slam the door again! Do you understand?" Her hand found my unsuspecting face, the physical hurt overshadowing what had anguished me moments before.

"I hate you when you criticize Papa. When he comes back, I'll go live with him," I shouted, trying, without success, to hold back the tears.

"Let me tell you something. If your father had not been such a gambler, maybe today we would be together and free."

"You didn't want to go to Poland, so he had to go by himself!"

"Stop shouting!" Mother screamed. She waited for her directive to sink in. Then in a normal tone, she continued, "You are right. I didn't want to go to Poland. Who knows what the Germans would have done to us by now? We would probably be dead. At least here we are safe from the Nazis. And did it ever occur to you that maybe your papa didn't want to go to France with us?"

No, that had never occurred to me. "What do you know about the Germans and what they would have done to us?" I asked.

"I know, I know." But Mamma never said more.

The thought that had we gone to Poland we could now be dead sent a screaming chill down my spine. Perhaps she knew something and didn't want to share it with me. Yes, it was better we had not gone to Poland. But even the thought of death didn't stop my resentment at that moment, and I told her so.

"*A kholeriye oyf dir*," I shouted, wishing that a plague should befall her.

When I realized the meaning of the Yiddish words, I pleaded with her to forgive me. She did so in her usual loving fashion. That night I added a line to my regular bedtime prayer. After praying to keep Papa, *Omama*, Aunt Stefi, and everyone else in our family healthy and safe, I added, "Please forgive me for upsetting my mother so often."

The events and uncertainties of the last three years were having an impact on us. Mother's nerves snapped at the slightest provocation and we ended in an argument and judging from some of the things I said, my emotional state was none too good either. I was feeling the strain of the uncertainty in our lives.

On the nights I had trouble falling asleep, my imagination roamed in the darkened room. I sensed my father's long-missed embrace and recalled that sparkle of joy in his eyes. Then my mind inhaled *Omama*'s scent as she stood by her open door and I felt the kisses her weak lips poured over my small face. I also tasted the homemade pickles my grandmother in Lwow stored in a cabinet on the cold stairwell, felt the softness of *Opapa*'s gray beard, and wondered if all this would ever be true again.

During the first winter in Ospedaletto, to alleviate the boredom, I learned to knit, sew, and use Dora's sewing machine. I also built a pair of wooden skis. The only time I had seen skis was in the park in Vienna and then only from a distance, thus what I made was a poor excuse for skis. They did have slightly bent tips, the only resemblance to the real thing. I cannot claim to have skied but only strapped the wood creations onto my feet and made an attempt at sliding about. I was thrilled. What anyone else thought of my skis was really unimportant. What mattered most to me was that I was the only person in the village who possessed a pair.

Don Giuseppe Sabatino, a young priest who had left Ospedaletto three years earlier to enter the seminary, returned home prepared to perform his first mass. He was lanky and pale, only the much-too-loose black tunic added some bulk to his frail body. His concave cheeks accentuated the lack of flesh, and the cartilage in his pointed nose was almost visible through the thin layer of skin, giving him a semblance of a dead man. Only his dark eyes glowed with vitality, in that otherwise lifeless face yet when he spoke, his zest for life was anything but lifeless.

Don Giuseppe had a certain charisma that made the local folks like him. Given the nature of the townspeople, so often bent on finding fault with anyone, liking this new priest was close to miraculous. Don Giuseppe had been back a few days when I spotted this new face sitting at the caffè on the small square. Prompted by my usual curiosity, I approached his table.

"Father, where are you from?" I asked.

"From Ospedaletto. I've been away for a while, but now I'm back to stay. What's your name?"

That morning, from our very first exchange, I sensed a bond. I was drawn to this man of the cloth, though I knew it would never meet with my mother's blessing. The glimmer in his intelligent eyes reflected that he enjoyed talking with me.

"What did they teach you at the seminary?" I asked.

"We learned many things. We studied the Holy Scriptures and also Hebrew. You did not know that, did you?"

"No. I also studied Hebrew but never liked it. Tell me something, why do priests always try to convert us Jews?"

"Because the New Testament tells us we cannot shed the original sin and be allowed into heaven until we have been baptized."

"What original sin?" I asked. I had heard similar invitations to become a Catholic and remembered how one of the internees had handled the debate. But I had not heard the part about the original sin.

"When God told Eve not to eat the forbidden fruit."

I wasn't sure whether to laugh or be serious. Was this man joking, or did he think I was a total fool? I knew the tale of Adam and Eve, but the thought that eating the apple was the original sin and that her sin was my sin seemed hysterically funny to me. Still, I held back from laughing for fear of offending my new friend. "Are you telling me that because she ate the apple, I'm guilty?"

"We all are. Eve disobeyed the Lord's command."

"I can't believe what you're telling me. I'll remain Jewish. We don't have these *bubbe mayse*," I said, throwing in some Yiddish for good measure.

"What was that you said?"

"*Bubbe mayse*?"

"Yes"

"It means a grandmother's tale."

He laughed. "You're a good debater," he remarked. "Where did you learn it?"

"From my mother and the other grownups. I don't have friends my own age."

Don Giuseppe's appearance into my small world created a ray of joy. I rushed home to break the big news to Mother. "*Mammina*, I just met this priest, Don Giuseppe. I like him. I think we'll become friends."

"*Eyn glik hot mik getrofen!*" That was *Mutti*'s favorite expression. She had used it so often that I knew its sarcastic meaning.

"No matter what I do, you have to criticize it!" I shouted.

"I only said I'm so lucky. How do you expect me to feel? I can't send you to a synagogue, and now you pick a Catholic priest for a pal. Do you want me to light a candle in church?"

Her humor disarmed me somewhat. "Well, I like Don Giuseppe and he's going to be my friend. You will like him, too."

Pietro was more understanding, but then he was Catholic. Catholic! For the first time this reality struck me. How can Mamma even think of being with a man who was not Jewish? That was inconceivable in our family. What was going on? Was everything upside down?

The time I spent with the young priest was never enough for me. Every get-together helped sharpen my mental agility. We had stimulating discussions even if occasionally I had to listen to his lectures on why I should convert.

Because I wanted us to remain friends, I asked him to let the religious argument rest and after a few more failed attempts, he did. Following his consecration, he invited me to be present when he celebrated his first mass. I was proud that this Catholic priest was willing to count me among his friends and never made me feel uncomfortable for being Jewish.

That year he invited me to spend Christmas night with his family. "Come to church and, after midnight mass, you'll come to the house. You don't have to pray or take communion."

Staying out all night needed Mother's approval. "Because it's Don Giuseppe, I'll give you special dispensation. I made a funny." She laughed at her own joke.

On Christmas Eve, I skipped church. Instead I took a short nap and, at about one in the morning, went to Don Giuseppe's home. The night was spent playing games and eating Christmas cookies until the early morning. As I was ready to leave, Don Giuseppe's mother invited me to come back for New Year's Eve.

What a difference between the companions I had left behind in San Remo and the youth I found in Ospedaletto. My old friends were well mannered and clean. I never heard them use vulgarities, while in this village cursing was the everyday language. Kids started early in life to repeat the profanities they heard their parents use. For the first time

I was exposed to words I did not quite understand but was too bashful to ask my mother or Pietro for an explanation.

But foul language was the least objectionable of the local boys' behavior. I found their cruelty intolerable. They routinely threw stones at dogs and anything that moved, and they enjoyed taunting the two mentally retarded young men who roamed the village. Reluctantly, I learned to stay out of the way of these urchins and, out of self-defense, I practiced pitching stones, limiting my throwing at inanimate objects.

The girls and young women of the village were not any less aggressive. They exchanged invectives and occasionally fought amongst themselves, which invariably included pulling each other's long hair. I couldn't help thinking about the lice crawling from the pulled hair onto their hands and arms. How disgusting!

"I don't want you to associate with those boys," Mamma said firmly after she had seen me walk through the piazza with two of the local kids.

Pietro, who was in the kitchen with us, agreed with my mother. "You must be careful about the company you keep. There is an old saying: 'Tell me with whom you go and I will tell you who you are.'"

I had a feeling they were both right, and furthermore, I wasn't about having any of those boys as my friends. Nonetheless, I resented being kept from doing so. "I'm sick and tired of always having to do what you want me to." I complained. "I go with you when you play bridge. But the adults won't let me play because I'm too young. Jimmy thinks he is too old for me and when I find my own friends you say they aren't good enough."

"You know Raffaele and his brother. Why don't you spend more time with them?" Mother said referring to the two Sanseverino boys whose father owned the one general store in the village.

"Raffaele has little time; he always has so much homework. And Giovanni is too old for me."

Mother also encouraged my friendship with Sabato Pisano, who was at least six years my senior. Because Ospedaletto's solitary school offered only the first five grades, those select few who owned shoes and the appropriate clothing could walk the four miles to Avellino to attend high school. The other villagers' children remained illiterate, since their parents were seldom able to feed their offspring, let alone worry about giving them an education.

One day in the post office, I saw someone place an X on a document. "What does the ex mean?" I asked Don Guglielmo, the postmaster.

"That's his signature. The man cannot write."

Raffaele belonged to one of the few fortunate families who could afford to provide an education for their children. His day began around 5:00, so he could make his four-mile trek in the morning darkness down the narrow footpath that led to Avellino. When classes were over at 1:00, my friend retraced his steps, sometimes through knee-deep snow.

"How come your sisters don't go to high school?" I asked.

He burst into a hearty laugh. "Are you joking?" he said. "Even in my family—and we are more modern than most—my father wouldn't think of letting my sisters walk to Avellino alone."

"Why not?" I asked.

"It just isn't done."

Because of old traditions, most young women in Ospedaletto never had the benefit of a better education.

Two years had elapsed since I had seen the inside of a classroom, and I became concerned about the education I was not getting. Without any objection on my part, *Mutti* approached Clara Gattegno, who was respected for her cultural background.

"I beg you, give Enrico some tutoring. He needs to study something. Anything."

"Lotte, I have never tutored anyone and besides, my eyesight has been getting progressively worse."

"Please, Claruccia. Anything."

Born in Ankara of Turkish parents some thirty years earlier, Clara Gattegno had moved to Italy as a child. Among her natural gifts were a strikingly sculptured head of short, black, curly hair, dark and fiery eyes, testimony of her Sephardic heritage as well as rounded cheeks and a well-defined mouth. Had she devoted a little time to her personal grooming she would have looked most attractive.

One day while Clara was visiting us, Mamma offered to help. "Let me fix your hair."

"No, no. I don't have time for such nonsense. I'd rather embellish my mind than waste time on my looks."

It wasn't just idle talk. She had a greatly embellished mind. I could listen to her talk and always be in awe. She was well informed and could discuss so many subjects.

Sipping tea in our kitchen, she confided to us, "I have never been religious. I don't remember the last time I saw the inside of a synagogue. When I asked the police commissioner in Naples why I was being sent away, he said because I was Jewish. Strange, though several of my Jewish friends are still in Naples living a normal life. Who can understand these Fascists?"

Succumbing to Mamma's pleadings, Clara relented and agreed to tutor me. I don't know who was happier at her capitulation, Mother or me, but I looked forward to the twice-a-week afternoon lessons. Clara taught me Italian literature, history, geography, and mathematics and rewarded my progress with postage stamps she had collected years earlier when she had worked at the American consulate.

I completed the daily assignments with enthusiasm and waited for my next lesson. Perhaps I had developed a crush on this gentle and beautiful woman and I loved the time we spent together.

16

Pietro Russo and Ettore Costa

The names of North African towns—Tobruk, Tripoli, Bengazi—were on every internee's lips. Was it Feldmarschall Rommel or was it General Montgomery who had struck a big blow the day before? It was impossible to ever get the truth from the state radio. If we were to believe what we had been told by the Italian newscasts, then British forces already had been annihilated and the only men left in that army were a few old cooks. I noticed Mother had become more vigilant when listening to the BBC. She confided that she was afraid Filomena would tell her husband and that it would turn into a major disaster.

Each morning, as my mother approached our gathering point in the piazza, the first question from the internees was, "So, hear anything new?"

"You will get me in trouble if you don't stop asking that question out loud," Mamma complained. "I am afraid someone will overhear you and that will be it."

Mr. Perutz, huffing and puffing, his weak legs straining to carry his portly body, was rushing up the incline to join the group at the regular meeting spot. Out of breath, he called for our attention. "Heard the latest? They bombed La Valletta again." He was referring to the capital of the tiny island of Malta. The island belonged to Great Britain and Axis planes bombed the island every single day.

"I don't understand something," Ettore said. "If, as they tell us, they have bombed Malta every day and I know the Fascist radio wouldn't lie to us, there can't be anything left standing. Then what are they still bombing? As a good Italian, I am indignant. They are wasting my money. I must write to Mussolini."

Mr. Perutz had more to report. Evidently he must have listened to the BBC. "The best news is that a large convoy of Italian tankers docked in Tripoli, but instead of petrol, the tanks were filled with salt water." As soon as that bit of news seeped in, everyone broke out in a guarded outburst of joy. "Can you imagine what this will do to Rommel? He needs this fuel to continue his North African campaign."

Pierce pointed his finger at Mr. Perutz. "The day will come when you will wish you had been on the right side."

"We *are* on the right side," Mamma said.

"You keep believing in your *Duce*," Perutz said. "We'll see who will have wished for what."

Now it was my mother's turn. "Signor Pierce, I cannot understand something. If you're such a great supporter of Fascism and Mussolini, how come you're here with us?"

Pierce waived both arms in the air while his face contracted in an ugly smirk. "Bureaucracy, bureaucracy. Just a simple bureaucratic error. And small errors will have to wait. I don't expect the people in Rome to find the time now to examine my case."

"Signor Pierce, you are a lost cause," Mother said.

On another morning, arriving at the corner earlier than usual, Ettore Costa was waiting for everyone to gather before divulging the rumor he himself had concocted. "Did you hear the latest?" he murmured. He bowed and pushed his slightly balding head into the group around him. Everyone stooped to bring their ears closer. He waited for a moment, then, with the tip of his index finger, pushed his thick glasses up on his forehead. "Last night hundreds of German planes bombed Tobruk. An absolute inferno." He stopped to let the news sink in. "Damage report: one flat bicycle tire."

"I guess you'll never change," Runia remarked as she joined the others, adding her self-conscious laughter to theirs.

As much as I enjoyed this man's sense of humor, I was even more captivated when Ettore was serious and spoke of his experiences as a correspondent. Sicilian by birth, gypsy by choice, Ettore graduated law school after his father had denied him the pursuit of music.

"I spent every waking hour with my artist friends," he said. "Never had enough sleep. It was a miracle I passed the exams."

After obtaining two degrees, law and journalism, he followed his call to travel. "I became a foreign correspondent, a sure way to see the world."

As a young man, he had covered North America and a number of European countries for an Italian newspaper. "Fabulous country, the United States. Immense farms, gigantic cities, and people of every race. I wish I had spent more time there."

In Spain he witnessed the civil war and in Germany the beginning of the rise of Nazism. He even admitted that, when Mussolini first came to power in 1922, he had been an ardent supporter of Fascism, only to become a passionate antagonist once he realized that his idol had become a dictator. "I have more than made up for my mistake of supporting Fascism. I have grasped every opportunity to write against

the regime and have paid a pretty price. Look at these thick glasses."
He had taken them off his head.

He told us of the many months spent in prison. How, while incarcerated, ignoring the ever-present censorship, he amused himself by writing anti-Fascist sentiments on postcards and sending them to friends. "They generally only censor letters because those idiots are sure that no one would dare express himself on a postcard." But a guard did read one of his cards and Ettore's audacity provoked a fierce beating that resulted in a severe loss of his eyesight. But for this idealist, being an anti-Fascist had become a crusade, a crusade he fought in the light of day unconcerned for his personal safety.

Cultured, intelligent, conversant in three languages, a confirmed bachelor, and a gifted painter, Ettore Costa fit the mold of the true Bohemian. Even his unruly hair—he seldom combed it except by running his fingers through it—matched his personality. "Life is to be lived," was a favorite expression of his. Then, casting his arm in the air, "Money? Possessions? Who cares?" And this man lived by his principles, for he hardly ever had money or possessions. Often he needed to ask his friend Pietro for a loan until his monthly government stipend arrived. He told us that before the war he could easily spend in one night all he had earned in one week. "Money burns a hole in my pants pockets." When asked why he didn't write about his life, he responded, "I'd rather live it than write about it."

Ettore was an absent-minded scatterbrain. Few mornings went by that he did not forget something—his watch, a handkerchief, to eat breakfast, or, once, even his socks. "You can't imagine what I forgot this morning," he announced. His impish grin betrayed him. "Forgot to call *Il Duce* to remind him there is a war going on."

Ettore lived life with great intensity. An abiding optimist and an inspiration to many who shared these times with him, he had the enthusiasm of a much younger man. For more than a year he brought humor, purpose, and hope to us all. Eventually, he was allowed to move to Fiesole, near Florence, because of his declining health.

"I hope one day I can be as funny as Signor Costa," I said.

"Maybe you will," Mamma replied. "I just hope you will not be as loud." My mother was still not especially fond of the man.

One day someone asked Ettore about Germany at the time Hitler came to power. "You want to know what went on in Germany in thirty-four and thirty-five? It was like nothing you could possibly imagine and I had the guts to write about it, but nobody listened. I saw people beaten until they couldn't move anymore. I saw the rise of anti-Semitism. The burning of books. I witnessed the beginning of the end of civilization. And no one cared. That's when I decided that I would not stand by silently if the same ever happened here in Italy."

"All your writing and talking. What good did it do you?" Karel Weil asked. "You ended up in jail. You got beaten. Look at Dottor Russo. He, too, landed in jail just for saying a few negative words about Fascism."

"But if we all keep silent, evil will have won its first victory and, even without going to jail, we will all be prisoners for the rest of our lives." I could tell from the agitation in Ettore's voice that Karel had touched a sensitive chord. "What's life worth when you're afraid to say what you think because your neighbor or perhaps your own friend will report you? Tell me, what is it worth? Only by raising our voices can we hope to bring sanity back to Europe. Today I speak, tomorrow you do and before long others speak and then soon the fervent hope we now have for justice becomes a reality."

I was so impressed by this man's mastery with words. Oh, how I wished I could speak like him.

Signor Pierce made the mistake of meddling. "You sound like the Communists. They use the same line: justice. Justice. What justice?"

"With due respect, you're an imbecile, *mio caro Signore*. Forgive me, but you are the most indisputably, matriculated, absolute imbecile I have ever met and I have met a few." Ettore was shaking and his voice was higher by an octave. "Comparing me to a Communist? That's a laugh." Then, turning to the others, he said, "This idiot has the nerve to call me a Communist. What do you know about Communism, Signor Pierce? You still believe anyone against your wonderful *Duce* has to be a Communist."

But Ettore's anger was short-lived. He had gotten it off his chest and within moments he was back in good spirits.

When John Howell asked what could have been done to stop Hitler before he embarked on war, Ettore, in his straightforward, undiplomatic manner, blamed Great Britain and France. He was certain Hitler would not have prepared for war in 1937 or 1938 had the German dictator been convinced of those countries' resolve. "But that idiot Chamberlain went to kiss Hitler's derriére. I hope you'll forgive me, Signor Howell. Let's not forget, tyrants have succeeded throughout history because good, naïve people just stood by and did nothing. Fear of war has never stopped despots; it only stopped decent people."

Pietro Russo offered his thoughts. "What's so sad is that, as decent people lose their courage, the others gain more of theirs. Right here in Ospedaletto there are many local people who don't support the Fascist regime or the war. They still remember the castor oil, which was used by the *camicie nere,* or Black Shirts, to silence those who opposed Mussolini. They're afraid to get involved or speak. Look what happened to me."

"So, is anyone suggesting we start a revolution?" Perutz asked.

"Not at all. Just to speak up whenever the opportunity presents itself," Pietro said. "Education is the greatest threat to any dictatorship. Fascism had succeeded in instilling in us fear of our own neighbors, friends, and even relatives. I no longer speak unless sure that only trusted friends are listening."

Ettore's sense of humor kept everyone's spirits high and his encouragement helped many to come out from their self-imposed censorship and be more outspoken. The Kamplers, John Howell, Runia Kleinerman, all generally timid in expressing their political ideas in public, became less apprehensive about verbalizing their aversion to Fascism. But Ettore had little effect on my mother. She insisted on remaining cautious in public about her political views. Anytime I risked saying anything that could be misunderstood as being against Mussolini or his government, Mamma was quick to shush me.

One morning Don Giuseppe, the young priest I had befriended, walked up to the corner where we gathered every day. With his usual friendly smile, he asked, "Do you mind if I join you for your walk?" No one did and, after ceremonious introductions, some of which I performed, we began our leisurely stroll.

Ettore seemed pleased at the priest's presence. "Great! We can put politics aside and talk about religion. I am a devout atheist." Whenever Ettore spoke, he savored his own words and this time was no exception.

"I was brought up as a Catholic," Ettore continued. "You know, Father, we Sicilians are supposed to be devout Catholics. What I cannot understand is this fanaticism to believe that ours is the only real religion. We go around the world trying to convert everyone so they can go to heaven. We preach about poverty and sacrifices, yet the Catholic Church is the wealthiest institution in the world. Father, forgive my directness, but when I became smart enough to see the true color of the church, I abandoned my early teachings and I'm happier for it."

There was a moment of silence. Only the soles of our shoes brushing the gravel road could be heard.

"These are strong words, my son," said the priest. He had fire in his eyes but his voice was calm. I had a close-up view of the two men since I had managed to walk alongside them.

"My dear father," said Ettore, "I've met many priests during my travels and the hypocrisy I've seen in many of them convinced me that my decision was the correct one."

"I will not question your experiences, but I want you to remember that priests are only human and subject to temptations. Only our Lord Jesus Christ is perfect and, if some of his disciples are less than perfect, that does not make our Lord so."

"What makes you think that only the Lord Jesus is perfect? How about Mohammed or Buddha?" Ettore asked.

"You know the answer, my son. There is only one God."

"Why could it not be Mohammed?"

"Because the Old and New Testament teach us who the only God is."

"If I remember my facts, the Koran says otherwise."

The group, fascinated, moved slowly, stopping every few moments to listen to the heated debate. We went only half the distance that morning and when we arrived back at the piazza, the contest had not yet stopped. It was nearly 1:00 and time for lunch, yet no one seemed eager to leave.

"My dear Father, you have not told me anything I have not heard dozens of times in catechism class, but these answers are no longer sufficient for me."

"Perhaps someday you will see the truth again," Don Giuseppe said.

"For sure not," Ettore said. "But let's remain friends. Now I must go get a good dish of spaghetti."

17

A Letter from *Omama*

T he last time we heard from Aunt Stefi was in 1940, when we were still living in San Remo. So when in early 1942 we received a letter from them, our jubilation was boundless.

At city hall I picked up the envelope, defaced by a number of Nazi swastikas. The black markings and the brown tape, used by the censors, intimidated me. Was this some letter from the Nazis? Even after I recognized the sender's name, my anxiety lasted all the way home.

Mother ripped the envelope with her forefinger and struggled to hold the three pages up straight. My aunt had obtained our address from the Swiss Red Cross and thanks to them, we were able to rejoice in this rare family communication.

Our joy was short-lived. From the three-page letter we learned Aunt Stefi and *Omama* were in a German labor camp. Starting in the early morning, before four, they dug potatoes and cabbage from the cold and wet ground. Life was good and safe. They were treated well, had plenty of food, and were happy to be together, my aunt wrote.

"I am sure only the last part of that sentence is true," said Mother, her eyes so swollen by tears that she strained to read the words on the paper. "She must have known her letter would be read by German censors." Then, pointing to the black marks covering a good portion of the letter, Mother added, "Look at it. This censor didn't like what Aunt Stefi wrote so they just covered everything with black ink."

In the half of the letter we were able to read, Aunt Stefi wrote how happy she was that, just before leaving Vienna, she had succeeded in getting a friend to send us some of *Mutti*'s personal possessions. She was sorry that she could not have done more, but our apartment had been emptied by the time she got there. We had received the package from the anonymous friend just before we left San Remo. Among other items, the package had included a down comforter that served us well during the cold winter nights in Ospedaletto.

By the time she laid the note on the table, Mother was sobbing. "Can you picture *Omama*? She is seventy years old, getting up at four in the morning, kneeling on the wet ground to dig out potatoes. But I thank God that at least they are alive and well."

I wondered why she had this fear of our family being dead. Did Mamma think the Germans were going around killing people?

We put our arms around each other and held ourselves tight. I felt my own tears mix with *Mutti*'s as they ran down my cheeks.

We received three more notes from Aunt Stefi, all bearing the unmistakable markings of the German censors. From my aunt's shaky handwriting we could tell that writing must have become difficult and painful for her.

"I want you to write a few words to Aunt Stefi and *Omama*," *Mutti* said. She handed me a blank sheet. "I will help you."

I still spoke German fluently but had never learned to write it well. By revising and correcting, *Mutti* helped me overcome my limited knowledge of the difficult Teutonic grammar. With great patience, she continued teaching me the language I would have learned to write if only I had been allowed to continue school in my native city.

Sitting at the kitchen table, I struggled to put together a few words from thoughts I had great difficulty formulating. After much writing and scratching out, I handed the sheet to my mother. In my short note, I wrote my aunt, among other things, of having a stamp collection and how happy she would make me if the next time she wrote she would use commemorative stamps. Her reply arrived about two weeks later. As had become my habit each afternoon, soon after the arrival of the coach from Avellino, I went to city hall to pick up the mail.

"Here you are," Don Pepe said, handing me an envelope. It was from Aunt Stefi. How many stamps! I was so excited.

I ran up the long, steep road all the way home and up the two flights of stairs. "*Mutti! Mutti!* From *Tante* Stefi. Look at all these stamps. Please be very careful. They're for me." The envelope looked as though it was covered by a mass of different postage stamps.

"Oh, my God," Mamma exclaimed. "Who knows how many weeks' wages this represents?"

I didn't quite understand what that meant, but, filled with anxiety to get to the stamps, I did not ask for an explanation. Mother, with shaking hands, was about to rip open the envelope.

"No, no, Mamma! Let me open it, please." At that moment my only concern was to protect those precious stamps. With my penknife I carefully slit open the envelope, pulled out the enclosed two sheets and handed them to my mother.

I was too busy examining the stamps to realize how upset *Mutti* was. Holding one sheet in each hand, through the abundant tears, she told me what my aunt had written.

"Aunt Stefi and *Omama* are being sent to another labor camp in Poland. She says that there they will have more work for them."

It would be their last letter. We never heard from them again.

The image of *Omama's* small figure in her black dress, the kind smile on her wrinkled face, the *sheytl*—Mother had explained the meaning of the wig—fused to the memory of her weekly visits when she had taught me how to play rummy. I remembered the times I had gone to her small, third-floor apartment on Ybbs Strasse in Vienna. My devoted Millie would walk with me there, down the Prater Strasse, past the amusement park. Somehow, although she had no telephone, *Omama* always knew when I was about to visit, for she never failed to prepare my favorite plum preserve.

Grandma would greet me at the door with a bright smile. "I have a surprise for you," then she wrapped me in her wide-opened arms.

I was only five or six and always knew what the surprise was and where she hid it, but I played the game anyhow. "*Povedl?*" I asked. "Where is it?"

"Ah ha. If you can find it, you can have some." *Omama* always hid it in the same place, down in the corner of a small cupboard under the kitchen window. Oh, how I loved the smell and taste of that plum preserve! In Ospedaletto I often asked *Mutti* to make me *povedl*.

"I can't," she explained. "I need dried prunes for that and I can't find any in this *verstunkenes* place."

One memory in particular gnawed and tormented me. I was not much more than five years old when *Omama* came to visit. My parents had gone out and I was in a bad mood. I refused to let her play with me and insisted she go home. Little did I care that it was Friday after sundown and my grandmother, in observation of the Sabbath, would not use public transportation but had to walk back home. Now, my greatest wish was to hold her close and tell her how sorry I was for having been so cruel that day.

Fate contrived another ironic twist. It allowed me only one possession as a memento of my beloved Aunt Stefi and my *Omama*: one stamp from that last envelope. A stamp with a large picture of Adolf Hitler.

A stamp bearing Hitler's image appeared on the envelope carrying the last letter from the author's grandmother and aunt, 1942.

In February 1942, Pietro received a special travel permit to visit his ailing mother in Sicily.

Pietro left immediately and returned two weeks later. Upon his return, he hired a horse-drawn cart to bring him from the Avellino train terminal. As the horse struggled around the last bend of the road, just before entering the village, I saw Pietro. I rushed to throw my arms around him, then ran back through the village to spread the news. "I have to tell Mamma!" I yelled as I ran away from him.

"Pietro is back! Pietro is back!" I shouted as I saw Mamma, then turned around and ran back.

By the time I got there, I saw the horse, visibly exhausted from the five-mile-long and difficult uphill labor, straining up the unforgiving incline. Pietro was walking alongside the carriage. The driver, using the whip on the defenseless horse, had jumped off the bench in the vain hope that lashing the animal from a shorter distance would produce some miraculous surge of energy. Instead with each blow, the struggling horse stumbled, losing more of what little strength it still possessed.

"Stop hitting it!" Pietro shouted.

The driver, with a mixed look of disbelief and annoyance, in a typical show of respect to his master, tapped the whip on the visor of his cap and, grasping the horse's metal bridle, walked on.

"Are you coming back to your room?" I asked.

Pietro hesitated. "Don't know just yet."

Those words saddened me. I didn't want Pietro to go somewhere else. I idolized this man. His two-week absence made me aware of how much I missed him.

As the horse, forcefully exhaling from its wet nostrils, labored up and around the last curve before entering the main piazza, Pietro directed the driver to our building.

"You fooled me!" I said and my gloom vanished.

I looked at the horse. The sad eyes of the worn animal spoke a language I could not understand. I looked and thought: How could any human treat a living creature with such inhumanity?

Three years had passed since we had received my father's last letter. Poland had been overrun in 1939, and partitioned between Germany and Russia, only to become a battleground a few months later when Hitler decided to attack his former Russian ally. News from that front was sketchy at best and only related to military actions. About the civilians, caught in the turmoil of war, we heard nothing at all.

Soon after Pietro's return, Mother and I were alone in the kitchen.

"*Erichl*, sit," she said. "I must tell you something. *Pupo* and I are in love with each other and I hope you can accept this."

At that moment I was more focused on how uncomfortable my mother looked uttering those words than on the words themselves. It was obvious that Mamma and Pietro were more than just good friends, but to be in love? Was Papa dead? He had to be dead. Otherwise, how could she fall in love with another man? My parents were still married and my mother could not be in love with someone else. My *Mutti* would not do that. Not unless she knew something she did not want to share with me.

I was afraid to ask. I trembled. I thought of Pietro. Oh, how I loved this man. I was also sure he cared for me and by now I knew him better than my own father. But I longed for my papa and didn't want to accept that Mother could marry another man. She had not mentioned marriage. What else did it mean when a man and a woman are in love? Pietro was not Jewish. Did my mother realize that? Papa would come back one day. I was sure of that. I wanted to scream all these thoughts so *Mutti* would know how I felt. Then, suddenly I realized what mattered most at that moment: Pietro loved me and he was there to show it.

Mother sat silently waiting for my reaction, but all she got was a blank stare.

Pietro Russo and Eric's mother in 1942.

18

Keeping Myself Occupied

Mother, seconded by Pietro, discouraged me from going to the billiards room where I had been losing my money. So, more to comply with Pietro's wishes than my mother's and to keep myself occupied, I stopped by the shop of one of the town's two cabinetmakers. Enrico, short of stature as well as temper, his curly hair untidy, his face most days unshaven, worked out of a small shop on the street level only a few paces from the church. He lived upstairs with his widowed mother and a younger sister.

His workshop resembled a storage shed—disorganized, with jumbles of remnants everywhere. A good look around his shop made me realize that Enrico saved everything. Old cabinets and planks of old lumber covered by thick dust, lay stacked against the back of the store. The walls were covered with hanging tools, sheets of paper, and even an old useless chair. The workspace was so reduced by all that clutter that it was impossible to build furniture in there. But, as I soon learned, Enrico had it all worked out, Italian style.

During the warmer weather, he moved his activity outside on the street. Since hardly any traffic ever came through the center of the village, blocking the road was not a concern. In the morning, on a well-abused blanket, he would place a furniture piece, only to bring it back inside at midday. Work never started before ten and between the time the item was laid out and the lunch hour, Enrico had just three hours to devote to his craftsmanship. That is, provided no one stopped by to chat or take him to the *caffè* for a much-needed espresso. The same routine he repeated in the afternoon. Watching this busy activity for the first time, I figured that more time was spent on getting ready to do the work than doing the work itself.

Enrico made only bedroom furniture and of only one style. He made the large items in the warmer weather when he could work outside, while the small pieces, such as night tables, were left for the colder days, when he could work inside.

Since the workshop was small, clients had to accept delivery as each piece was completed and because most of the furniture was made for newlyweds, getting married in Ospedaletto d'Alpinolo included strategizing when to place the order.

Enrico used only hand tools.

"How come you don't use an electric saw?" I asked. "The other cabinetmaker in town has one."

"Costs too much and I can do it better my way," he replied. "The old methods are still best."

Enrico sawed, planed, and drilled everything by hand. Even the lumber he purchased was not milled. He preferred to cut it himself. He had a thirteen-year-old boy, Pasquale, who, for the privilege of learning a trade, worked for no pay. For Pasquale learning was not easy, for each time he made a mistake or was slow to respond to instructions, Enrico tended to hit him rather than show him what to do.

"You idiot! You'll never amount to anything. *Si na bestia!*" Enrico would scream, calling him an animal and hurling a chunk of wood at the boy.

Three times I stopped by the shop before I dared to stick my head inside. Enrico walked up to me. "Do you want to give me a hand?" he asked. I wanted to, indeed and was eager to learn woodworking, but I was intimidated by the way the cabinetmaker abused his helper.

"I'm not sure. What do you need?"

"I need to cut this plank down," he said, pointing to a thick trunk of tree, bark and all.

With trepidation, using a feeble excuse in case I wanted to leave early, I said, "I have very little time today."

I helped Enrico cut several thin, uneven planks. Standing on opposite sides, we pulled and pushed a large saw, scraping its toothed blade back and forth against the hunk of lumber firmly clamped to the bench. The steady rhythm of the serrated blade cutting into the resisting wood produced a pleasant pitch that made the five-hour tedious labor a bit more tolerable. By the time I left the shop in late afternoon, I was covered with the delicious-smelling sawdust. Thus was that I became Enrico's second apprentice. Back I went the next day, anxious to learn but still somewhat hesitant.

"Come in! Come in! *Buon giorno!* What's your name?"

"My name is also Enrico."

Without asking, he handed me a heavy plane made of a solid block of wood with a metal blade. I had seen him sharpen it with meticulous care the day before.

"Know how to use this?" he asked.

"Not really."

He took the plane from me, gave me a short course on how to use it by digging into a scrap piece, then handed the tool back. The tone of voice he used with me differed greatly from the one he used to yell at Pasquale. "When you tire, you tell me," he said.

For the remainder of the day, except for going home for lunch, Pasquale and I took turns letting the curved blade dig out the hard chestnut plank Enrico and I had sliced the day before. Thirteen hours we worked, when we added the sawing to the planning, to bring the board down to Enrico's desired thickness. It was arduous labor with little reward, since it was hard to see any progress we made from hour to hour.

When Enrico concluded that we had removed enough from the plank, he shoved us aside and took over for the next phase. Using a different plane, he reduced the board to about one inch. More than half of the original lumber ended in a waste pile. The labor, which took two days, could have been done in one hour with power tools had Enrico not insisted on remaining entrenched in the nineteenth century.

Enrico did make beautiful furniture but took forever to make it. After cutting each piece by hand, using different planes to produce groove and tongue fittings, he would prepare a special glue, a glue that came from fish bones and had to be heated every time he needed it. To tighten the glued parts together, Enrico used a homemade cord contraption, which acted as a vise. Nothing he built ever came apart.

After the glue dried, the cabinet was given a final sanding. That took at least one full day or more. Last came the finish. For days, hour after hour, with an old worn rag wrapped around a wad of wool and soaked in stain and mineral spirits, Enrico rubbed the cabinet with a circular motion, alternating from hand to hand until the surface glowed with the luster he wanted. This little man took great pride in his workmanship and the finishing steps were his alone to do.

Mamma and Pietro were happy to see me so involved and, knowing where I was spending my hours, they never complained about the time I spent away from them.

Quartered in nearby Avellino was the officers' cadet academy, which used the forests of Ospedaletto for target practice. Each morning, rain or shine, one or more companies of ninety cadets marched up the main road and through the village followed by the ever-present barefoot urchins.

My only indelible memory of the military was of the terrifying experience at the Vienna train station when we were surrounded by the black uniformed Nazi soldiers. Yet, not smart enough to know better, I remained fascinated by soldiers, especially officers.

So, when the cadets came marching by, I rushed to watch them from our balcony. I soon learned their schedule and, instead of looking from a distance, each morning waited for them outside our building. I wanted to approach the lieutenants, but was intimidated by that smart uniform and polished leather boots. I had seen some officers chase other boys out of their way and I didn't want to suffer the same indignity. For days I stood by the side of the road trying to build up my courage. Then, one morning, pushing my fears aside, I fell in step alongside the officer at the head of the column.

"Could I march with you?" I stammered.

He looked me over from head to toe. "You're not from here, are you?" he asked.

"No."

"I thought not. You look too clean. Sure, come along."

In seconds I felt ten years older. Looking straight ahead, I made an effort to match his stride as my vanity exploded with every stretched step I took. How those local urchins would envy me and for certain my mother would be so very proud of me.

"What is your name?" the officer asked.

"Lifschütz, Enrico. And yours?" I never changed my pace nor looked at his face.

"Benedetti. Lieutenant Benedetti."

The fear that had permeated my whole being only moments before was gone. I felt perfectly at ease marching at the head of those cadets.

"What song is this?" I asked my newfound friend. The cadets were singing a tune I had not heard before: "*Sotto la caserma mi metto ad aspettar . . .*"

"'Lilli Marlene.' A gift from the German army."

When we approached the spot where the cadets entered the woods to reach their target-practice area, the lieutenant stopped me. "You cannot come with us. Too dangerous. Wait here."

At the edge of the road I waited a long time, four hours according to the bell tower clock, until the troops came marching out of the woods.

"Come back with us," Lieutenant Benedetti ordered.

The cadets seemed glad to see me judging by how they welcomed me back. I would have liked to sing along with them but knew none of their songs. They seemed such a cheerful bunch and I was so happy to have become part of them.

As we passed my building, still a bit reticent, I addressed the lieutenant. "This is my home. I have to leave now."

"Don't forget tomorrow. Same time!" the officer shouted.

I shot up the two flights in a state of euphoria, two steps at a time, dashed through the doors of both bedrooms and, losing my breath on the way, shouted, "Mamma! Mamma!"

"You scared me half to death with your screaming," she said. "What are you so excited about?"

"You should have seen me, Mamma. I marched with the cadets and the lieutenant asked me to march with him again. And you know all the kids from here? He chased them away. Isn't it exciting?"

"Sure is. *Eyn glik hot mik getrofen!*" Mother mumbled the sarcastic remark referring to the good luck I was bringing her. "Wonderful. Now go wash your hands. I have lunch ready."

From the day we first met, I bonded with Lieutenant Benedetti and our friendship grew through summer, winter, and the next spring. I also became acquainted with other officers, but none of those relationships became as warm or lasted as long as the one I enjoyed with Benedetti. Six days a week the cadets marched up the road. Even though I did not join the cadets every day, I resented Sundays, their day off.

Most mornings I waited outside our building anxious to lead the platoon. There were some disappointing days when another lieutenant led the company or when Benedetti signaled that the captain was present and for me to stay away. But I was grateful that those days were few. More with apprehension than with glee, one day Mamma watched from the balcony as her son led a platoon of officer cadets.

The weeks went by and I was adopted as the company mascot. Even the supposedly grouchy captain was not opposed to my presence and I learned he was not grouchy at all.

"Do you want to try one of these machine guns?" Benedetti asked me.

I looked at him. He could not possibly have spoken to me, so I did not reply.

"Well?" he said. "Do you want to or not?"

He *was* speaking to me. "Did you ask . . . if I wanted to do what?" I blabbered.

"Yes. Do you want to shoot a machine gun?"

"Yes! Oh yes!" I shouted.

"Let's wait until the old man leaves," he whispered, referring to the captain.

When it was safe, a sergeant handed me an ammunition clip, gave me the military salute, and left me to walk alone to the dirt platform where six guns were lined up on the ground. Trying to remember what I had seen the cadets do, I copied every step. I lay on my stomach behind the weapon, legs spread wide, resting my elbows on the hard ground and placing the gun on my shoulder. If only my friend Jimmy or Mamma or anyone I knew could have seen me. I could sense the cadets' eyes on me and, between my pride and tension, I couldn't find the calm needed to load the gun.

For a never-ending moment, I remained motionless. As the tremor diminished, I was able to push the clip into the gun, draw back the lever, and hear the first bullet enter the chamber. My cheek leaned against the gun's butt as, aiming at the target across the narrow ravine, I pulled the trigger. Nothing had ever equaled the experience of that moment. The vibration of the rapid firing, the kickbacks against my unsuspecting shoulder, the bullets rushing through the barrel and leaving the gun all filled me with an awesome sensation of strength and apprehension. The discharge was fast and furious and, before my brain could gain control over my finger that pulled the trigger, the clatter of twenty bullets was followed by the quiet click of the pin hitting the empty chamber.

I waited in my prone position. Soon the target man across the ravine would identify the hits. One, two, three, four . . . twelve, thirteen, the flag signaled. Thirteen hits out of twenty? I couldn't believe it. I heard cheering behind me. "*Bravo!*" the cadets yelled. Just a kid, I was being applauded by mature men. The surge of power of those few minutes gave me the feeling that I could have conquered the world.

As we came down from the mountain, keeping in step with the lieutenant at the head of the platoon, I began to sing in my boyish voice: "*Sotto la caserma, mi metto at aspettar, una volta ancora ti voglio salutar, addio piccina dolce amor, ti porteró sempre nel cuor, con me Lilli*

Marlene, con me Lilli Marlene." I had learned the complete lyrics of the song that by now was filling the airwaves several times a day.

The cadets joined in the tune and the singing helped keep my excitement at bay. When we reached home, with the blood pumping at my temples, I forgot to properly salute my friend and his men. From the doorway I turned, waved my arm and shouted, "*Ciao!*" In nonmilitary fashion, many responded in kind.

Bursting with breathless enthusiasm, I ran upstairs. "Mamma, you won't believe what I did today. They let me shoot a machine gun!"

Mother was not in the least interested in my military accomplishments. On the contrary, she acted irritated and covered her ears with both hands before I had a chance to say another word. "I don't want to know!"

She did not want to know. She was a woman and couldn't possibly understand military pride. I forgave her. Pietro was not home, so I had to wait to share my enthusiasm with him.

One day, before leaving the shooting range, I took a small souvenir with me; a tracer bullet. I needed to know how it worked. Why did these bullets burst into flames when they hit the target?

Facing our courtyard was a small tool shed filled with hay. Other than Vincenzo, I had never seen anyone else use it. Unseen, I sneaked into the shed and searched for a tool to open the cartridge. I saw a large eyehook fastened to the doorjamb. This would do fine. Inserting the bullet into the hook, with all the strength I could muster, I broke the bullet off at its tip and, without warning, the portion still attached to the casing, caught fire. It was a violent and wild fire with sparks flying everywhere. Visions of explosions and buildings going up in flames filled my mind. This was my end. I did not want to die. How was I to know the bullet would catch fire? Oh, my God! All that hay! I was nailed to the ground with the flaming cartridge firmly in my hand. Filled with panic and not smart enough to know what to do, I tried to snuff out the wildly burning flame by pressing my naked palm on it. Looking down, I saw my hand on fire, but so overwhelmed by fear, I was not aware of the pain. As I saw the skin peel off my hand, I tossed the burning cartridge quickly into the open courtyard and, screaming from the now excruciating pain, I darted into the house.

Mother, seemingly calm, helped soothe the hurt. She placed my hand in cold water, then broke open a precious egg and tenderly covered my hand with the slimy white stuff. "Is this better?" she asked.

"A lot better, almost painless," I said, trying to regain my newly learned military bearing and at the same time commend *Mutti* for her effort. That's when she let loose and gave me a few well-aimed whacks on my behind to keep company to the ache of my scorched hand.

One day the cadets were being introduced to a new automatic weapon. At each of the six positions on the platform was a soldier struggling to take apart and then reassemble the new gun. There were only three instructors to help them.

Lieutenant Benedetti, hands tightly clasped behind his back, his eyes transfixed on the ground before him, and wearing a grave facial expression, paced slowly back and forth. The fallen autumn leaves crunched under his polished boots. "This is taking too long," he mumbled. He looked up and walked toward me. "You think you can help those fellows put the gun back together?"

"Are you talking to me?" I asked, not sure I had heard him correctly. I felt my legs shake under me. From the time I was three or four, I had enjoyed tinkering with mechanical toys, but this was way over my head.

"Yeah, you. You want to play sergeant?" he asked, a tinge of annoyance in his voice. "Here is your chance. Do you think you can put it back together? This is taking too long. You think you can do it?"

Totally confused, I didn't know what to say. "I'm only twelve."

"I didn't ask for your age. Can you help them?"

I had never handled the gun. What I had put together as a kid were toys. "Sure. Yes, sir!" My voice conveying infinitely more confidence than I felt.

Benedetti gave me the military salute. "Then go to it, soldier."

I returned the salute, then running instead of walking, got to the first cadet. While he sat on the ground looking baffled by the presence of a kid, much to his surprise as well as my own, I took the weapon apart.

"Here, follow me," I said and began to guide him through the reassembly process. But when he became discouraged by his inability to do so, he let the pieces fall into my hands. I reassembled the weapon and, now experienced, walked to the next position to help another cadet.

The three instructors, who had been helping the cadets, left the platform, a signal for me to do the same. Quickly, I put together the last gun, gave the soldier a pat on the back, and left.

"Not bad. Not bad at all," said Benedetti.

Flushed with conceit that gave me an air of invincibility, I circled about with arms behind my back, using up my overflowing energy. As a twelve-year-old boy, my greatest pipe dream had been realized that morning. I didn't want the moment to end and, when it did, I couldn't wait to get home. I found Pietro and Mamma in the kitchen and excitedly blurted out what had happened.

"Enrico, slow down. I can't understand what you're saying," Pietro interrupted.

"As a small kid, Enrico always loved to take apart every new toy and then put it back together," Mamma told Pietro. "I don't know where he learned it. His father couldn't hold a hammer. You should have seen the trolley car he once built."

Pietro asked me about my experience and he too expressed his pride. For several days hereafter, I felt untouchable by common people and probably acted that way too.

Time prevented me from getting to know many cadets. They came and left so fast, as Benedetti explained, they were rushed through training so they could be sent to the ever-demanding battlefields. Several of the officers I had befriended also were called to join their fighting brothers. Many of them, I learned from Benedetti, had laid down their young lives for Mussolini. The captain, whom at first I had feared but eventually got to know as a gentle man, also was killed in North Africa.

At twelve I learned to grieve in the way most kids that age did not. Knowing that so many men I had known were no longer alive dampened my enthusiasm for soldiering. I spoke to Benedetti about my inner conflict. "You should not have told me that so many of these cadets have died. I don't think I can continue being with your men knowing they may be going to their death."

He looked me in the eyes. "I'm sorry, but I understand. I enjoyed having you as a friend. Remember, whenever you want to come back, you will be welcome." He shook hands with me, then, taking one step backward, gave me the military salute.

May 10, 1942 marked Mother's forty-first birthday. I had always done something special for her on that day. Many years before, when I was only five and we were living in Vienna, I had run down to the courtyard to ask a group of roaming singers who went from building to building to earn a few *Groschen*, to sing the Austrian song for all mothers: "*Mutti*." Mother had tears in her eyes when she learned I had paid for the song. On other occasions, with Millie to help me, I baked a miniature cake, or when Papa took me out shopping, I picked out a gift for her. Even while we lived in Nice and San Remo I had been able to buy her a small something to show how much I cared for her.

This year, in a small mountain village and with few resources, my options had been greatly reduced. I didn't want to speak to Pietro, for having him buy the gift would have hurt my pride. Instead I spoke to Dora. "What could I give Mamma for her birthday?"

"How much money do you have to spend?"

"I have three lire."

"That won't buy much. How about making her something?"

Make something? I had never made a gift for my mother.

"Like what?" I asked.

Dora had a few ideas: a scarf, a hat, a wallet.

"That sounds best, the wallet," I said.

I went to Raffaele's family general store to look for material. I didn't know what I needed and at first was too embarrassed to explain the gift I wanted to make. In the end, realizing what little progress I was making, I told my friend's mother my plan and asked for her advice.

From one of the shelves she dragged down a large roll of shiny cloth. "You need this."

"But I need a very small piece. Can you cut it for me? I only have three lire."

The old woman had a puzzled or perhaps annoyed look. I couldn't tell. "Maybe I have a small piece somewhere," she said. She looked in every corner and rummaged in the rear of the store, but found nothing. "Just because you're Raffaele's friend, I will make an exception. I never cut such a small piece. If I did this for everyone, I would have to close the store. Never could I feed my family. The least I can cut is half a meter. Even that is too small." I suffered through all of her lamentations, a common practice in Ospedaletto. Perhaps by speaking a lot, people thought the day would slip by faster. The woman did cut a small piece from the oilcloth and handed it to me. "Just remember, only because you are a friend of Raffaele."

I gave her the money and ran back to Dora. "I got it!" I shouted exuberantly.

"What did she charge you?"

"Three lire."

"What a thief. Half would have been too much."

Dora suggested first making a paper pattern. This I did and the next few days were spent secretly cutting, gluing, and taking apart pieces of paper in order to make a model of the wallet. I made many mistakes, but, thanks to the paper pattern, I did not ruin the actual material.

After I'd cut the oilcloth to match the pattern, Dora, with a saintly patience, let me use her sewing machine. "Don't forget to leave enough material at the edges so that the needle won't tear through." After much agonizing, fearing I could not finish in time or that Mamma might not like the gift, I completed the wallet with two days to spare, thanks to Dora's invaluable help.

For two long, never-ending days I waited for her birthday. Would Mother appreciate what I went through to make her gift? Then, early on the morning of the day, I slipped into her bedroom, hoping she would still be sleeping. She was awake. "Happy birthday, *Mammina*. Here, this is for you."

As she examined my labor of love, I added with much pent-up enthusiasm, "I made it all by myself. Dora helped me a little, but I designed and sewed it together."

"It's beautiful! Absolutely beautiful! Just what I needed. Mine is so old already. Thank you, my *Schatzele*." A few kisses, a big hug, and a promise of a chocolate cake, but mostly the way she held the wallet to her breast made all my work worthwhile.

Later that morning, when Pietro presented my mother with an embroidered nightgown. There was hugging, kissing, and many furtive glances between Mamma and Pietro, but by then I had learned to accept their secretive messages.

19

A New Suit

W e were living in San Remo in 1939 and war had not yet broken
out when Mussolini spoke on the radio. He promised to make Italy
independent from what he labeled the imperialistic countries, where
buildings were constructed out of cardboard. I was astounded to learn
that in America houses were built out of cardboard. The Italian dictator assured us that Italy was going to produce enough grain, rubber,
and armament to make all its forty-five million citizens self sufficient
and to have an army of eight million bayonets. I wasn't quite sure what
he meant. I asked Mamma, "Does he want just an army of bayonets?"

Three years had passed since that famous speech, but judging from
the rationing that began during the early days of the war, his plan was a
dismal failure. Flour, the most essential staple for Italian families, was
the first item to be rationed, followed by bread, pasta, and sugar. Soon
the long list filled two printed pages. Only the pure mountain water
was still freely available. From soap to candles, jams to oil, almost

nothing could be bought without a coupon, and often not even if you had one. Wool fabric was not rationed, for it was useless to issue coupons for items that could not be found anywhere.

While visiting his family in Sicily, Pietro had sent us a gift package. With a bit of luck, we found a neighbor willing to bring the large—and it was massive—wooden crate from Avellino on his horse-drawn cart. Three men were needed to carry the crate up to our kitchen, where, with cheerful anticipation, Mother and I gazed at the huge container.

"Oh, no! I wonder what broke?" Mamma exclaimed, looking at the oil oozing from the crate.

With borrowed tools, I removed the cover. Cautiously we searched through the straw. Pasta, pasta, and more pasta. Not store-bought but special, homemade pasta. This was like finding gold. Pietro had sent us enough pasta to last us a year and even share some with Dora.

We searched and found the broken bottle at the bottom of the crate. The rich, priceless olive oil had soaked every item except, miraculously, a bolt of woolen cloth Pietro had sent for me. With care, Mother pulled the material out.

"Do you realize how rare this is?" she said. "Look here. 'Made in England,'" she read from the edge. "Pietro must have had this from before the war."

"Now you can get a new suit. Pietro is so good to us."

After sharing the secret of the fabric with Dora, Mother asked if she knew a tailor in Avellino. "If I show the material to anyone here, the whole town will know about it."

"You are right," Dora agreed. "I know someone in Avellino."

When Mother confided in Runia Kleinerman about the material and our impending trip to Avellino, Runia asked to come along. "I never told anyone. I have been holding on to a piece of cloth to make George a suit. This is a good opportunity."

Runia and my mother went to the police station to ask for a permit to leave town. The next morning, the two mothers, Giorgio, and I, met in front of the post office to catch the bus to Avellino.

"I have not been to a city in more than a year," Mamma said. "I feel so free and we haven't left yet."

While the two mothers held a lively conversation for the thirty or more minutes it took the bus to reach our destination, eighteen-year-old Giorgio wanted nothing to do with twelve-year-old me.

In Avellino, with Dora's directions in hand, Mamma led the way down the narrow street and into a small, bleak, unlit shop, where a short man, working beneath a faint lamp, came forward to greet as though he was welcoming a long lost friend. Runia and my mother, looking around the shop and toward the door, guardedly removed the two bolts of cloth from their paper wrappings. "*Bello, molto bello*," the tailor exclaimed. Then, lifting my cloth, he exclaimed how beautiful he found our English-made cloth: "*Bellissimo. Fatto in Inghilterra. Per bacco!*"

My mother told the man we wanted two suits, one for each of the boys. "I want you to give us a special price," she said.

The man, dropping his head to his chest and placing one open hand on his chin, peered into emptiness. He was looking over his glasses and I noticed they were broken and held together by a black thread. He stared at Giorgio first, then at me, then went into a long self-consultation and finally, looking at both mothers, mumbled a price for his labor.

"Oh, no. That's much too much," Mamma said. "We couldn't possibly afford that."

He scratched his head and volunteered a reduction. "I'll take off ten lire from each suit since you're ordering two."

Mother looked at Runia. Considering the textile shortage, the man could not possibly have been too busy. "You'll have to do better than that," Mamma said.

The man cleared his throat and with a dramatic tone that he must have practiced for years, conveyed this gem: "If I do it for one *centesimo* less, I'll be losing money."

"You'll have to take off fifteen lire for each suit because that's all we can afford."

As per local practice, the tailor put on a small performance. He grasped a piece of partially used paper and a pencil stub and, with his arm extended, he waved it through the air in a grandiose theatrical gesture. Then, holding it out of the women's sight, he brought the pencil tip to his tongue and scribbled something. Again peering over his glasses, he looked at the two women. "If I keep doing this, I'll be ruined. You're such lovely ladies." A flirtatious smile brightened his unshaven face.

He rubbed the corner of one cloth between two of his fingers as though looking for some magical inspiration. "But you must promise you will tell no one. I swear I wouldn't do it for anyone else at this price." Swearing was big in these parts of the world but meant very little—unless one swore in the name of a divinity, then it meant a little more.

The bargaining over, the tailor began to take our measurements. This, too, he did with dramatic gestures. Squeezing the tape between two fingers to mark my waist size, he pranced around looking for something to write on. Still holding the mark on the tape, he pulled a badly worn booklet from a drawer, leafed through it and, as I looked in disbelief, picked the corner of a page already filled to write my measurements. How would he be able tell the sleeve from the leg? Or was my information from that already there?

Mother seemed to have the same concern. "Excuse me. Did you want to put our names on the sheet?" she asked. Her diplomacy was obvious. She was not about to arouse his southern Italian temper.

"Don't need to. Keep everything in my head. Never make a mistake." His grin and tone of voice showed great confidence. He pointed at me, asked for my name, and marked it in the same corner. "Here, to make you happy, *Signora*."

Finished with me and, after taking Giorgio's measurements, the tailor asked us to return in two weeks for the first fitting. Out on the street, my mother expressed her concern that the man never marked which measurements went with which cloth.

"I wouldn't worry," Runia said. "He must have been doing this for years. I'm sure it will be all right. What I find strange is that everyone loses money in this country."

Mother laughed. We had been in Italy longer than our friends and Mamma understood the local mentality better. "Don't believe a word. He isn't losing money. I just hope we're not overpaying. I'm more concerned that he will be able to find the page, read his writing, and know it's us."

Two weeks to the day, with a new permit from the *carabinieri*, the four of us boarded the bus to Avellino. I was in high spirits, looking forward to my new suit. The ride on the Irpina Coach was always an adventure. One always knew when he left but never knew when he would get back.

The coach, looking as though it had been pressed into service from a museum, was the only means of public transportation to and from Ospedaletto. In normal times it might not have even qualified for junk, but now, since factories had been converted to the war effort, this dilapidated, battered, and rundown vehicle was being used to prevent our village from becoming totally isolated. And because fuel was in such short supply, the bus had been modified to run on methane gas. A tall cylindrical contraption looking like a torpedo and mounted on the rear of the bus burned the wood that would hopefully produce the needed gases to run the vehicle. If the driver made sure he had enough wood and if the wood burned and produced enough methane and if the gas reached the front of the vehicle and entered the engine, then the trip would be trouble-free. But the ifs didn't always materialize and, on the days when the bus stalled and, stall it did often, the passengers were asked to push it along and help it get to its destination. One was always certain to get to Avellino, for the road was downhill, but on the return trip, one would consider oneself fortunate if the coach lasted long enough to stall within walking distance of our village.

The day of our trip, we arrived in Avellino on schedule.

"It would be asking too much to get back without a breakdown," *Mutti* remarked.

"I have not seen a film in so long," I said. "Do you think we could go see a movie?"

"If we have time, after the tailor," Mamma replied.

Since I remembered the road to the dingy shop, I walked ahead of the others, trying to urge a faster pace. The tailor was ready for us, a miracle in southern Italy. He brought out the two suits and Giorgio and I tried the jackets first.

"What is that?" Mamma asked. "This jacket will fit my son in three years!"

The man, who claimed a faultless memory and prided himself on never making a mistake, had not made my jacket too big. He had switched fabrics and used my material to make Giorgio's suit and his to make mine.

I had rarely seen my mother so angry. She looked at Runia and in German shouted, "I should never have asked you to come along. This would never have happened. Mine was a pure British cloth. How am I going to replace it?"

"I shouldn't have come with you," Runia shouted back. "Giorgio didn't need his suit now. You are the one who told me about going to a tailor and now I get the short end of the stick."

"You got the short end? What about me? What about Enrico? He is the one who is getting an inferior suit."

Watching the two mothers quarrel rather than focus their rancor on the one who had made the error, I couldn't help but chuckle.

"What are you laughing about?" *Mutti* screamed. "You thought I was a worrier. There you have it!"

By now I was smart enough to realize that my best move was out to the street. As for the two suits, the damage had been done. I was smaller than Giorgio by at least four inches and nothing could be done to the suits. Nevertheless, the two mothers bickered as though establishing who owned the more expensive fabric would make a difference in the outcome. In the end, they settled their quarrel by leaving matters as they were. I got a navy suit with two thin pinstripes, Giorgio got a suit of the same color with only one stripe, and the two mothers remained friends. But we never did get to the movies.

To survive on the government's meager rations would have been difficult if not for the supplies we were able to find from local farmers or, when one could afford it, the black market. Living in a small village gave us access to much of the Earth's produce and, thanks to the chicaneries of the townspeople, we were able to share in some of the locally raised meats.

With communication limited to the one telephone inside the post office, it was amazing how fast news spread within the village. Thus, when a farmer was preparing to butcher a young calf, everyone in town knew about it. To kill an animal was illegal unless it had been injured, for all livestock had to be handled by a special government office in charge of meat distribution. But rarely did an animal injure itself and, after a farmer killed a calf, he would quickly break one of its legs, thus skirting the existing laws.

At the time and place of the slaughtering, more people would show up wanting meat than one animal could possibly provide. The ritual was always the same. Everyone had to wait until the veterinarian concluded his examination and certified that the killing had been done according to law. Only then could the carcass be cut up. The few times I witnessed such a killing, the first cuts were always shared among the *maresciallo*: Don Pepe, Dr. Sellitto, and the pharmacist.

During late summer, fruit was plentiful in this fertile stretch of the Italian boot. This was the ideal time to make preserves for the winter months, the only drawback being that sugar was in short supply. The priceless coupons were hardly sufficient to provide enough of the sweetener for the daily coffee, let alone make jams and jellies. As did most Jews, we did not eat pork products, so Mamma was able to trade lard coupons for sugar ones. Whenever we found someone willing to make a swap, my mother would bring home the sugar while I went on a frantic search for fresh fruit. I rushed from farm to farm to pick pears, apricots, mulberries, cherries, plums, peaches, figs, or whatever else I could gather. Because I did my own picking, I was able to save my mother some money. My homecoming from these trips was always a joyous occasion for Mother and me. We would examine what I had brought home; then for hours I would help stir and watch the fruit turn into a soft jelly.

When Mother declared *"Pronto!"* announcing the jam was ready, I stopped the stirring and helped pour the delicious preserves into special glass containers. I then waited for them to cool so I could seal the jars with their airtight caps. On those rare occasions when she had extra sugar, Mother made enough jam to last us until the next season—unless some *internati* had none of their own and my softhearted mother shared some of ours.

Of all the rationed products, the most difficult to find was soap. The two shops that sold groceries were always out of the precious item and the few crude homemade bars we were able to buy from the local people were never enough. We also enjoyed another advantage. With Mother in command of the kitchen, our consumption of pasta was a fraction of a typical Italian family. That gave us some extremely valuable paper squares which our Italian friends were eager to exchange for other items. The villagers would happily do without soap. I had seen ample proof of that. But pasta? Never.

Everyone had an ample supply of coffee coupons, certainly not for lack of wanting the brew, but because the aromatic beans were nowhere to be found. Barley was the popular substitute and the first time our landlady roasted this grain, I yelled, "The house is on fire!"

Mamma called out from the kitchen, "It's nothing. Signora Filomena is roasting *orzo*."

I went to see what Filomena was doing. In the kitchen, with one hand protecting her eyes from the acrid smoke, she was turning a metal cylinder positioned over the open stove. This strange circular contraption spewed smoke throughout the house, making it reek like the charred remains of a fire.

When nothing else was available, there was always the black market. Although hardly anyone acknowledged it, everyone knew of its existence. The *mercato nero* was attacked with regularity by the government radio, labeled a crime against the Italian war effort and all its citizens. But few Italians took their government's view seriously. Once in a while rumors circulated that someone had been arrested for selling rationed items, but mostly they were only rumors and rumors there were many.

While Mother did not have the money to enjoy the luxuries this illegal market had to offer, she seemed to enjoy going along with Dora whenever she went where someone had goods to sell. When she came home, excitement was written all over her. "Erich, they had everything. I couldn't believe what I saw. All there in the open, like they didn't care about the *carabinieri*. Not just soap, but good smelling soap. Even real coffee, sugar, olive oil, and all sorts of pasta. I wonder where they get all that stuff?"

Pasta and bread had been the basic staples of the Italian table forever. The average adult needed at least two pounds of pasta every week, and the first ration, at the beginning of the war, provided that much. But when the ration was reduced to a bit more than one pound, there were such loud protests that Mother feared there would be a revolution. But nothing serious happened and people adapted.

By 1943, the black market all but vanished, cutting off anything other than what could be obtained with coupons. The well-known Italian generosity was cooled by a sense of self-preservation, a determination to stay alive. No longer did I hear the ritual invitation to "sit and eat with us." People had become fearful that hunger might induce someone to accept. Even with so little resources, my extraordinary mother never failed to provide me with the basic necessities. Through all the war years I never went hungry.

The deprivation of our freedom was more painful for the adults in the group of internees. For me, however, it was just a different lifestyle. While hoping for the end of the exile, many turned to bridge, *boccie*, reading, and knitting to break the monotony. Many internees, especially those who came from affluent families, lived with their memories. Recalling what life had been before Mussolini's alliance with Hitler seemed to make it easier for some to accept their present condition. But whatever else one might have been doing at the time, a good debate was forever a puff of fresh air, electrifying the otherwise dull days. I especially welcomed these verbal exchanges and, thanks to them, my vocabulary expanded greatly. I began to understand more of what adults were saying and thinking. Mother tried to point out the benefits I was gaining from being around mature, cultured people.

Ospedaletto had two *boccie* fields. Internees used the one in the communal garden at the opposite corner from where the group had its morning meetings. Before each game I silently prayed for an uneven number of players to show up so they would have to ask me to be part of one team. Jimmy, though only two years older but two heads taller, was always the first one included. Oh, how I envied him! I wished he would catch a cold and have to stay home.

We played *boccie* in the afternoon, after lunch and the customary nap, so it would not interfere with the morning walk. The internees were amateurs compared to the local men. I had watched those villagers throw a wooden ball forty feet through the air and hit their opponent's ball dead center. Smack! The balls would go flying every which way as I stood in awe admiring their skill. We all tried to emulate those shots, seldom succeeding and then only by sheer luck.

Group playing boccie in Ospedaletto, June 1942; from left, Giorgio Kleinerman, Antonio Dello Russo, Pietro Russo, William Pierce, Luigi Michelgnoli, Willy Weil, John Howell, Karl Weil, and the author.

In addition to the regular players, there was Jimmy and I. On occasion, Antonio Dello Russo and Sabato Pisano would join in, while Ettore Costa came along occasionally, but his poor eyesight ruled him out.

Boccie was restricted to the warmer months, while bridge was played all year. During spring and summer, playing cards was limited to a few evenings and Sunday afternoons, whereas in the cold weather, card games went on every day, usually at the Howells'. The hosts, Agatha and John and Mother and Pietro were the regulars, while Mr. Perutz, Willy and Karel Weil, Giorgio Kleinerman, Jimmy, and I made up the second table.

I was eager to play but still learning the finer points of bidding, which was why the others wanted to keep me on the sideline. With the exception of Jimmy, who played bridge fairly well and had told me how he considered me a pain in the behind, most adults tolerated my youthful zeal. But tolerating did not translate into letting me join in the game except when they needed a fourth. Occasionally, my mother intervened and came to my rescue, and I was allowed to replace Jimmy for a few hands.

The Perutz Family.

Watching and not playing was boring, so when no one was looking, I arranged the second deck of cards so that one of the partners would be dealt all the high cards. Oh, what fun watching the face of the lucky person whose finger stopped at each card. Two or three times the player counted the points with an expression of disbelief. "Seven no-trump!" It only worked that one time. Someone figured out that I was the culprit and the cards were reshuffled and dealt again.

From the intense concentration of the players, it seemed that bridge was not a game for fun. That is, except for Signor Perutz, a born actor. When his wife was not around, he was unwilling to maintain a serious demeanor, thus bringing a bit of cheer to the game. With a long silver cigarette holder between his two well-manicured fingers, he leaned his head backward to blow out small puffs of smoke, an elegant flair he had acquired from his wife, who claimed to be a descendant of Russian nobility. At all times debonair in his attire, he did not wear a suit but a contrasting jacket with the ever-present kerchief in his breast pocket and a tie held down by a diamond pin. He had a friendly face with eyes that always smiled.

This man had the uncanny ability to see all thirteen tricks unfold in his mind and was willing to rely more on luck than on accepted conventions. With each hand, win or lose, he was in equally good humor to the audible annoyance of the other players. I liked his style even if, most times, I was the only one who did.

Signor Perutz added levity to the bridge parties. He was an avid storyteller and to me it seemed he always had a new story to tell. But most of his jokes flew right over my head. When everyone laughed, it was irritating not to understand what he had said, yet I was too proud to ask for an explanation and let anyone know I didn't understand what was going on, so I joined in the laughter anyhow.

One day Mother asked me about my laughing at one of his remarks. "Did you understand what Signor Perutz said?"

I hesitated. "No, not really." My face flushed. From the heat on my cheeks, I knew they were crimson red. Embarrassed for having to admit my ignorance, I never again laughed unless I understood what was being said.

Whenever Mrs. Perutz was present, her husband became sedate and serious. No more funny comments, only interesting thoughts. In some ways he reminded me of Ettore Costa, just a few years older but definitely not a Bohemian.

An afternoon at the Howells was more than just a card game. Tea and cookies were always part of the custom. At a given time, everything stopped. "*Eccoci. È tempo per un po' di tè*," Signora Agatha would say.

At home Mother and Pietro made tea in a glass. The Howells served it in delicate porcelain cups. At home we dangled a small metal tea-ball in hot water, whereas here making tea was an art in a traditional British way. The dried leaves were put in an unglazed ceramic teapot, placed on top of a kettle of boiling water, and left to steep.

Mrs. Howell would return with an assortment of homemade sweets, the tea, and the kettle of hot water, which then served to dilute the concentrated beverage to one's own taste. Whether or not I got to play, I was always included in the snacks.

Occasionally someone mentioned a subject that was more important than bridge itself, bringing the game to a halt until the topic had been resolved, sufficiently discussed, or put to rest.

"If the German forces can survive the Russian winter, things will be hard for the Allies. I don't think the Russian army is strong enough to halt the German advance." Judging from the people's head-shaking, Signor Perutz, in that one single thought, had expressed everyone's concern that summer of 1942.

"And we don't seem to be able to learn the truth about the Russian front. We need a second front in Europe," John Howell said.

"That goes without saying, but only American forces can create a second front and it does not seem that America is ready yet," Pietro Russo said.

"And if Russia wins the war, does anyone think this will be better in the long run for Europe?" Agatha asked.

"Well, at this point anything is better than Nazism. Later we'll cope with the Communist problem," Mamma added.

"Does anyone think America and Great Britain will eventually have to fight the Russians?" John asked.

"Possibly," Pietro responded. "This is the first time Communism has been given the opportunity to export its philosophy by using someone else's money. America is providing what Russia needs. What a coup for Stalin."

"In the meantime, Hitler is putting all the Jews into labor camps. I have not received mail from my sister in months, not since she wrote that she and my mother were being sent to Poland," Mamma said.

"For me, this is the greatest puzzle," John said. "How can the Nazis find time and energy to seek out Jews? What are they really doing with these people anyhow? No one has been able to get any information."

I was always eager to follow what was being said, though occasionally the arguments were beyond my ability to comprehend. Each day was boringly like the previous one, and I was becoming intolerant and resentful of our confinement.

While I enjoyed the enriching experience of growing up in the midst of adults, what I missed most was being a child. I thought of San Remo and the many games I played with my friends there. One morning I expressed my feelings to *Mutti*. "By the time this is all over, I won't be a kid anymore," I moaned.

From the sad look in *Mutti's* tearful eyes, I believed those words hurt her more than the reality hurt me. "I wish I could do something," she said. "I can't, *Hasele*. It will end soon. You'll see."

So much had changed. No longer did I take pleasure in the sunsets I so loved. Even the spring flowers blooming all around stopped bringing any joy.

Only Sundays were different, not so much for us but certainly for most of the people of the village. Missing were the clamor of the lumber mill and the erratic engine noise of the mail coach with its clouds of dust. The townspeople put on their finer wear, and the urchins disappeared from the dusty village roads. Even we dressed in our best clothes.

One morning, during our walk, I spoke to Jimmy's father. "Time seems to stand still."

"It goes very rapidly as you get older. You'll see," he said.

His words were of little solace. Already the twelve or more months I had spent in Ospedaletto felt interminable. Ultimately, for twenty-nine months I would remain in this village and be deprived of things I had previously taken for granted. For twenty-nine months I would not see a movie, hear a telephone ring, go to a theater, have an ice cream cone, use a trolley car, take a full bath or shower, brush my teeth under running water, eat a candy bar or a banana, go to a dentist, see the inside of a classroom, or pray in a synagogue. Since crossing the Italian Alps on that March day of 1938, I had not tasted a *Frankfurter* or sunk my teeth into an ear of corn. In a country where there were as many salami varieties as there were dialects, *Frankfurters* were unknown and corn was snubbed as animal fodder.

When torrential rains stopped us from venturing out one evening, Pietro, Mamma, and I remained in the kitchen. I liked the hours we spent together. I especially liked getting to know more about Pietro. "Tell me something about Sicily," I said.

"The Greeks called Sicily 'Trinacra.' It's a beautiful, fertile land. The people are hard-working, living either off the land or the sea."

"Trinacra?" I asked. "What does it mean?"

"It goes back to the time Greece occupied the island, but I don't know the significance. It's the symbol of a woman's head with three legs."

When Pietro spoke of Sicily, the words had a particular musical ring. His eyes sparkled and his face was radiant. He adored his native land. It made me want to know about the place where he was born.

"Mazara has one large industry: fishing. All around are plants that process sardines, tuna, and other fish. We also produce much wine and olive oil, grain and, oranges. One day you will both come to visit and you'll see how beautiful my country is."

"I would love that," said Mamma, her face aglow, as she sat quietly listening to Pietro speak.

"I promise you. When the war is over, you and your mother will come and be my guests in Mazara."

"That's fine with me." I wanted to know more, so I asked him about his family.

"It is a large family," he said. "Nothing like here in Ospedaletto, but my dear mother had eight children. I am the youngest boy and my sister Giovanna is the youngest of all. My father died when I was about your age and we all had to go to work on the farm to support the family."

"I'm sorry about your dad. Do you have a picture of him?" I asked.

"Not here. I do have a picture of my mother. I'll show it to you tomorrow."

"When were you born?" I asked.

"Enrico?" My mother reprimanded me.

"That's just fine. In 1909. April 18, 1909." Pietro, at thirty-three, was eight years younger than Mamma.

"Did you ever marry?"

"No. Only one of my sisters, Masina, is married and she lives in America. We all have been too busy working our land."

When I asked about the farm, his face lit up with pride. "We have several farms but only one is dear to my heart. It was nothing but rocks and sand until my brothers and I turned it into a splendid garden. We call it 'Palio' and we grow many kinds of vegetables. At least we never go hungry in our family. When I go there, I also go hunting."

This man, who read poetry like a god, was speaking of killing. What happened to his gentleness? "Hunting?" I said. "I've never gone hunting. I don't think I could ever kill an animal."

"When you shoot an animal for food, you do it for survival, not for sport. It's not being cruel. We hunt for rabbits and birds. Then we cook them right away."

"I just don't think I could do it."

"If hunting is part of your upbringing, it becomes a normal part of your life."

"Maybe when I come to visit, you'll take me hunting." Looking at Pietro that moment, I detected his strong physical being. I noticed his large arm muscles, his sun-darkened skin.

"You know what I would like you to teach me more than anything?" I said.

"No. What?" he asked.

"To read poetry like you do."

"I don't have to teach it to you. All you need is feeling in your heart. Penetrate the poet's soul and it will come naturally."

I wasn't sure I understood. Penetrate the poet's soul? It sounded terribly difficult and I said so.

"Read the poem to yourself," Pietro said. "Understand it, then feel what the poet meant. Poetry comes from the heart, the soul. Try it."

"Not now, maybe tomorrow." Then changing the subject, I asked, "Did you ever play billiards?"

"Sure. I shot my way through school. I was really good at it, too. Made enough money so I didn't have to ask for money from my mother every month."

"Would you play with me?"

"Only if we play for money." That was not the answer I wanted to hear. To play for money? I didn't have enough money for that. I saw that grin on his face and couldn't tell what it meant.

"You're probably too good for me," I said.

"I was only joking. Of course I'll play a few games with you. And no money."

What a relief to hear that.

"I'll only allow you to go with *Dottor* Russo," Mamma interjected. "You understand?" Mother insisted on being formal when she spoke of Pietro.

I understood, and every week we played once or twice. He paid for the table fee, and I learned a lot from the many times he had the upper hand.

"You are getting better," Pietro said. He had placed his arm around my shoulder. "I'm proud of you."

The only time I ate in a restaurant during the Ospedaletto period was when Pietro, with a permit from the *carabinieri*, took me on a one-day trip to Naples. We rode the bus then took the train at Avellino for the forty-five minute ride to the big city. What an exciting day! I got to ride the train, see a new city and, best of all, get out of that lousy village.

In Naples, upon my request, Pietro took me to stamp store.

On Via Roma we entered a shop and, by some strange circumstances, the owner, Signor Ravel, had also been interned in Ospedaletto. Of French descent, he had been released after France surrendered.

Though we did not know each other, we were linked by our shared experience.

"Pick what you want up to twenty lire," Pietro said. "I have to run a short errand and will be back in time for lunch."

Twenty lire! That was a small fortune, almost half our rent of fifty lire. He must be wealthy.

"Go ahead, pick more," Signor Ravel said. "I will give you a nice discount, my fellow *confinato*."

Leaving the Ravel shop with a large envelope stuffed with more stamps than I had ever handled at one time, we walked down Via Roma, passed the *galleria* and the enormous and impressive Royal Palace. We continued toward the waterfront, where Pietro treated me to lunch at the world-renown Zi Teresa. Located where Via Roma meets with the bay, the restaurant was a few steps down, closer to the water than to the street level. One could easily walk on Via Caracciolo, which runs alongside the restaurant and miss seeing the many tables below the retaining wall. Only the high neon sign announced the restaurant's presence.

It was 1:00, the customary hour when Italians have their midday meal, yet only two of the thirty-odd tables were occupied. We picked a table outdoors, right at the water's edge, where we could hear the repetitive waves slap against the seawall and where the salty smell of fresh fish did much to increase our appetites. A waiter approached and handed us the menu. "You can have anything you want," Pietro told me.

Before even looking at the short list on the menu, I had decided what I wanted. "I'll have spaghetti with clam sauce and for seconds a *milanese*," asking for the Italian version of the *Wiener Schnitzel*. Then turning to Pietro, "Mamma always says, 'All you get is bread crumbs and no meat.' But I love a *milanese* and I don't care."

A lone fisherman broke the rhythmic sound of the splashing waves by maneuvering his small boat and docking it alongside our table. The man's face was burned by the sun and his parched skin made him look much too old to still be rowing a fishing boat.

Leaning over the low railing, Pietro addressed the man. "Have any fresh fish?"

"*Certo, padrone.*" From a water-filled bucket he lifted a fish by its tail. "Just caught this nice yellow tail and a splendid looking sole." He wasn't lying, for the fish was still flipping in his hand.

Pietro motioned to the waiter. "Buy that sole and sauté it lightly in butter. Can you do that?"

"If the cook has butter, no problem," the server said.

Pietro handed the waiter our food coupons for the pasta and bread. The man took a quick look around, then bent to Pietro's ear. "If you prefer," he whispered, "we could do it without them."

"That's all right," Pietro said.

I asked what the waiter meant by his remark.

"He wants to get some money under the table. Then I can keep the coupons."

Why would anybody put money under the table? I asked myself.

The waiter served the spaghetti. How disappointing. Such a small portion. I had not been to a restaurant since rationing began and did not realize portions were limited to three ounces, hardly enough to fill a plate. In spite of the few strands in my bowl, my mouth began to salivate when I saw the tiny clams peeking through the thick sauce. I looked for Pietro to make the first move and was glad he did not hesitate. I picked up the fork and spoon and dove into that delicious dish.

"This is even better than the pasta Signora Dora makes," I said. The cook found butter and Pietro savored the fresh sole. His eyes ate each morsel before his mouth did. I saw how he lost himself in the flavor of that fresh fish and was amazed at his taking such delight in eating. Fascinated, I stared, letting my own food sit before me.

"You like fish?" I asked.

"This is what I miss most. At home I have fish every day. But you better eat or your food will get cold."

Our train back to Avellino was not due until 3:00, allowing us to linger at our table in the April breeze. We enjoyed Mount Vesuvius in the distance and the Isle of Capri rising from the shimmering blue waters of the gulf. I saw firsthand the splendid panorama of Naples and understood the popular saying I so often had heard: "*Viri Napule e po' mori.*"

That one-day trip to the Parthenopean city was my first and only holiday from our confined and Spartan life.

20

Don Antonio

From the small village square one morning, I heard a choir practice. Always curious, I followed the sound, walked up the little knoll, and into the church.

Don Pasquale noticed me from the balcony. "Do you like to sing?" he asked.

"I love to. I sang in a synagogue choir in Vienna."

"I need boys in my choir. Only seven come regularly. Why don't you join us?"

I hesitated. Me sing in a church? A Jewish boy? It had to be better than doing nothing. Mamma would not object. It would keep me off the street. "Sure. When do you want me to start?"

"Come tomorrow for a tryout. Four o'clock."

Without telling my mother, I went back to the cold church the next day and found Don Pasquale playing the organ. "Don Pasquale," I called out. "I'm here!" My words echoed in the cavernous space.

"Come up," he shouted from the organ balcony.

The few thin rays of light peeking through the high windows, darkened by age and by dampness from years of unheated air, created a ghostly feeling. This gloomy church would not have been my first choice of where to spend time. On days when boredom weighed heaviest, I grasped at any new experience. Up I climbed the narrow, circular metal steps, following the direction of the priest's voice.

"Welcome, welcome, Enrico! I'm so happy you've come. I always need people for my choir. It's so difficult to get boys to come. They would rather run on the streets." He handed me a well-worn music book. "Can you read music?"

"No. I've never learned. When I sang in a synagogue, I just followed the music."

"Well, just look through it. You'll be able to learn."

A vision of *Mutti* leafing through the book with all the references to the Holy Mary, Jesus Christ, and the Holy Spirit flashed through my mind. Loud and clear I could hear her caustic comments and, even funnier, I imagined the eloquent facial expressions she would make. A big grin crossed my face. It was too dark for the priest to have noticed or surely he would have asked me to explain. As long as he didn't ask me to make the sign of the cross and take communion, I could live with the words in the book.

He asked me to sing a few notes to his accompaniment. "That will do just fine," he said. "I'm happy to have you join us." He informed me when rehearsal time was and with an enthusiastic handshake, sent me on my way.

I had turned six when *Mutti* heard me sing in the synagogue in Vienna. Would she now come to church to hear me? Never! When I told Mamma, her reaction was milder than expected.

"I'll make believe I don't know anything about this. My son singing hymns in a Catholic church. This is worse than when you almost joined the Italian army." Then, with hands held together in prayer, she fixed her eyes to the sky. "Dear God, please forgive my *meshugene* son."

I would have liked for my mother to have heard me sing and see me wear my embroidered white cassock, but maybe it was better she didn't. It was unthinkable to have her Jewish son sing in a church, but, to see him dressed as an altar boy and hear the names of Catholic divinities come from his lips would have been like planting a dagger in her chest.

For several months I donned the white cassock and sang with the all-male choir. The weekly choir practice occupied a few hours and helped develop my rapidly changing voice.

Among the many people who befriended me in Ospedaletto, Don Antonio was the most provocative. The priest was strolling through the village with Pietro when I first met him and at once I was captivated by the tall man's charisma.

"Enrico has become a friend of Don Giuseppe," Pietro said. "Isn't that true?"

"We have good debates," I added.

"Well, perhaps you and I should get together and have a debate," Don Antonio said.

Don Antonio, born into an old-fashioned religious family, had been honored to become the village monsignor at the young age of twenty-four.

"It was my greatest dream come true," he said. "In those days I wanted nothing else but to be a monsignor. I wanted to do homage to my father's memory and make my mother proud."

But his life's dream was no sooner realized than this intellectual rebel began to distance himself from the constrained lifestyle of his family, the village, and the church.

His mother and sister always dressed in black as a sign of mourning for the priest's father, who had died many years before. Their hair, neatly combed into a chignon, was in stark contrast to the dirty feet that showed through the open *zoccoli* and which matched the accumulated dirt under their fingernails. Every day they walked to church down the unpaved, dusty road, nodding discreet greetings to those they passed on their way. Their religious ardor and attire were typical of women of a southern Italian village.

Don Antonio differed so much from his mother and sister that it almost seemed they could have been born in different eras. Nothing about him was characteristic of this village. Not his proud bearing. Not his secret wardrobe. Bright, intelligent, he had caught the attention of someone from the Vatican when still a novice and was transferred to a job in Rome. "I was delighted to go to the Eternal City." He also confided how he soon found an apartment and a lover, not necessarily in that order.

I wasn't quite sure what a lover was and, after his cautious explanation, my curiosity overrode my better instinct and I risked asking, "Isn't that against the laws of your church?"

Perhaps as a subtle rebuff, Don Antonio ignored my question, making me realize that I probably should not have asked.

During one of his visits to Ospedaletto, with youthful enthusiasm, this thirty-year-plus Catholic priest showed me a suit he had recently purchased. Index finger on his lips, he whispered, "Shhh. No one is to know about this." As a kid of twelve, I felt uneasy being this sophisticated man's confidant until I found out that most of the *confinati* already knew, for this *simpatico* man was incapable of keeping his own secrets. A tall, good-looking, affable, and quiet rebel, he loved to wear civilian clothes in disregard of the church's precepts, for, as he had boasted to some, he had cast off his celibacy long before.

I enjoyed spending time with Don Antonio. His exquisite Italian, without a tinge of the local dialect and the worldly knowledge he was willing to share made up for the musty odor in his mother's house.

"Where do you wear your civilian suit?" I asked.

"When in Rome."

"Oh, tell me about Rome, please."

"*Roma. Bellissima! La Città Eterna!*" He let out a sigh as his eyes gazed at the ceiling. "There, antiquity merges with the present. It's incredibly magnificent. A majestic city that would be even more majestic if Mussolini were far away from it."

"You don't like *Il Duce*, do you?"

"Why should I? Because he drained the Pontan swamps and made the trains run on time? What about Ethiopia, Eritrea, Libya? But I better stop before I get myself in trouble. Tell me, what do you remember of Vienna?"

"Not much. We owned a hotel. I loved going to the Prater, the Vienna amusement park. Oh, yes. I enjoyed going to the Lilliputian village there."

"What's that village?"

"In the Prater there was a whole colony of midgets, Lilliputians. They lived in their own tiny houses, had their own shops, a church, and a little theater. The houses were so small that even, when I was six, I had to stoop to get through the doors. Once I saw a couple get married and in their tiny theater I learned a skit. Do you want to see it?"

"Of course. Go ahead, show me the skit."

I mimed sewing an invisible garment and then losing the imaginary needle. Rising from the chair, I looked for the needle and, unable to find it, sat again. The needle, hidden in the chair, implanted itself in my behind and made me jump up with a scream. We both laughed.

"That was good, very good," he said.

Don Antonio was great to be with. He spoke to me as an adult, always ready to enlighten me on many subjects. That day I got him to tell me how Mussolini, without provocation, had attacked Ethiopia, Eritrea, and Libya.

Clara Gattegno was tutoring me, yet Mother still worried I was not studying enough. Alfredo Michelagnoli had arrived recently in our midst, and before long my mother asked him to teach me English.

Never one to accept without question what my mother had chosen for me, I raised my objection. "I'm studying with Clara and that's enough for me. Besides, Jimmy doesn't have a tutor."

"I really don't care what Jimmy has or doesn't have. His parents will have to worry about that. I want my son to have as much knowledge as possible. Just remember one thing," Mother said, pointing a finger to her head. "Nobody can take away what you have in here. When we left Vienna, we had to leave everything behind. Do you remember? But what I learned as a child I took with me. Learn, *Schatzele!* Learn all you can, for your knowledge will stay with you for the rest of your life!"

A professor at Oxford at the outbreak of the war, Alfredo Michelagnoli was forced by British authorities to return to his native Italy, where the Fascist government, citing his British connection, interned him, his wife, and his two young daughters. Wearing tweed knickers, a matching beret, and riding boots, he looked the part of an English country gentleman. He changed his clothes often, but his beret remained the same, serving as a cover-up for his premature baldness as well as a stylish article of clothing.

His walk was more like a duck's waddle. Adding to this learned man's almost comical image, Alfredo also suffered from a nervous twitch that made his nose quiver and his shoulder snap upward toward his cheek. I had never seen anyone do that and, finding it funny, bit my lip to suppress the impulse to laugh.

Although not as debonair as John Howell, during his stay in Great Britain, Michelagnoli had adopted a British demeanor. "The British say I look Italian. The Italians say I look British. If they could have agreed on this, they wouldn't be at war."

Alfredo was more serious than most *confinati*, although at times he tried telling a joke or two with little success.

"You're still the professor at Oxford," Mother remarked. "Now you are part of us. Our sense of humor is what keeps us going. Without it we would all go crazy."

But Alfredo Michelagnoli, as long as I knew him, remained the pedantic Oxford professor.

I enjoyed the twice-a-week English lessons with the professor. Patient and skillful, in a short time taught me a working knowledge of English, enough to understand and respond when Jimmy Howell made one of his condescending remarks to me.

From left: William Pierce, Pietro Russo, Alfredo Michelagnoli with fountain in background in Ospedaletto, 1942.

21

Pietro Russo Is Freed

My mother's involvement with Pietro had become common knowledge among both the internees and the locals. I was getting annoyed that Pietro was now her favorite conversation topic. I couldn't understand why anyone would keep talking about one person so often and so much. Once, when Mother was in Dora's apartment, I put my ear against the door to listen. Again, she was babbling about Pietro, how much she loved, how she wanted nothing else but to spend the rest of her life with him, and on, and on. She also used many peculiar words I could not understand.

Without knocking, I stormed into the room. "I heard what you were saying. What about Papa? What's going to happen when Papa comes back to us?"

"I will have to deal with that," Mamma answered.

"But I want to know!" I said loudly. "Is Papa going to be living with us, too?"

"I don't know." Suddenly my mother had lost her self assurance.

Dora answered. "It will be all right, Enrico. I'm sure your mother will be able to make the right decision when your father comes back."

I wanted an answer from my mother but got none. Dejected, I left the room and ran downstairs. My mind was in such turmoil. Pietro, Mamma, Papa, me. I did not know what I wanted to happen. I knew I wanted my father to come back to us. Of that I was sure. Or was I? I was happy being with Pietro, but did I want him to replace my father? Was Mother going to leave me to spend the rest of her life with this new man? I had heard of parents abandoning their children. Would I be roaming the streets without a parent or a place to live? Who would feed me? I could stay in Ospedaletto. Dora would take care of me. I may not go hungry but never again would I eat my favorite meal, Mother's *Wiener Schnitzel*!

Mamma and Pietro spent more hours behind closed doors. Once or twice I tried to open the bedroom door, but it was always locked. Mother had never kept secrets from me, which made these strange goings on even more strange. My mind was so confused that I didn't want to be angry. Not at my mother and certainly not at Pietro. If only they would tell me what was happening.

In June 1942 the postman delivered a telegram to Pietro Russo. We were in the kitchen when Mamma read the message on the narrow paper strips glued to the canary sheet. The telegram slipped from her fingers as both arms fell to her sides, eyes downcast and her expression grave. After a long silence, she whispered, "When do you plan on leaving?"

Pietro didn't look any happier. "I guess soon. I don't really know when."

Mother asked me to leave then closed the door behind me. They remained alone while I waited in the hallway. I tried to listen but heard only mumbling. When Mamma opened the door, her red, swollen eyes clearly spoke of her feelings. Pietro sat at the kitchen table, his forehead slumped between his cupped hands.

I did not know what message the telegram brought. Perhaps the upsetting news was about Ettore Costa who, because of his failing health, had been allowed to leave some weeks before. Before I could do any more guessing, Pietro lifted his head and pulled me close.

"I will be leaving soon. Going home. I just received the news."

I had grown to love this man and although I still called him Pietro in public, within the walls of our home I started calling him *Pupo*. "Why is *Pupo* leaving?" I asked.

Mamma handed me the yellow piece of paper. "Pietro has been pardoned," she said then read the message: "GREAT PERSONAL PLEASURE TO GRANT YOU FULL PARDON STOP FREEDOM RESTORED AT RECEIPT OF TELEGRAM STOP BENITO MUSSOLINI." Most official notices in those days were sent Mussolini's name. It was impressive but not unusual.

As with all local news, Pietro's pardon spread quickly and the next morning the group of *confinati* remained at the corner unwilling to start their walk on time. This was an extraordinary event and the *internati* reacted with joy. As the telegram moved from hand to hand, everyone showed their excitement and made congratulatory remarks. Even the cantankerous William Pierce wished Pietro well.

"Well, I think this calls for a celebration," John Howell said.

"Absolutely," everyone said in chorus.

"Maybe we can get a permit to go to Montevergine," Willy suggested.

"I'll talk to the *maresciallo*," Pietro said. "I'll show him the telegram. He'll be impressed by *Il Duce's* signature."

I went with Pietro to the police station and, as he had predicted, Maresciallo Marchetti was impressed with the telegram and delighted to grant the permit. "You can take as many people you want, Dottor Russo. I'll send one of my men with you. Just let me know when."

As we left the small building, the maresciallo stepped out into the street. "*Auguri! Auguri*, Dottor Russo!" he shouted.

Two days before the planned celebratory hike, Pietro asked me if I wanted to go with him to Avellino. Of course. To go anywhere with Pietro was exciting. The following morning I woke up earlier than I needed to, but stayed in bed until Mamma came into my room. "It's time," she whispered in my ear, and I jumped out of bed.

After breakfast, which I forced myself to eat, we kissed Mother goodbye and walked to the small square to board the broken-down bus. In Avellino we stopped at the police station, where Pietro had to complete his release papers. First he spoke to one person who sent him to speak to someone else, who sent him to another floor, where we sat and waited.

"Nothing is ever simple with bureaucracy," Pietro whispered. After a long while, we were ushered into a small office, where a man emerged from behind an open newspaper. Methodically, he folded and placed the paper on the desk corner, then acknowledged our presence. Pietro concluded his business in less than five minutes, but that did not include waiting, the obligatory niceties of the handshake, asking where the man was from, and showing admiration for his office. When we walked out of the building Pietro remarked, "We were here more than an hour."

As we strolled down the main street, we passed a jewelry shop. "Let's go inside," Pietro said. In the store, he asked to see some men's watches.

After spreading black velvet on the glass counter, the shopkeeper picked a tray of watches and, as though handling some delicate living creatures, with theatrical gestures, placed each watch on the cloth. "Here you are, *Signore*."

Pietro lifted one of the watches from the black velvet and held it close to my face. "How about this? Do you like it?"

"Very nice," I said. What did I care?

He held my arm and placed the leather strap around my wrist. "How does it fit?"

"I guess all right." I couldn't imagine why he was asking these questions. Getting out of that shop would have been my choice. This was boring. Whether I liked it didn't mean the person for whom Pietro was buying it would have liked it too. Anyway, what did I know about watches?

"Well, you better make sure, since you'll have to wear it."

Those words were so overwhelming that my tongue got glued to the roof of my mouth and refused to respond. I stood there feeling foolish and unable to utter a word.

"Let's start again," Pietro said. "Do you like it and does it fit?"

I gathered my thoughts and tried applying the brakes to my runaway emotions. Finally I found my tongue. "I don't believe it. You're buying me a watch?"

"Stand still for a moment. Do you like it?"

Still moving about the store, my eyes transfixed on the shiny round instrument on my wrist, I answered, "I love it." Then, with some hesitation, I pointed to another one lying on the counter and said, "If I could, I like this better."

The clerk removed the timepiece from my wrist and replaced it with the one I had pointed to. The strap was a bit too large. "No problem. I can adjust it to fit him perfectly," the man said.

As if someone had shot a handful of sharp needles into my buttocks, I was hopping in circles about the store. Waiting for the jeweler to put two holes in the leather strap drove me up the wall. Getting a watch had been the furthest thought from my mind, and now the reality of this new, beautiful shining timepiece made me lose control. I had just turned twelve and this was my first wristwatch. The one my *Opapa* had given me in Poland six years earlier was a pocket watch.

I waited until we exited the store before flinging myself at Pietro. "I love you, *Pupo*. Oh, thank you, thank you, thank you!"

"It's your birthday gift. Now, every time you look at it you'll think of me."

Little did Pietro realize that I didn't need a watch to think of him. He had become a large part of my life. As excited as I was about my gift, I would have been happier to relinquish my new watch in exchange for him remaining in Ospedaletto with us.

The day of the planned hike to Montevergine, twelve internees and Sabato Pisano, whom I had befriended and also had become Pietro's friend, planned to come along. Mother woke me at two-thirty that morning. She was already dressed, wearing her walking shoes and ready for the long hike. Outside it was pitch black. Faster than usual, I washed my hands and face, then reached for my new watch to see the faint phosphorescent glow. How amazing! I could tell time in the dark. Oh, how much I loved my beloved *Pupo*!

Breakfast was ready. *Mamma* came to my room. I was not dressed. "What are you doing? You've been up for more than twenty-five minutes. Hurry up!"

How could she know, how could anyone know how long it took a twelve-year-old to sufficiently admire a new timepiece?

When I entered the kitchen, Pietro was already there waiting. We ate in silence while the outside darkness added a sense of sadness to our somber mood.

In the piazza, by the pale light of early dawn, everyone got to see my glowing watch. I made sure of that. My only regret was that only twelve people were going on the climb. I would have liked a greater number so I could show my new gift to more people.

"Has anyone ever been to Montevergine?" someone asked.

No one had except for me. When alone in one of my rebellious moods, I had run up to the monastery, never revealing the escapade to anyone.

A little past 4:00, the lone *carabiniere* joined us and we started the ninety-minute, uphill hike. The gravel footpath cut through the woods where only traces remained of what must have been steps, perhaps from Roman times. Clara Gattegno had taught me that this area of Italy had been part of the Roman Empire.

For the first thirty or more minutes, shrouded by the dense forest, we walked in total darkness. Unable to see where to put our feet, we found staying upright on the rocky path to be a challenge. When the fluorescent glow from the watch told me it was 4:40, the sun's early light filtered through the thick foliage and we could almost see where to step. The playful rays danced about the ground creating magical sparkles as the leaves high up in the trees moved to the tempo of the mountain breezes. I joined in the dance, trying to stomp on the rays of light before they vanished, only to seek them out in their next spot.

For almost two hours we climbed the steep road. Someone cut a tree branch to make a walking stick. Pietro, attentive as always, made one and presented it to Mamma.

When we reached the monastery, none of us looked as tired as we should have.

"I feel free like a bird," Pietro said. "Just being out of Ospedaletto."

We spent most of the day under the watchful eyes of the solitary *carabiniere* assigned to us to foil any planned escape. Of course, the maresciallo knew that, if escape was what any of us wanted, we could easily have done so right under his very nose. But no one ever tried to escape. We had nowhere to go.

That day, for the first time in more than two years, Mamma allowed me to use the camera Papa had sent with Aunt Sally when she passed through San Remo on her way to America. Owning a camera was a serious infraction, and Mamma had forbidden the mere mention of it. But now, with Pietro leaving, it was an opportunity to use it and have him take it to Sicily. Besides, no one, including the *carabiniere*, would report it. But Pietro told William Pierce that it was his camera. "I take no chances with that imbecile," he said.

The monastery of Montevergine was an imposing structure. Situated five miles from Ospedaletto by way of the serpentine road, but much closer by the path we had taken, Montevergine was 3,600 feet above sea level.

"How did they bring all these stones and bricks up the mountain?" I asked.

"Donkeys and horses, I guess," Pietro answered.

The mountain *basilica* was three times larger than the church in Ospedaletto. Four rows of tall, white marble columns gave it an aura of grandeur missing in the village church but also a coldness not felt in the much smaller house of worship. Monks in white or brown habits moved briskly across the portico. A gift shop sold a variety of trinkets, key chains, postcards, viewers with photographs of the monastery, and pictures of the Madonna. Just as in Ospedaletto, the church's walls displayed hundreds of aged photographs and silver replicas of human limbs representing the claimed miracles. I shared with Pietro and Mamma the knowledge I had acquired from Don Pasquale. "You learned a lot in Ospedaletto," Pietro remarked.

In respectful silence, we walked through the interior of the sanctuary. Only the echoes of our steps could be heard. Those who were

Catholics genuflected as they stepped across the splendid altar; then all of us, following the signs on the wall, went to look at the body of Beato Giulio displayed in a glass case.

A friendly monk passed by and, satisfying our curiosity, explained that the monastery had been built around the beginning of the thirteenth century, then rebuilt and enlarged in subsequent years.

"When did Beato Giulio die?" I asked.

"In the year of our Lord 1801."

"Eighteen hundred and one?" I repeated. "That makes him one-hundred-forty-one years old."

I got chills staring at the embalmed corpse of the priest, dressed in his stark white tunic. The flesh shriveled by time and the skinless nose gave the remains a less-than-human appearance.

"Is this how we're going to look after we die?" I asked. But no one answered my question.

"Who would have thought I'd be celebrating an event in a monastery?" Mamma said.

"Why?" someone from the group asked.

"Well, Jews don't usually frequent a Catholic church. But these are crazy days and everything goes."

After visiting the large cathedral, we walked to the fountain in the courtyard to fill our containers with cold mountain water. We looked for a place to escape the hot midday sun, found it on the monastery's front steps and sat down to have our picnic in the shadow of the basilica. Everyone in our group had brought lunch. Mother had prepared sandwiches consisting of a single slice of hard-to-find salami and one tomato between two slices of Dora's homemade bread. Simple but delicious. Just being out of the village was a jubilee of sorts. If only the reason had not been Pietro's leaving us.

The steps to the entrance of the altar in Montevergine.

Finished eating, I pestered the people to pose for a number of group photographs. I remembered little of how to use the camera, but my enthusiasm compensated for my lack of knowledge. Everyone was in a happy mood, and no one complained that I made them stand, sit, then stand again. Taking pictures and seeing new sights had me so engrossed that I forgot why we had made the climb. Only on our way back to Ospedaletto did my sadness return. Not even my shiny new watch was of any solace.

As I was kicking up dust on the narrow path, Pietro caught up with me and placed his arm around me. "What goes?"

I struggled out of his friendly hold. "Nothing."

"Eh, I know you too well. Something is bothering you."

"Leave me alone," I shouted.

I was brusque. He didn't deserve my rude reaction, but I was angry and couldn't help but feel that, just as my papa had done before, Pietro was abandoning me. I was only twelve, just a boy, yearning for that special paternal love.

Drowning in my misery, I trotted all the way down to Ospedaletto, crying and kicking stones.

Back in the village, I raced across the municipal gardens and up our two flights to take refuge in Mother's room. My room was too accessible and, the way I felt, I didn't want to see anyone. I turned the key to lock the door and threw myself onto the bed. Not long after I heard a faint knock followed by Pietro's gentle voice. I unlocked the door and kept it ajar and his large and friendly face, with that captivating smile, peeked through the narrow opening.

"Can we talk?" he asked.

I made some kind of noise in response and fell back on the bed.

He pushed open the door, entered and sat next to me. "I would like to know what's bothering you."

It was impossible to resist his love-filled voice. I buried my face into his chest and wept out loud. "Will I ever see you again?"

Group of internees who climbed to Montevergine to celebrate Pietro Russo's release from internment in June 1942.

With his strong arms around me and his large hand gently stroking my hair, he shared his gentleness with me. "Of course you'll see me again. I love you and I love your mother." It was the first time I had heard Pietro express this feeling. Love. What a warm, beautiful word! What splendid emotion! At that moment I could only think of the word but didn't quite grasp its full meaning.

Four more days before Pietro would leave, us and of those days I tried to steal as many of the hours as he and Mamma would allow. I even spent one night in his room, something I had done occasionally.

"Do you remember the night when you showed off how you could hit the ceiling with your spit?" I asked.

"Of course, I remember. I also remember how cold it was and the brazier we placed between the sheets didn't do much to keep us warm. We did such silly things just to keep our blood flowing."

"I like when you read Pirandello. I'll miss that much more than the spitting contest." We both laughed. Not a happy laughter.

"I'll read to you tomorrow. When I get home, I'll send you an anthology of Italian poetry and you'll be able to read them by yourself."

"It won't be the same."

The next morning Pietro found a volume of poetry. I watched how gently he fondled that book. He loved Italian literature and had a unique fondness for Carducci, Foscolo, and Leopardi.

Partially from the open book held in one hand but mostly from memory, Pietro recited the words of a grieving father: "*Sei nella terra fredda, sei nella terra negra, ne il sol piú ti rallegra, ne ti risveglia amor.*"

My eyes were swollen as I shared in the pain and anguish of the poet Carducci, who had penned the verses for his dead child. The day before leaving us, *Pupo* gave me that book of poetry. I have reread those same verses many times but never recaptured the feelings Pietro created with his reading.

22

Tragedies and Grief

Since the start of the war, death occurred frequently in Ospedaletto. Most adult males had been drafted into Mussolini's army and, some of the internees remarked, if luck was on their side, they were sent to Africa; otherwise, they were shipped to the Russian front. As young men turned eighteen, they were drafted, stirring up emotions in their respective households. But the news of a soldier killed or missing in action caused hysteria among parents, relatives, and friends, bringing misery and sorrow to the entire village. Most of the 1,800 townspeople were related to one another by blood, by marriage, or by being a *cummare*.

To an acquaintance, who grieved a recent loss, I asked, "What is a *cummare?*"

"A *cummare?*" She hesitated a bit. "He was our best man when I got married. It could be someone who helped name your baby or just a good friend."

In a village where grief became a public spectacle and death a frequent visitor, war caused much visible agony. I remember well the large, disheveled woman, clad in black, a large cross swinging from her neck and dirty hair slipping out from under her black scarf, who came running from her home, arms waving over her head. She stopped, looked up and down the narrow road, then, as loud as any human lungs allowed, cried out the terrible news. "*Maronna mia! Hanno ammazzato Peppino.*"

Because half the men in Ospedaletto d'Alpinolo were nicknamed Peppino, bedlam erupted in every family, whether they had a soldier by that name or not. It followed that, as the woman's howling spread the news of Peppino's death, a mob frenzy engulfed the village, piercing the placid mountain air with distraught screams.

"Which Peppino?" someone shouted.

"Maria's son." Not much help, since Ospedaletto had as many Marias as Peppinos. The mass wailing increased, spreading down the dusty road, to the narrow alleyways and into every home. I kept turning in the direction of the new sounds and, if not for the tragedy of the moment, I might have been witnessing a well-rehearsed *opera buffa*.

During a similar episode, I discovered how contagious weeping could be. Several women, in the same black attire with crosses hanging from their necks, emerged from their homes and joined in the communal wailing. I got the impression that sobbing could only be performed in public or, possibly, that no one wanted so much noise inside their own house.

These open displays of grief became more frequent as the fortunes of war turned against Italy.

In the fall of 1942, I went to visit the postmaster's twenty-year-old son, Carmine, who lay dying of tuberculosis. Though I was much younger, I had befriended him and wanted to pay him a last visit.

"I don't want you to get too close to him," Mamma admonished me. "TB is very contagious. I let you go because it's the right thing to do."

When I went to the apartment above the post office and entered Carmine's room, I found his parents, Don Guglielmo and his wife, by his side. I kept a distance from the bed as I had promised my mother and thus was unable to hear the dying young man's soft whispers. His father conveyed the message that he was grateful for my visit.

On that same day, a telegram from the Ministry of Defense arrived with news that the dying young man's older brother had been killed at the Russian front. In a compassionate gesture, the mailman, acting as assistant postmaster, kept the telegram from the grief-stricken parents for several months.

Each new tragic announcement from the defense department created absolute havoc for Dora Dello Russo. Antonio had been shipped to occupied Albania and, though he wrote frequently, his letters were more than a week old by the time they arrived.

"Lotte, I'm going mad. Men are dying everywhere. If anything happens to Totonno, I'll kill myself." Dora no longer spoke. She only shouted.

"And you'll leave your children orphans? That is really clever. Nothing is going to happen to Antonio. I feel it inside. Nothing. Do you hear me?"

I loved listening to my mother talk. Her soothing melodic voice calmed Dora. I admired Mamma's talent to put words together. They simply flowed. But I never understood how she could be so certain of her almost psychic premonitions.

23

Lello Is Born

Lello Dello Russo was born in the winter of 1942, and showing how much confidence she had in my mother, Dora encouraged her to share in the care of the newborn.

Since Pietro's departure in June, Mother had shown little interest in anything. Even her contact with other internees had been reduced to a bare minimum. Knowing how much she thrived on interacting with people, I was disturbed to watch her become a recluse. Lello's birth was the event Mother needed. She soon became involved with the new baby and, when I saw how her spirits were lifted, I realized that Lello's arrival was a truly blessed event for us all.

Mamma began wearing dresses she had not worn in months and cooking more elaborate meals. Everything about her spoke of the pleasure she took in sharing Dora's maternal duties. Perhaps at one time in her life my mother might have wanted more children, although she had never openly expressed that desire. As for me, a brother or a sister would have been a welcome comfort in those trying days but, for whatever reason, no other children ever enriched our family.

During our first days in Ospedaletto, Mamma had noticed the practice of swaddling children before they were put to bed. Frowning, she had mumbled, "How barbarous. Have these women never heard of diapers?"

On the evening when I watched Filomena, our landlady, wrap her baby's feet, legs and buttocks in an endless binding and turn the child into an inflexible living mummy, I had described the incident to *Mutti*.

"How long do they keep a child in this inhumane state?" Mamma asked Dora, after having watched the thirty-month-old child being bandaged for the night.

"Until the child learns to use the toilet."

Mother looked horrified. She shook her head in disbelief, as though the shaking could bring a better understanding of what she had heard. "Even if the baby learns to tell you it has to go, by the time you unravel these *fasce*, the child will no longer need a toilet. Besides, I wouldn't be surprised if the stench in what you call a toilet will not make the child wish to stay wrapped forever."

Nothing could change the old ingrained habits and customs in Ospedaletto d'Alpinolo.

Observing a woman breastfeeding an older child, my Mamma asked, "How old is he?"

"Three."

I knew my mother well enough to recognize the meaning of her facial expression. Mamma was outraged. Her grimaces were more expressive than a hundred words. I often told her she should have been an actress. On another occasion I was baffled to see a child, who had been playing in the street, run up to his mother, unbutton her dress and cling to her breast. The boy seemed even older than three. Nor was it uncommon to see a woman, sitting on her front steps, with two children of different ages busily sucking from her fully exposed breasts.

Once my mother asked a woman how long she breastfed her children.

"It depends," the woman replied. "I still nurse the last three."

To Dora Mother said, "You know how I feel about *fasce* and breastfeeding. If you want me to help, it has to be my way."

"I'll try. Whatever you say, Lotte."

So, at age forty-one and without giving birth, my mother became Mamma Lotte for the Dello Russos and practiced her earned title for the remainder of our stay in Ospedaletto. Reluctantly, Dora stopped breastfeeding when Lello was six months old.

"I stopped when Enrico was six months. Look how healthy he is now," Mamma said.

Lello was never bandaged and, instead of *fasce*, my mother introduced Dora to more modern methods. "I need a sheet to make diapers for Lello."

No one in Ospedaletto had ever heard of diapers and Dora was no exception. Nonetheless, she gave Mother everything she asked for.

Except for breastfeeding, Mamma Lotte performed with enthusiasm most other maternal roles. I also enjoyed the presence of that little fellow and never felt jealous of the attention we now shared. For me, Lello was the baby brother I never had, although it occurred to me that the fraternal relationship was only for the duration of our stay. Mamma was so devoted to her new charge that, during Lello's first two months, she even abandoned her regular bridge game. Caring for the baby was great therapy for her lonely heart.

When Antonio was discharged from the army for medical reasons in December 1942 and went back to his commercial activities, most stores had empty shelves and welcomed any merchandise anyone was able to deliver. Antonio earned more than the family could spend.

With both Dora and Antonio, Mother shared what she had experienced at the end of the first Great War. "You must take your money and buy things. Buy anything. It doesn't matter what. All your money will not be enough to buy one pound of bread. After the last war, people carried their money in wheelbarrows to buy just one small bag of potatoes. Paper money had so many zeros, people didn't know how much it was worth."

Dora looked frightened. "What are you saying? *Madonna mia*, we are honest people. Totonno works hard to earn this money. What can we buy? The stores are empty."

Antonio was less swayed by his emotions. "I think Lotte is right."

"Go down to Avellino," Mamma said. "Look in the stores. The first thing I would buy is the best radio I can find. Buy two or three. You'll be able to sell them later."

"Three radios?" Dora repeated in a whisper. "That's crazy. We don't own one now. What would we do with three radios?"

"Your money will be worth nothing, Dora! Nothing, believe me. With all your money you won't be able to buy one pound of pasta." My mother's voice was forceful and convincing.

Antonio understood and, a few days later, he attached the horse to the long cart and took Dora to Avellino, where they purchased a console radio with a built-in bar as well as several pieces of furniture. Upon their return, my mother was so excited with the purchases that one would have thought the items had been bought for her. Meanwhile Dora kept repeating, "We've spent all our money. All of it!"

By the time we left Ospedaletto d'Alpinolo in 1943, the Italian currency had lost most of its value, and the Dello Russos could not find adequate words to show their appreciation for my mother's far-sighted financial advice.

Mr. and Mrs. Wovsi were older than most of the internees and seldom joined in our physical activities. In times when gossip and criticism helped the days slip away, no one ever uttered a critical word about them. Indeed, most internees spoke with a certain reverence for this refined and dignified couple.

One morning, soon after we arrived, Mr. Wovsi invited Mother and me to join him and his wife for tea that afternoon. "It would be nice to get to know you," he said. "The Howells will also be there."

Located on the slope where the footpath to Montevergine had its beginning, their second-floor apartment, furnished with a delicate touch, was much larger than what most of us could afford. For the Wovsis, Ospedaletto was a comfortable, even if hard to tolerate, retreat.

As we sat on the soft and elegant sofa, admiring their living room, Mrs. Wovsi rolled in a cart carrying a shiny brass samovar.

"That is absolutely lovely," *Mutti* remarked.

"We brought it from Poland," Mrs. Wovsi said. Then turning to her husband, she asked, "Was it 1927 or '28 when we first came to Italy?"

"I think it was 1928, dear." I got the impression he felt ill at ease to remember what his wife had forgotten.

While Mother admired much of what she saw, I soon became bored by the conversation about furniture. What did I care what they had brought from where and when?

"Italy was such a marvelous country then," Signora Wovsi said. "We felt welcome. People were so friendly. Remember, Morris? We didn't speak a word of Italian."

He chuckled. "I still don't speak it too well."

"We sent all our boys to *Yeshiva,* and nobody bothered us. Those were wonderful times. Mussolini left everyone alone until he made that stupid friendship with Hitler."

"Signora Wovsi. Everything is so nice," *Mutti* remarked.

"We were fortunate. They allowed us to bring our furniture from Milan. It makes being far from home a little easier to bear."

"Have you heard anything about your request?" Agatha Howell asked. She was referring to their petition to return to Milan.

"Our children are working on it. We are very hopeful. How long have we been here, Morris?"

"It will be two years in November."

"I miss my grandchildren terribly," Mrs. Wovsi said.

Among the other restrictions, racial laws prohibited Jews from hiring servants. This same rule applied to all *confinati*, yet the Wovsis did employ a young woman who did their house chores. In Ospedaletto, regulations did not matter much, because those responsible for watching for violations seemed not to care.

The Wovsis told us why their sons had been able to remain up north. "In their business they have made many contacts and through them they are able to remain in Milan." Now these contacts were trying to get the sons' parents out of Ospedaletto.

"You are so fortunate to have family who can help," Mamma said. "We have nobody and I guess we'll stay here until the war ends."

Several months passed before the long-awaited telegram arrived. "WITH GREAT PERSONAL SATISFACTION I HAVE INSTRUCTED LOCAL AUTHORITIES TO RELEASE YOU FROM INTERNMENT STOP BENITO MUSSOLINI." Their sons' efforts had paid off, and the Wovsis' dream to go back home to be with their grandchildren came to pass.

Most of the internees went to congratulate them for their good fortune and perhaps express a bit of envy of their returning to civilization and to all that we missed so much: running water, heat, a bath, and a real toilet.

Mr. and Mrs. Rozental, Runia Kleinerman's parents, were in their seventies and seldom ventured out to join the other *internati*. "We don't like these dusty roads and stony paths," Signora Rozental said, speaking for her husband as well. "We feel very insecure walking. Besides, we would rather stay in and read a book."

Books were every internee's constant companions. When going on the morning walks or to play bridge, more than one person brought a book along, looking to steal a quiet moment. Finding books, however, was not easy. Seldom did anyone get to a bookstore in Avellino. From time to time, a new book reached us from the outside world.

"It's an unwritten rule," Runia said. "Whoever gets their hands on new reading material should share it with other *confinati*."

I too was able to take advantage of the circulating books, thus expanding both my vocabulary and my impressionable mind. Though *Mutti* tried hard to find me some German books so I wouldn't forget my mother tongue, her efforts succeeded only a few times.

While Mr. Rozental exercised his mind with his translations, his wife, also an avid reader, devoted a small part of the day to cooking. I never had a chance to evaluate his work as a translator, but I did have occasion to taste her cooking. As often as I accepted one of her dinner invitations, whether in winter or summer, the first course always seemed to be the same: a watery cabbage soup suitable for prison inmates and served so blisteringly hot that I thought my teeth would melt. It was strange that the old lady could bring the soup to such high a temperature on a stove that strained to bring water to a boil. Of greater wonder was seeing everyone else at the table finish their portion before I could place the first spoonful in my mouth. I suspected that the soup's scorching heat was her secret way to conceal its lack of taste.

Each time I had dinner at Runia's, I tried to develop a friendship with Giorgio, but the boy, six years my senior and much too serious for his age, I thought, showed little interest in me. Thus, after my several attempts had met with rejection, I finally abandoned the efforts.

Although none of the internees expected visitors, the arrival of the bus from Avellino held the greatest expectation of the day. It carried the mail and perhaps an occasional letter for some lucky *confinato*.

Every day at 2:30, I began listening for the huff and puff of the dilapidated coach struggling up the steep mountain road. It arrived seldom on time, but, in those days hours were plentiful and filling them with waiting was part of our daily life. Starting from home at one end, I'd run the length of the village to meet the bus as it stopped after its first turn into town. The coach, avoiding the village center, traveled on the main road from where the mailman, or anyone else waiting there, picked up the village mail sack, the size of a small paper bag. With me in tow, the sack was carried into the post office, where, after separating the items addressed to the internees, Don Guglielmo handed those pieces to the mail carrier to take to city hall for the required censoring. The process was quick, for the man, entrusted to read our letters, never did but immediately handed the mail to the waiting internees.

To me it was a matter of pride to be first at city hall. With a feeling of self-importance, I had elected myself the internees' courier and seldom neglected my self-imposed duty. Several *confinati* were happy to let me pick up their mail and spare themselves the round trip on the dusty, steep incline.

When my mother wondered how they expected Don Pepe to read letters written in German or English, Ettore had replied, "That's why Italy will never win the war." Despite Mother's personal feelings for the man, she often quoted that line.

One afternoon while distributing the mail, Don Pepe handed me a letter from the Swiss Red Cross. It was an invitation to become a pen pal with a Jewish boy somewhere in Italy. Enclosed was a list of names from which to choose. A chance to correspond with a Jewish boy was a novel and exciting event in my life.

The boy I picked, Dino Levy, was also twelve and lived in Venice. Thrilled and driven by my impetuousness, I wrote him a long letter that very day telling him about myself and my mother. I described our confinement, our needs, our frustrations. He replied a week or so later telling me about his private school and his imminent summer vacation in the Alps. No mention of how he and his parents had remained untouched by the Fascist regime and why his family had been allowed to continue pursuing whatever business they were in. I was disappointed he had not understood my plight, but Dino was generous, often sending packages of clothes, books and food items along with a measure of good cheer. He was the only person who wrote to me. I had never thought of getting addresses from my friends in San Remo, so I couldn't have kept in touch with them.

"Look, Mamma! Two books." A package from Dino had arrived that day and I wasted little time immersing myself in one part of its contents: *The Rains Came*, by Louis Bromfield.

"Can you put the book down to eat something?" Mamma complained.

"Mamma, this book is so good." Both the writing and the subject I found fascinating.

Dino's letters and the knowledge that someone my own age cared were great morale boosters during those days in exile. I harbored the hope to meet my penpal one day to tell him in person how much his kindness had meant to me.

During the months in Ospedaletto, I matured faster than a boy of twelve should. Of all my experiences, the one that left the most lasting mark was the day I witnessed death.

I was visiting my friend Raffaele and as luck would have it, found myself in his parents' bedroom just as his ailing father decided to exhale his last breath and let go of his life right before me. What an audible last breath in the otherwise quiet room! Why did he have to do that while I was there? Raffaele and his sister were at their father's bedside, while I, in shock, stood far away and in a bizarre reaction found myself imitating the man's last sound. I stared at that motionless body, alive only seconds before and now dead. Dead. Totally dead. It brought on the jitters. How could a man be alive one instant and dead the next? I couldn't remember how I had imagined someone dying, but this certainly was not the way.

Suddenly, I found myself surrounded by a wailing crowd of town folks who, as though by magic, had arrived to see the dead man. The new widow with her other three children entered, followed by a number of women dressed in black. While the family threw themselves on the body, shaking and caressing it, some women flung themselves on the bed. Some screamed, others rolled their eyes toward the ceiling as if trying to pierce through the roof to reach some supreme being in the hope of bringing the dead man back to life.

The children tried to console their mother, whose emotions were out of control. Though small of stature and slim, she was strong and it took all five children to restrain her from throwing herself on the floor.

In the midst of this pandemonium, I watched the pudgy figure of the village barber enter the room with a Napoleonic strut. He was bald and shorter than most people there and soon got lost in the taller crowd. Ceremoniously, the fellow placed a well-worn bag on the bed, removed his shabby jacket, and slowly rolled up his shirt sleeves. Then, as though preparing for some joyful task, he vigorously rubbed his hands. In slow motion and with concentrated attention, he pulled his utensils from the bag and laid them next to the corpse. Methodically, one item at a time, he pulled out a straight edge razor, a soap mug, a leather strap, and a limp brush.

"I need a glass of warm water," he whispered.

With elaborate posturing, the man reached for the brush, raised it over his head and as if practicing an ancient rite, dropped it into the mug. He seemed poised to entertain the crowd with some magic acts. His calm performance in the midst of all that turmoil was truly an accomplishment, as though he was in a trance or had left his feelings at home on the mantlepiece.

Transfixed, I stayed put as the man pulled from his worn bag a frayed and dirty towel, which he tucked under the dead man's chin. Then, wetting the tired brush in the warm water that one of the sisters had brought him and rubbing it into the soap mug, he twirled the lather onto the face of the corpse with a well-rehearsed gesture of his hand. He rotated the brush and stroked it up and down, for just to lather was not enough. He was bent on creating a work of art! And, like the artist steps back to judge his painting, so did he after every few layers of the lather. Tilting his head to one side and then to the other, he studied his subject. After a few more strokes of the brush and a final examination from a distance, he tied the leather strap to the bed frame and sharpened the blade with a back-and-forth motion.

Returning to the bed's edge, he stood on his toes to reach the body, yet no matter how much he stretched, he was unable to get to the far side of the dead man's face. With a hop, he jumped onto the bed and kneeling on its edge, with two fingers pinching the cheek, *whuff,* he shaved off the stubble.

Standing to one side, moving from here to there to keep out of the way of people busy with their own histrionics, I had a problem keeping a straight face as I watched the pompous barber at work. To my relief, Raffaele was busy comforting his mother, for I would not have known how to explain my silly behavior.

Looking at the freshly shaven, bloodless cheeks, I kept wondering whether his soul had floated out with that last sonorous breath. Why else would the man's last breath have been so loud? I pondered life and death, spirit and body, and thought about heaven and hell. There had to be eternal life. At that moment all my misdeeds flashed through my mind. So many! Could I ever be forgiven? I was terrified. I certainly didn't want to go and meet Lucifer.

Though surrounded by all those noisy mourners, I felt lonely in that large, crowded room. Couldn't at least one person comfort me? But no one noticed. The mid-July afternoon was intensely hot, yet my shoulders shivered with cold wetness flowing from my skin. My conflicting emotions made it difficult to decide whether to stay or leave and, because I could not take my eyes off the dead body, my feet remained glued to the floor.

Don Pasquale entered with an altar boy, who was swinging an incense holder. The room began smelling like a church. The priest started to chant and, except for an occasional "*Così sia*" response from the mourners, a respectful hush descended on everyone present.

The calm broke the spell. I had seen enough for one day. No need to stay for more of the religious rites. Slowly I backed out of the room and, as if chased by some wild animal, flew down the stairs, wanting to be out of that house. As I hit the dusty road, the fresh air relaxed my tense body. I drew a long breath and ran home.

Up the two flights I raced and, gasping for air, yelled from the hallway, "Mamma, I just saw someone die!" I had hoped that getting the words out would finally calm me down. It did not.

Mother met me at the door. "Oh, my *Schatzele*. Come here. That must have been terrible. Let me hold you, then you can tell me what happened." She put her arms around me and held me tight to her bosom.

"Signor Sanseverino just died. Just like that. He let out a big breath and *puff*. What a spooky sound! It was scary."

"Try not to think about it. Maybe we'll go out for a walk."

I freed myself from her embrace. "It was Raffaele's father. I didn't know dying was so easy. One moment he was talking to his daughter and then he was dead. You should have been there to see what went on afterward."

"No thanks. Just tell me what happened."

"There was such screaming and yelling and crying. They came from everywhere. I don't know how they knew the man had died. Some people tried to shake his body to bring him back to life. Can you do that, Mamma? Bring someone back from death?"

"I don't think so."

"The barber came and shaved the man. Why do they do that?"

Mother had a puzzled look. I sensed she knew as little as I did about the barber. "He did what?"

"He shaved him."

"I don't know why."

Death occurred often in Ospedaletto and was not restricted to the elderly or the military. While playing bridge one afternoon, my mother learned of the death of a newborn baby that day.

"With so much ignorance and superstition, it's no wonder so many children die here," she remarked. "The women have more babies than they can care for."

"And no one wants to call a doctor or go to a clinic," Agatha Howell added.

The nearest clinic was in Mercogliano, about two miles down the road to Avellino, but the local women preferred relying on Maria, the village midwife, to help with their childbirth. I saw Maria a few times. She resembled a gypsy fortune teller rather than a professional midwife. Her hands, the first to touch every newborn, looked wrinkled, not from her forty-some-odd years but by years of layers of encrusted dirt. Even I had learned that the lack of running water and the people's ignorance of hygiene could cause the infant population to dwindle rapidly.

At the Howell's one afternoon, Mamma related the experience of seeing a woman, sitting outside her house, the blouse unbuttoned and feeding two children from her naked breast. Mother repeated the conversation she had. She had given birth to twenty-five, the woman said and thanked the Holy Mary for the seven she lost soon after birth.

24

Pierce's Betrayal

After Pietro's departure for Sicily, Mother devoted her time to bringing up Lello and writing long letters to her love. Seven days a week she wrote, sometimes even twice a day.

My time was divided between Enrico's shop, the billiard hall, tutoring, reading, and my stamp collection. I stopped singing with the church choir. Although not as observant as my grandfather would have wanted me to be, I was developing a strong feeling for my Jewishness and was less comfortable spending that much time in a Catholic church.

Mother began to smoke again, a sign of her increased nervousness. To save money and totally out of character, she bought a pack of cigarette paper and a package of bulk tobacco.

"What are you going to do with that?" I asked.

"I'll start making my own cigarettes."

The first time she tried to roll a cigarette, I saw her destroy more than half of the paper booklet without making one cigarette.

Runia, who was visiting, watched too. "Wouldn't it be cheaper to buy cigarettes?" she asked. "Look at all the tobacco you've dropped on the floor."

Mother looked frustrated. "Erich! Stop laughing!" she yelled. "If you think you can do better, here, you try it." With a large smile, she shoved the torn sheets and the bag of tobacco my way. "I guess you can tell I wasn't born to do this."

"Lotte, I admire your vitality," Runia said. "I often wonder how you keep that sense of humor under these circumstances. I get so depressed sometimes."

Internees loved having my mother around for her *joie de vivre*. Her optimism helped them raise their own spirits. Only when alone with me did she sometimes show her inner foreboding.

A few days after the failed cigarette-making incident, I watched a man make cigarettes using paper tubes and a plunger. "It looked simple, Mamma. Something even you could do."

"I am thrilled you have so much confidence in your mother. And where do I find these items?"

"I guess at the tobacco shop."

The next day, Mother brought home a box of cigarette sleeves and the metal stuffer. "Would you do it for *Mutti*?" she asked.

"Sure."

I had watched the fellow and was pretty confident I would have no trouble. But I soon learned the tubes were hard to fill. "The paper keeps splitting, Mamma." I used almost a full box of one hundred tubes before succeeding in making the first cigarette. But by the end of the first week, the cigarette machine worked flawlessly and seldom did I ruin another tube.

One morning Mother and I noticed Karel Weil saving his cigarette butts. Leaning against a wall, he crushed the cigarette tip against the sole of his raised shoe. Then, rolling the tip between two fingers, he let the ashes fall to the ground, felt the butt for any remaining fire and slipped it into his inside jacket pocket.

"What do you do with those butts?" *Mutti* asked.

"I use them to make cigarettes. Cheaper than buying new tobacco."

From that day, Mother began saving her own stubs. She did not crush the stub against her shoe but stepped on it instead. "Not very ladylike to raise my leg," she said. A week later she handed me a handful of butts. "Use these."

In 1942, Allied planes began flying over our heads on their way to bombing Naples and, by the end of summer, the raids had become a daily occurrence. Listening to some of the internees speak of these air raids, I became convinced that we had nothing to fear from these friendly planes.

"What would they want to bomb here in Ospedaletto, between two wooded mountains?" John Howell asked.

Yet, the deep rumble of wave upon wave of these large and noisy planes made everyone uneasy.

One morning I watched a group of American bombers being intercepted by Italian fighters. I heard the *rat-a-tat-tat* of machine guns, the sound muffled by distance. Watching those little planes chasing the big ones was an electrifying spectacle. I had only seen that at the cinema. Now I was witnessing reality. I was rooting for the Americans and, without realizing it, stirred by my heightened emotions, I was talking out loud. "Watch out, he's on your tail," I yelled in Italian. "Let him have it. You're much bigger." I glanced around and, to my relief, saw no one there to hear me.

Rat-tat-tat and a puff of smoke spurted from one of the giant American planes. It felt like a bullet had hit me in my chest. The plane started to fall. Oh, my God! Suddenly, small dots jumped from the plane's belly seconds before the crippled craft, nose turned downward, ended its flight in a long, lifeless, pathetic spin. These men were fighting for us, trying to liberate us. What would happen to those unfortunate aviators?

The parachutes opened. One, two, three . . . seven. I lost track. I saw the dots float toward earth until the chutes disappeared behind a distant hill. My concern was tempered by the knowledge that these Americans, falling from the sky, were touching down in a country of good-hearted and generous people.

Hypnotized, I stood on the dusty road. This had been the real thing. No cops and robbers, no target-shooting. These were people, flesh and blood, being killed and real planes shot down. The palms of my hands were cold and clammy.

With every passing day, the number of planes flying over us increased in number. I made a game of counting the aircraft flying overhead. Fifty, sixty . . . ninety-five. The raids escalated and as the numbers increased, we felt the earth's tremors responding to the impact of the tons of bombs. My own anxiety increased, and Mother was constantly jumpy. We never got used to the loud drone of the big engines.

Then one day the Earth shook. Mamma and I were in the kitchen having breakfast. We looked at each other.

"That was no bomb," Mamma said.

"What was it?" I asked.

That same question was on everyone's lips that day. There was no one to ask, no one to contact. For the first time since we had settled in Ospedaletto, I saw real fear on the faces of the local citizens

Weeks passed before we learned the mystery: A munitions ship had been hit by Allied bombs in the Bay of Naples. Struck while in port, the burning ship was piloted into the open bay by a few brave Italian sailors, where it exploded, carrying those valiant young heroes to their final resting place. But this was only the rumor. The information came from refugees arriving from Naples. They told us that windows of every building facing the bay were shattered, but not a single civilian death was attributed to the doomed vessel. The truth, as we learned it later, differed greatly from the rumor. The ship, *Caterina Costa*, exploded at the pier, causing tremendous damage and killing hundreds. Several ships nearby caught fire and sank, while heavy tank parts were found as far away as Il Vomero, several miles from the port.

For months some internees had expressed their suspicion that William Pierce had been sent in our midst to spy on us.

"I can't believe it," said John Howell after he first heard it. "Not even the Fascists would pick someone that dumb."

But if anyone had doubts, what happened next must have certainly dispelled them. A day or two after the big blast but before anyone knew any of the details, Pierce reported to the *carabinieri* that Giorgio Kleinerman was somehow involved in that whole affair. Pierce claimed to have heard the boy make mention of the event before it ever happened. These were times when facts did not have to match fantasies, nor did accusations require proof.

One morning at the roll call, Maresciallo Marchetti invited Runia Kleinerman into his office and told her of Pierce's accusation. Desperate and out of breath, Runia came running to us.

"Pierce has accused Giorgio of being a spy."

"That swine. He's a mean, crazy man," *Mutti* exclaimed.

"He accused Giorgio of knowing ahead of time about the mysterious explosion. I told the *maresciallo* that it was utterly ridiculous. My son is only eighteen and could not have known anything about that. He has never set foot outside Ospedaletto."

"No one knows anything about it. We're still trying to find out what it was," Mother said.

"The *maresciallo* said we must go away from here. I am beside myself. He apologized, told me that no charge can be ignored. I don't know what Pierce told him. What do I tell my parents? This might kill my father."

"Calm down. Let me make you a glass of tea. We'll talk." In those days a glass of tea was a cure-all for anything that ailed us. It was the first thing anyone offered when you had a cold or a tragedy.

Mother used the small electric immersion heater to prepare the tea for her trembling friend. "Maybe someone can talk to the *maresciallo*."

But no one could. The *maresciallo* gave everyone the same answer, "You know, spying?"

The day this news spread, Pierce showed up for the morning walk.

"You should be ashamed of yourself," Runia said.

William Pierce strained to offer an explanation. As a loyal Italian, he justified exposing anyone who was against his country.

"You are a mean old man!"

"You are a beast!"

"A bastard!"

These and other invectives were hurled at the man until they chased him from our midst. From that day, Pierce was ostracized by all the *confinati* and was left to spend the rest of his internment period by himself.

Runia and her family were ordered to move to Paternopoli, another internment village not far away.

25

The German Occupation

In the spring of 1943, our sleepy village awoke to the sudden and massive arrival of a contingent of German troops. Military vehicles were everywhere, creating the kind of traffic Ospedaletto had never experienced before. Motorcycles roared back and forth and the multitude of armed soldiers walking through the village made me think that at any moment we were going to be in the midst of war. The troops set up camp in the surrounding forests and, in the short span of one day, we found ourselves encircled by the full force of the German army. Since that fateful day at the Vienna railroad station in March 1938, I had learned enough to be alarmed at having soldiers this close.

Mother was visibly shaken. "I hope the SS won't follow."

"Mamma, are you afraid?"

"Of course I'm afraid."

"What can they do to us? We haven't done anything."

"With the SS you don't have to do anything. You only need to be Jewish."

During all the years of our wandering, my state of mind very much reflected my mother's demeanor. When she was relaxed, so was I, but when she was scared, I was terrified. What were the soldiers going to do? I wanted to ask but feared the answer, and in my fear I remained in the dark, allowing my thoughts to wander wildly. And wander they did. The memory of *Turandot* at La Scala opera house with its severed heads pierced on long poles and paraded on stage created a gruesome image of my own head at the end of a German bayonet.

"Do the Germans cut off people's heads?" I asked.

Mother was deep in thought and did not answer right away. "I don't know. Don't think of such things. Just stay away from them."

The townspeople were busy selling their wares to the newly arrived soldiers. None of the villagers were intimidated by the new military presence. But we all, villagers and internees alike, suffered pangs of envy as we watched the soldiers enjoy foods none of us had tasted in years. We felt the indignity of our small ration while they ate sausages and fresh farm bread, spooned butter from large cans, or plunged their bayonets into a plump, canned chicken. The soldiers strolled through the village gorging themselves before our envious eyes without any regard to our dire condition.

Two German soldiers walked by a group of villagers.

"Did you see how they sneered? Those bastards!" a woman said.

"Watch them eat the salami. They're goading us like saying 'You can't have it!' I could just gouge their eyes out, those sons of bitches!" A man cautioned them to remain silent.

One woman spread her legs and with her hand made a vulgar gesture suggesting they should re-enter their mother's womb. "So what are they going to do to me?"

"My kids haven't had a piece of bread in days and these swine walk around our town teasing us?" another woman snarled. By then our bread, what little we had, was but a concoction of yellow corn that had the shape but not the taste of bread. It was impossible to slice, for no matter how much care one took, it crumbled into yellow granules.

Otherwise, the soldiers seemed amiable. They strolled through town unarmed. Didn't look dangerous and I started to question why my mother was afraid of them. I was twelve, almost thirteen, old enough to tell if someone was dangerous.

I went upstairs. It was as though *Mutti* had read my mind. "*Erichl*, don't start speaking to the soldiers. Promise me."

"I promise." As I spoke I could taste the good German bread on my tongue.

Pietro wrote every day, some days twice. Although war was raging all around Europe, the mail moved with regularity and we received his letters each day. Pietro's writings were poetic. The salutation, varying with each note, left an indelible mark on my young mind. "My most adorable, sweetness of my life, unique, intelligent, beautiful *mammina!*" was just one of the many poetic salutations he used to start his letters.

A few times Mamma let me read the entire letter but, even when she didn't, she always showed me the amorous greetings.

"Why won't you let me read that letter?" I once asked.

"Because it's just between *Pupo* and me."

"How can you find so much to write every day?" I asked. "And to fill four pages?"

"I hope one day you will fall in love with someone as good as *Pupo*. Then maybe you too will write poetic letters, four pages long."

During those desolate months, Pietro was our lifeline. At a time when it was strictly forbidden to ship items that were rationed, he risked imprisonment by sending olive oil, canned tuna, sardines, flour, anchovies and wine at least once each month. Antonio Dello Russo also took great risks by picking up the wooden crates from the railroad station in Avellino. But with food supplies getting scarcer with every passing day, people were prepared to take risks. Mother gladly shared her gifts with the Dello Russo family and a few internees.

Twice Pietro came to visit and each visit was a festivity for our group of *confinati*. Mamma was a woman transformed almost into a little child. The secret talks with Dora took place once again, piquing my curiosity to the point that I had trouble falling asleep. Then there were those muffled noises and laughter coming from Mamma's bedroom. I was almost thirteen; why could I not be told what was going on?

Thanks to the provisions Pietro had brought with him, Mother was able to prepare dinners for friends. The kitchen was small and only accommodated six at the most, so my Mamma would have two dinners on separate days to make room for all of the more intimate friends she wanted to invite. When Pietro was with us, our small home was overflowing with love and laughter. War and the German troops surrounding us seemed a faraway threat.

After Pietro and the Wovsis were freed from Ospedaletto and Ettore Costa transferred, an air of gloom descended upon our small family of *confinati*. In a short period we were deprived of the poetry of one, the spiritual guidance of the other, and the satire of the third. For me the morning meetings lost their appeal, and I stopped going to the gathering spot on the piazza.

With the German army so close to our homes, my mother didn't dare listen to the BBC, thus cutting us off from the only reliable news of what was happening in the rest of Europe. Runia's forced departure ended Mother's opportunity to converse in Polish as well as the companionship of her best woman friend. Much of what had sustained us during the previous months no longer was. Despair seeped into our lives. Mother lost the spirit so indispensable to me, and my mood slipped to an all-time low. I stopped going to the billiards hall, knowing how much it displeased her. We argued more often now. Everything and anything irritated us. Mamma's only serenity came from watching Lello, until the Dello Russos moved to a building belonging to Dora's family, located in the center of the village. Though Mamma Lotte kept caring for Lello in his new home, it was not the same as having him next door.

One morning I found Mother in the kitchen crying.

"What happened now?" I asked.

"Nothing and everything," she said, using her apron to dry her eyes. Mamma tried to compose herself, perhaps only for my benefit. It was a useless attempt. Her voice was shaky. "Erich, I don't know what will happen to us. But whatever it is, I want you to know that I love you more than life."

"I know that, *Mutti.*"

"I often worry that there will be no one left to say Kaddish for us."

"You mustn't think that. Everything will be all right."

"If anything happens to me, I want to be remembered as Szyfra. Don't forget!" She grabbed me by the waist and pulled me close. "I think you'll be fine when you grow up. I just hope I'll be around to see it." Only our labored sobs broke the silence.

For a moment, as she let go of me, I had the feeling that Mother's spunk may have come back for an instant. And if indeed it was back, I believed she did it only to raise my own morale and give me courage.

Mamma began smoking even more than usual and, while in the past smoking made her lose weight, this time, despite smoking, she gained some. A box of a hundred paper sleeves vanished every three days.

On the morning of May 27, 1943, Mother slid under my covers. "Do you know what day it is?"

I was still half asleep. "I think it's my birthday," I said.

"You're thirteen today." She hugged me. "You can't even be *Bar Mitzveh'd.*" The room, except for our heartbeats, was wrapped in silence. Her voice was soft. "I do have a gift for you. Wait here."

Back from her room, she handed me a book of Italian poetry. Pietro had sent it with one of his monthly packages. Somehow it had escaped my inspection. The dedication read: "May you grow up always surrounded by love, beauty, and poetry!"

"This is better than any Bar Mitzvah," I exclaimed. I pressed the book to my chest. "I love you and *Pupo* so much!"

"We love you too, very much. What do you want to do today? Do you want to go with the group for a walk?"

"Since *Pupo* and Ettore left, the walks have not been the same. It's like the body is here but the spirit is gone."

"I couldn't buy you anything. But I will bake your favorite cake."

No longer was I a kid. The discomfort of being among adults had disappeared. By now I felt at ease with older people and had stopped seeking the company of boys my age. I also started to appreciate my mother in ways I never had before, realizing what a master she had been in balancing strictness with her consistent love.

Most of that day I spent reading my new treasure and composing a thank you note to *Pupo*.

When in July of 1943, Mother was suddenly deprived of the joy of Pietro's writings, we did not know the cause. Each day Mamma insisted on going to city hall to check the mail personally. I felt so sorry for her and wished I could have done something to cheer her up. Back from her daily mail trip, she dragged herself up the stairs looking dejected.

"Can I do anything?" I asked.

"No. Nobody can do anything."

"Why don't you go and visit the Howells? I'll go with you."

"I don't feel like seeing anyone. I have never told you, but *Pupo* and I talked about getting married. After you, he is all I want in life. Now I have lost him. I don't blame him. Why should he burden himself with a woman who is older than he, who will probably never understand his family and will not go to church with him? And why should he burden himself with. . . ."

"With what, Mamma?"

"Nothing, really nothing. I just wish . . . I don't know what I wish. Why don't you go out and play? What happened to your Italian soldier friends?"

Lieutenant Benedetti had stopped coming since the German troops had set up camp in Ospedaletto. "I don't know. They haven't been here in months."

"If I didn't have you, I would put an end to it," she murmured.

"*Mammina*, don't talk like that. You scare me." I wrapped myself in her arms.

"Don't be scared, *mein Hasele*."

This was the only time I saw Mother in such a state of depression. I started wondering if Pietro would ever come back and read to me or warm me with his infectious smile. I could see his chipped tooth and the twinkle in his eyes. I thought of my father. We had not heard from him in years. Four years, to be exact. Was he still alive? How could my mother think of marrying someone else, even if it was Pietro? She was still married to Papa. I questioned if I really wanted Pietro as my father. No, I wanted my real father to come back. Maybe Pietro could remain our friend. I was sure he and Papa would get along and I could have both.

"I don't understand how you can think of marrying *Pupo*. What about Papa? He is your husband."

Mother did not respond. "I guess I won't worry about that any longer," she said. "Pietro is not coming back."

During the first half of 1943, Mussolini's presence was felt everywhere, more than ever before. Each day his voice filled the airwaves with exhortations to victory. When he was not on the radio, his dogmas, painted on most unencumbered walls, could be seen silently shouting at us. *"Se avanzo seguitemi, se indietreggio uccidetemi!"* This slogan, one of dozens, appeared on one of the village buildings.

We knew nothing of what was happening in the outside world. The Italian radio reports could not be trusted. Newspapers were not available and the BBC, more than ever before, was too dangerous to listen to with so many German troops surrounding us. Internees gathered more frequently at the Howells'.

During a bridge game with a number of other internees crowded in the living room, John Howell said, "I have a feeling things are not going well for the Germans."

"Why? Did you hear anything?"

"No. I didn't hear anything in particular. I just have a feeling. Why is Mussolini on the radio every day?" John asked.

"My daughter Gaby used to hear from her fiancé regularly. Lately, nothing," said Perutz.

"Do you think they may have sent his fighter group out of the country?" Mamma asked.

"Who knows? Remember when he used to fly his plane over Ospedaletto and tip his wings to send greetings? Gaby doesn't talk all day. She is so depressed."

"I can understand that very well," Mother said.

"Any word from Pietro?" Agatha asked.

"No. I pray to God he is well."

"We all hope so," John added.

The question caused a somber air to invade the room. The bridge game paused.

"Do you want to finish the rubber?" someone asked.

There was silence. "I don't think so," John said.

"Just stay there," said Agatha.

Bridge, so important to people during these times, was replaced by a simple cup of tea.

Many days would pass—days of despair—before details about Sicily finally reached us. We heard the news on the Italian state radio in our landlord's kitchen. Allied forces had landed, occupied the island and cut off all communications with the rest of Italy. But the announcer, with great confidence, assured us that soon these imperialistic occupying forces would be pushed back into the blue Mediterranean, signaling the beginning of Mussolini's march to the final victory. Mamma threw her arms around me. "I knew it! I knew it!" she exclaimed. "I was convinced of his love. Oh, Erich, how could I have ever doubted him?"

Filomena stood in silence. I was still too young to fully comprehend my mother's emotions.

I had gone to visit my friend Raffaele when word spread that the bakery had just made a fresh batch of bread. We had been unable to get bread in many days. "I don't get flour," the baker complained. "How can I make bread?"

When I heard the rumor, I ran home. "Mamma, there is fresh bread at the bakery. Give me our coupons."

Quickly, she handed me some money and the bread coupons. Down the stairs I dashed, coupons and money clenched in my hand, then down the incline through the village toward the center square. Little clouds of dust shot up from each step, showing how fast I was running. When I got to the bakery, optimistically exhilarated and out of breath, I found dozens of people already waiting in line.

"How much bread can we get?" I asked the woman standing in front of me.

"Who knows? The bread is still in the oven."

The line was getting longer and, as more people joined us, the murmur grew louder.

"Eh, Giuseppe," someone yelled at the baker. "What's going on? By the time the bread is ready the war will be over."

"Yeah and we'll all be dead from starvation," someone added. There was laughter in the crowd.

Giuseppe appeared at the door. "I'm working as fast as I can. But bread has to bake and that takes time. Please be patient." He reentered the shop and closed the door behind him.

The crowd was growing and so was the murmur. "He's taking the bread out of the oven," a woman shouted. A man at the front of the line pushed the door open and everyone shoved to squeeze through the narrow opening. Surrounded by this mass of people, I was carried inside by the herd. There was no bread anywhere. Where did that woman see bread being taken out of the oven?

Instead of waiting outside, most of the people now waited inside the small shop. Nothing else had changed. Finally, as Giuseppe opened the oven, the smell of freshly baked bread floated into the air. The fragrance was inviting, but the sight of the bright yellow bread reminded me of its taste. Why was I here?

"What is this garbage?" one woman screamed. "You call this bread? Did you use piss instead of water?"

"Here are my coupons," someone shouted.

"I can give you only one loaf!" the baker called out above the clamor.

"I've got seven kids at home. They haven't had a piece of bread in days. I want three loaves."

"Sorry, Anna. Only one per family."

A man jumped on the counter. "Give them what they want!" he shouted.

Another man darted behind the counter. A woman followed. Giuseppe, ashen, stepped out of the way and hid toward the rear of the shop. People reached for the bread and filled their shopping bags, then threw a few loaves to others standing in line. Soon all the loaves were gone. I didn't see anyone pay for the bread or turn in their ration coupons.

I had tried to push my way to the front of the line, but I was just a kid and all the adults, bigger and stronger, kept shoving me from one side to the other. By the time I got close to the counter, the ersatz bread was all gone.

September 8, 1943, brought cheer but also new fears into our lives. We had finished our evening meal and descended the one flight to the Guerrieros'.

"Do you mind if we listen to the news?" Mamma asked.

The landlord invited us into their kitchen. *"S'accomodi, Signora!"*

Instead of the regular newscast, the radio announcer informed us he was about to bring us a special bulletin.

"Another bulletin," Mamma remarked. "They have so many of these bulletins and never anything important."

We waited in silence. The radio was still. Then a male voice: "This is Maresciallo Badoglio. Having been entrusted by His Majesty Victor Emmanuel III, King of Italy and Emperor of Albania, to form a new government, on behalf of Italy and the glorious Italian army, I have signed an unconditional surrender with the Allied forces."

No one moved. The only sound was Badoglio's voice, but after the initial statement, much of what he said afterward was lost on us. Our silence expressed everyone's reaction.

Mother broke the hush. "Antonio, what's going to happen next? Does this mean we have a new government?"

He shook his head. His eyes were glazed and stared in the distance. "I don't know. I really don't know. With all the German troops around us, this could turn nasty."

"I am concerned about your safety," Mamma said. "Everyone knows you are a *Camicia Nera*," reminding him of his black shirt, a symbol of the Fascist party.

"I've never hurt anybody. I'll just have to have faith in the Lord."

"Why is she talking about our safety?" Filomena asked.

"*Niente, niente*," Antonio said. Then looking at my mother, he said, "This should mark the end of the war for you."

"I'm not so sure," she remarked. "I do believe that now we are in the same boat."

"Why?" he asked.

"To the Germans both of us are now their enemies."

Through the open window, we heard what sounded like cheering.

"Somebody has to go tell these people to stay home and be quiet," Mamma said. "When the Germans find out that Italy has surrendered and they hear people celebrating, it could provoke a massacre."

Antonio got up from the chair and reached for his jacket. "I'll go talk to them."

"I don't believe you are the right person to go," Mamma said.

"Then who?"

"How about if we both go?"

"I'll come, too," I said.

"No. You stay here," Mamma ordered.

Mother and the landlord were back in minutes after having calmed the people in the street. I did not grasp the dangers brought on by the new events, but, judging from Mother's reaction, I was uneasy and that night asked to sleep in her bed.

In the middle of the night I awoke to find my mother sitting near the open balcony door. The room was pitch black. Still half asleep, I failed to hear the commotion outside. "Mamma, what's happening?"

She rushed to the bed. "Shush. Quiet. The German soldiers are down there and something important is happening." She bent over to kiss my forehead, pulled the covers over me and, without making a sound, returned to the chair she had placed far back from the balcony to avoid being seen from the street.

The continuous loud roar of motorcycles sounded menacing. Over the din, a commanding German voice announced in a grave tone, "The Italian government has surrendered and as of today Italy is our enemy. You will consider yourself in unfriendly territory and will have to act accordingly. We will continue our just struggle until our final victory."

Thus, a Jewish woman and the German troops received the information of the Axis breakup at the same time. Even after the troops dispersed and silence returned to the road below, Mother remained sitting absolutely still in her chair. Her worst fears were coming true. The silence that fell the night was foreboding.

Afraid to be alone, I whispered, "Come back to bed."

Mother stretched out next to me. "I can't sleep," she said. "I'm just too nervous. I'm afraid of what this will mean for us. Do the Germans know there are Jews in the village?"

With her words echoing in my ears, I succumbed to a restless and troubled sleep. When I awoke in the morning, I had more reasons to be frightened. Spying through the slits of the balcony shutters I saw the road below. Ospedaletto d'Alpinolo had turned into an armed camp. German soldiers were everywhere. These same soldiers, who the day before had strolled casually through the narrow streets laughing and joking, now marched in full battle gear. Helmets, bayonets mounted on rifles, and hand grenades stuffed in their black leather belts brought me face to face with the reality of warfare. In the months gone by, I had seen bombers overhead and heard distant explosions, but that had been too far away to make a meaningful impression on a thirteen-year-old. Even the small bombs, dropped during the first air raid over San Remo and which I had seen explode, were just a faint memory. Nor did the war stories my papa told us on the train to Italy create anything more than gruesome pictures conjured up in a childish mind. Now things seemed different. Even I grasped that.

"Are they going to start shooting?" I asked.

Mother, staring in the distance, didn't answer. The thought of getting caught in the midst of battle crossed my mind. I didn't have the slightest idea what a shooting war was all about and not knowing made it that much more alarming. I feared for my safety, but most of all I feared for my mother's.

"*Mutti*, I'm so scared!"

Her arms wrapped around me and her chin rested on my head. "I'm scared, too."

"What will you do if the Germans take me away?" I asked.

"They're not taking children."

"What if they take you?"

"They won't."

"But if they do? What will I do?"

"You run to Dora and she'll take care of you until I get back. I must speak to John. I must tell him what I heard."

We got dressed in a hurry. That day, for the first time in months, Mother did not make breakfast. I was not hungry anyway. "I'm going out," she announced.

Although she ordered me to stay home, this time I would not obey and followed close behind. Perhaps her tone was not authoritative enough, or perhaps my fear of what was happening was far greater than the fear of my mother.

"Where are we going?" I asked.

"To the Howells'." When we arrived, other internees had already gathered.

"I guess everybody has heard about the armistice and the new government. Last night, under my balcony, the German commander was informing his troops what had happened. Then he told them Italy is now their enemy. That's why you see all these armed soldiers."

"Now I understand," John Howell said. He looked around. In the room were Perutz, Clara, the Spaechts, the Kamplers, and the Weil brothers. "This is grave, especially for our Jewish friends," Mr. Perutz said. "I believe this is the beginning of the end of the war, but until that time comes, we must be very careful not to add to our problems." It was the first time I had heard Signor Perutz make a serious comment. His face was drawn, his voice grim. "If none of the villagers talk, we will be all right." He looked older than I had ever seen him look. As I glanced at all the faces, everyone seemed older. Even the Weil brothers had lost their dapper look.

Karel Weil had always seen danger, even where there was none. He moved about nervously. "But if someone does talk . . . ?" His voice quivered.

"They'll kill us all." someone answered. "What else did the German officer say?"

"I was afraid they would discover me if I got any closer to the window," Mamma said. "I didn't hear much else."

"First of all, we must remain calm," John said.

"How can we stay calm?" asked David Kampler. "We're surrounded by Germans who now view Italy as enemy country."

"Any suggestions?"

"If only we could hide somewhere. Why don't we talk to some townspeople? Let's find out what ideas they have."

"That's another problem," my mother said. "The villagers. Some can't be trusted."

But everyone agreed it was a good idea. Mr. Perutz would talk to Dr. Sellitto, Mother to Don Pasquale and John to Don Pepe at city hall. The Kamplers, the Spaechts and the Weil brothers looked relieved not to have been selected.

"One more suggestion. We must stay out of sight. Let's all stay inside and have just one person be the contact among us." Willy Weil volunteered to be the contact.

Events began to happen rapidly. The following day Willy brought news that a German officer had requested from Don Pepe a list of all Jews living in the village. John Howell went to city hall to meet with Don Pepe and after would relate the details of his encounter.

"When I asked him what he was going to do, he exploded at me: 'Nothing!' He was obviously annoyed by my question. He started shouting. Not at me. In dialect, he said he didn't have to give anything to those '*figli di puttana.*' He wanted to suggest they should get the list from Mussolini."

In less than three weeks, the Germans made the same request four times and four times Don Pepe told them he was trying to oblige but never did.

Some of the internees had lived in that village for almost four years. We were known to the townspeople. Anyone could have easily pointed out where each of us lived, yet, except for one isolated incident, no one did.

Knowing Germans were looking for Jews kept us in a state of constant alert. Mother and I stayed home and out of sight. The tension was more than I could cope with. Mother made a poor attempt at trying to hide from me how terror-stricken she was.

I broke down and in tears mumbled, "Are they going to kill us?"

"I don't know. I really don't know," *Mutti* murmured. Had she realized how these words affected me she would have said nothing.

My mind went to places I didn't want it to be. Lying on a street, I saw my dead father's body covered with blood while people in black uniforms danced around his corpse.

"Do you think they killed Papa?

"I hope not. I don't know."

"Let's run away," I cried.

"Where?" The tone reflected Mama's own inner agitation. "I wish I could speak to Antonio or Dora, but that means going out." Then a moment later, she said, "How could they help? What do they know about the Germans?"

That night Mother must have been spying from the door. She found me sitting in bed and came over to sit next to me. "Why aren't you sleeping?"

"Mamma, I don't want to die. I'm not yet Bar Mitzvah'd. I have not lived."

"You're not going to die. Go to sleep." I heard no conviction in her voice.

My mother slept very little the next few nights. For hours I heard her walk about and the strain showed on her once-beautiful face. The certainty that my life was ending just past my thirteenth birthday chased every rational thought from my mind and deprived me of sleep while keeping me in constant turmoil during the waking hours.

Nothing Mamma said could soothe me. A deep-seated anxiety had taken hold. Every day I stayed home, determined to spend my final hours next to the person I loved most. Day and night I hardly left her side and even spent the nights in her bed.

We were fast asleep when shooting in the distance woke us. I pressed close to Mother, dreading what was happening.

Antonio Guerriero had disappeared and Filomena didn't know where he had gone.

"It's a good idea he left," Mamma said.

Filomena was hiding in her own apartment and had taken from us the only life link we had with the world: the radio. Having lost touch with the other internees had dropped us further into a black hole.

Dora came bearing dreadful news. In the middle of the night, a German patrol had broken down the door where the Kamplers lived. Someone must have informed the Germans. Their landlord reported that just before the patrol entered the house, Gusti and David jumped from their window one flight up and escaped in their pajamas.

Dora was wringing her hands. "*Madonna mia*! Who could have reported them? Such a terrible thing!"

"Dora, promise me one thing," Mamma said in a veiled voice. "If anything happens to me, you will take care of Enrico."

Dora started to wail. "*Gesu Cristo mio*. What can happen?"

"They could round up all the Jews. There is no way we can jump from the here."

"No one knows you live here," Dora said.

"Everybody knows we live here."

As I listened, I felt my insides burning. I lost track of how many days I had not left our apartment and suddenly realized that staying inside could become an inescapable trap. My words exploded: "I have to go out! I don't care where, but I've got to go out."

"We must stay put," Mamma said. "Going out is worse."

Dora hugged us both. "I left the children alone. I have to go. Enrico, you listen to your mother! You hear?"

The room remained wrapped in silence for the longest time. I needed some protection, some comfort. "Would you pray with me?" I finally asked.

Mother took my hand as she guided me in a prayer. "Oh dear God, give us peace, guard over us and protect us from the Germans. Please forgive us for not being as observant as we should be. And please protect the rest of our family. *Umen*." As she whispered these words, I pictured my father's unique waddling coming toward me on a sidewalk in Vienna. I saw my *Opapa* performing his morning prayers, my grandmother preparing a Friday supper, my *Omama* adjusting the hairpiece on her head. I wanted all of them to be safe and in His care.

For the rest of the day, I tried but was unable to read my book. Visions of jail cells, torture chambers and death crowded my head. I saw Papa in his gray, double-breasted suit, *Opapa* with his sculpted white beard, Grandmother in her kitchen, *Omama*, and Aunt Stefi. I remembered the Seder in Poland, my silver watch. The happy and trouble-free days in Vienna, the coffee house the small birthday cakes I had baked with Millie.

No longer did single soldiers stroll in the village. Now they marched in twos or threes, their heavy boots pounding the dusty road, a dreadful reminder of the scary echoes in the Vienna railway station. With each sound of a passing motorcycle, my nerves tightened. And Mother's looks failed to calm my nerves.

"Mamma, do you think William Pierce will point us out?"

"Everything is possible. He reported Giorgio Kleinerman," she said. "Aren't you hungry?"

I had not eaten a full meal in two days. Food was the farthest thing from my mind. "No, Mamma. I'm really not hungry."

"*Hasele*, you should eat something. I'll make you something special."

"Like what?"

"I could try a *palatchinka*. I have a little flour left. Would you like that?"

"Oh *Mutti*, I sure would love that."

Except for John Howell, who had brought the ominous news of the German list request, we had not seen any of the other internees. For days we didn't know if anyone else ventured out. We had become reclusive. The safety and protection we had felt in this primitive village were suddenly gone. Vienna came to mind, the five days in March 1938 when I was also kept inside the house. I worried whether what happened then was going to happen all over again. Where could we go? Would we have to start running again?

I grew up rapidly during those September days, never to be a child again.

With every passing day, our lives became more chaotic. Mother ignored the routine reporting to the police. We didn't eat a cooked meal, only that which could be eaten raw. But then, neither of us thought much about food.

While the days were bad, the nights were worse. The slightest noise awakened me. "Mamma, Mamma! I think I hear footsteps on the stairs. They're here!" I muttered.

Mother would come running from her room and place her ear against the door leading to the corridor. "There is no one there, *Schatzele*" I heard relief in her voice. "Go to sleep, *Hasele*."

Living in constant fear and unable to sleep through the night distorted my ability to judge the passing of time. What I thought had been weeks were only days. The bed became my escape. Nightmares followed nightmares. I relived the final moments of Raffaele's father. I saw the dead body, but it was not his father, it was my father I saw. I pushed myself through the crowd and, as I reached the bed, I found that it was my mother who was lying there. In shock, I looked through the room. Those were not the townspeople I knew. These were soldiers in black uniforms, high boots, and the dreaded red and black armbands, glaring down and leering at me.

The apprehension of finding my mother dead in the next room kept me from opening my eyes for the longest time. When I finally did, I eased myself into her room. With more force than I wanted, I shook her still body. "Mamma! Mamma!" I shouted.

Startled, she sat up. "Yes? What is it, *Schatzele*?"

"I just had this terrible dream that you were dead."

My trembling was visible. Mamma pulled me close to her. "It was just a dream."

During that period I had many such dreams. Often I saw my Papa dead. Shot! Hanged! Frozen! I struggled to chase those thoughts from my mind. On the few occasions when I did, I saw *Omama*, *Opapa* and Aunt Stefi. Every morning and every afternoon, Allied squadrons of big planes flew overhead to drop their bombs on Naples. We had become so used to seeing the formations of those large birds that I stopped looking skyward.

An endless flow of people came from the direction of Avellino. Dressed in modern clothes, wearing leather shoes (not *zoccoli*), we knew they were not on a pilgrimage to Montevergine. Mamma wanted to know where these people were coming from but would not go out of the house to ask. The German army stayed in town and neither Mother nor I dared venture on to the street. Standing back from the balcony, we watched the mass of humanity tramp through the village, wondering why they were all walking up the mountain.

There was hardly anything to do. We ate little during that period and were grateful to have an ample supply of water to drink.

"We will do without washing ourselves," Mamma said, "but we can use a little for brushing our teeth."

And so, twenty days crawled by. Twenty painful days.

Then one morning I looked at Mother's face. It looked drawn and wet from crying. I caressed her hair and wondered what was going through her head. Suddenly I saw how beautiful she was as she announced, "We're going up to Montevergine."

Mother had recovered her ability to think. Although this meant we were on the run once more, I felt a great sense of relief. She was in charge again! My hallucinations ceased!

That morning in late September 1943, rushing to pack a few essentials into a small bag and without the required permit from the *carabinieri*, we prepared to flee Ospedaletto.

26

Montevergine

Flying fortresses droned overhead as we walked out of the house. We passed through the piazza and continued up the narrow gravel path to become part of a flood of people who seemed driven by their own individual fears. We mingled into this endless column of humanity. Hundreds, perhaps thousands of refugees had walked from surrounding towns and villages: whole families, infants carried by siblings, grandparents struggling up that arduous path and parents carrying what they were able to salvage at the last moment. We all walked at the same pace, bodies touching bodies, bringing us the small comfort of shared misery. The scraping of feet on the gravel path mixed with the sounds of battle in the valley below.

"Does anybody know what's going on?" Mamma spoke. "We haven't heard a news bulletin in days."

"The Americans have suffered a bloodbath in Salerno," a voice in the crowd replied. Salerno was less than twenty miles away.

"Salerno? When did the Americans get to Salerno?" Mother asked.

"Haven't you heard? They landed three weeks ago," someone from the crowd responded.

"Are you coming from Salerno?"

"We're coming from there," a woman joined in the shouting.

"Can you tell me what's happening?"

Twenty years of intimidation by the Fascist dictatorship had shaped the people's behaviors, but now the concern of being overheard and denounced by one's neighbor seemed gone. People were eager to talk to anyone, even to strangers.

"There is shooting all over. We just ran away. We left everything behind."

A limping old man vented his anger. "*Che lo pozzino ammazzare, quel benedetto Mussolini.*" As was often the custom in this part of the country, the man had combined dialect with pure Italian. "The Allies are going to beat the crap out of the Germans. I once believed in Fascism and fought for the bastard in Ethiopia. Even lost a foot. Now look what he did to us. May he rot in prison. They should give him castor oil like he did to Matteotti." Giacomo Matteotti was head of the Socialist Party at the time Mussolini came to power. His strong opposition to Mussolini brought on his death in 1924.

Someone else in the walking crowd aired his frustrations. "For years I've been afraid to open my mouth," he shouted. "It has poisoned my spirit." Then, making up for lost time, he began yelling at the top of his lungs, "May the Fascists rot in hell!"

Many applauded. Mother asked more questions while we made slow progress up the congested pass. The people, attempting to hurry the pace, pushed and shoved and created such confusion on the narrow, overcrowded trail that they accomplished the opposite. Our energies, which we needed to climb, were dissipated by our efforts to keep from stumbling off the sides of the path.

"Don't push! Slow down! Let's not kill each other!" Someone made an attempt at restoring order.

The trail narrowed and became even steeper as we approached our destination. The wider mass of human beings was forced to squeeze to half its size, making our last twenty minutes of the tedious trudge even more difficult. My nostrils were filled with dust. My eyes were burning. I looked at *Mutti* and was proud at how well she was holding up.

The approach to the summit was signaled by a surge of energy emanating from the people ahead of us. Suddenly we reached the top and came out of the tree shadows into the midday sun's heat. We had reached the monastery high on that mountain crest.

The picnic to celebrate Pietro's restored freedom had been in June of the previous year. Yet now, overwhelmed by different emotions, I could hardly recognize the place. So many people filled every available space.

Quickly my mother, with me in tow, approached the protective wall that surrounded the monastery and walked through the gate heading to the courtyard. Mamma stopped a passing monk. "Where can we stay, father?"

Without slowing his walk, with his arm pointing toward the building, he replied, "Just go inside and find a room."

With fresh energy, Mother grabbed me by the hand and together we traversed the large courtyard. Facing us in the corner was the entrance to the church enclosed on each side by a large, two-story stone structure. We entered a side door of the building and, pushing ahead of the crowd, rushed up one flight of stairs, then down a long corridor.

Dozens of doorways opened into the corridor and Mamma, peeking her head into every opening, asked, "Is there space for two?"

"No, *Signora*. You have to go all the way down the corridor," one voice replied.

People were passing us by. "Let's run," said Mamma. Holding my hand, she pulled me down the narrow hallway past the numerous cubicles and around its ninety-degree turn. The crowd had not yet reached here.

"Is there space for two of us?" Mamma asked.

"Sure. Come in," a woman answered.

The dimension of the barren cell was defined by the size of the bunk beds set against two opposing walls. About the smallest room I had ever seen. There was no mattress or a pillow. The double-tier bunks were bare planks of wood. Even the entrance door was missing. After a careful look, I saw no sign of hinges and realized there had never been a door. A solitary chair rested against the far wall and above hung a dusty wooden cross. A single small window, way up high on the wall facing the entrance, allowed just enough light to give the alcove a sinister appearance. A tiny light bulb, dangling from a bare and dust-encrusted electric cord, reminiscent of the air-raid shelter in San Remo, hung from the high ceiling. At night the light, with its faint glow, would have the impossible task of relieving the absolute darkness.

A young couple, clutching each other, sat to the side on one of the lower bunks. We sat on the wooden plank on the opposite wall.

"*Buon giorno!* Where did you come from?" Mamma asked.

"Naples," the man replied. The sadness in his voice was reflected on his face. His eyes were sunken and vacant in an otherwise young-looking face. His hair was uncombed and the bottoms of his pants, as well as his shoes, were covered with dried mud.

Naples was more than twenty miles away. "How did you get here?"

The slim, young woman started to cry. "Over the mountains. We've walked all night. We lost everyone in our family during the last air raid. It was hell."

"I am so sorry," Mamma said.

The man was stroking the weeping woman's disheveled dark hair. "And where are you coming from?" His voice had a listless, emotionless ring.

"Everything will be better, you'll see," Mamma said. Often I had heard my mother encourage others with inspiring conviction. This was not one of those times, for the words I just heard had a hollow ring. "Where are we from? Ospedaletto, just down the mountain."

I sat next to Mother on the lower bunk facing the couple. We were exhausted, due more to our emotional state than physical fatigue. I had just leaned back against the wall and closed my eyes when Mamma let out a shriek that made me jump. She bolted from the bed.

"What is it?" I asked.

She turned and pointed to the cot. "My God, my God." She kept repeating. I looked in that direction and wanted to throw up. A mass of ugly insects was crawling to and fro between the wooden planks and the wall. So great was their number that the little brown bugs were crawling over each other.

The couple from Naples made a forced sound almost like laughter. Mamma, in a shaky voice, asked, "What are those things?"

"Bedbugs," the two answered as one. They never looked in the direction of what had caused my mother's anguish. They just seemed to know. "You don't know what they are?"

For three weeks we made our home in that odious room and slept on the infested boards. Every night before stretching out on the bare wood we roasted those bugs using precious paper, lit by even more priceless matches. "I don't know which is worse, the live bugs or the nauseating burned smell," Mamma said. Necessity helped us overcome our revulsion. What really mattered was that we had a place to lie down.

In Montevergine we could not find anyone with a radio. However, because of people coming and going, we got more news than in the last three weeks in Ospedaletto. We heard that, after the initial stalemate on the beachhead in Salerno, Allied troops were now moving in our direction. Within days of our finding refuge at the monastery, the valley below had become a battlefield. The *boom* of big cannons and the *rat-a-tat-tat* of machine guns echoed off the mountains. At night, when the sound of small arms ceased, the fiery blazing of the artillery pierced, if only for short instants, the darkness in the valley and the clamor of war shattered the eerie silence. Yet, in spite of the tension the clamor created, I remained at the edge of the cliff embraced by the mountain gazing in awe at the spectacular fireworks-like scenes below.

The action in the valley was far enough removed for me to recover a bit of tranquility. At last I no longer had to hide from the menacing armed German soldiers nor stay confined in our two-room apartment. From where I stood, a few feet above the monastery, I had an unobstructed view of the whole valley, making me an unexpected spectator of what a battlefield was really like.

The fighting went on for most of the three weeks we stayed on the mountain. We had heard that the battles had been fierce, but we did not realize, until much later, how precarious the beachhead had been or how close the Allied troops had been from being pushed back into the sea. Many evenings I stood alone thinking of the foreign soldiers who were giving up their lives so that we might regain our liberty.

From our balcony in Ospedaletto, I had been able to see the Monastery of Montevergine. It appeared to be built on the mountain's ledge, almost at its peak. Now, being here made me realize that the abbey was built on a narrow flat space, much below the peak, from where one had a clear view of Avellino and the area around it. As birds fly, the distance to Avellino could not have been more than four or five miles. Aside from the officers' cadet school, there was no other military target there, but that did not seem to matter, for the city suffered days of relentless and horrible bombings.

A few days after we climbed up the mountain and had settled in, I faced the full, gruesome picture of war when wave after wave of British planes appeared over Avellino. At first I thought these planes, as they always had done in the past, were going to continue their flight toward Naples. Not this time. The double-fuselage bombers, flying at my eye level, started their dive to within a few hundred feet from the ground before restarting their ascent. At that very moment the planes' bellies opened and bombs, many, many bombs, left their bowels and fluttered in the air before achieving a spiraling speed. As the bombs hit their targets, I stood there near the cliff, spellbound.

Because of my vantage point, I could see as each bomb hit a house, some family's home, how it pierced the roof and how a three-story building crumbled in a cloud of dust. Structures that took months, perhaps years, to build collapsed faster than I could comprehend what was happening. I saw people, children, and animals escaping into the streets. Did I see them or was it my imagination? They were just little dots. I thought of those people dying only because they were there and was reminded of what Mother once had said when I asked why the Nazis were persecuting us: "Just because we are Jewish."

The horror of what I saw made me shudder. And though my mind registered what my eyes were seeing, my brain was incapable of accepting it as reality. I followed each plane's maneuver and sometimes could even see the pilot's face, the leather cap, the goggles, the earphones. I had a front-row seat for this dreadful spectacle.

The air attack of that day and the ones that followed the next two days caught the city's populace by surprise. Later I heard that more than 4,000 innocent souls were snuffed out from a total population of about 30,000.

Within hours after the attack on Avellino, dazed survivors joined the hundreds of us who already had taken refuge in the monastery. They struggled up the mountain, a journey four miles longer than ours, in their nightgowns, robes, and slippers, or shoes without socks. Their eyes reflected the shock of what they had seen and, despite our own poor state, many of us looked at these pitiful folks, exhausted and disheveled, with compassion. I watched as strangers embraced each other and exchanged kisses and tears. Some of these refugees told us how they had been exposed to air-raid alarms for years, but, since no bombs had ever been dropped on the city, they had stopped going to air-raid shelters.

It was October and the weather was turning cold on the mountain. Without blankets, we slept in our clothes. The day we escaped Ospedaletto, Mother measured need versus practicality when selecting what to take with us in our small bag, taking little of some things and nothing of others. Except for a week's change of underwear, most of our clothing was left behind. We brought not a book nor a pencil, only one pair of shorts and no jacket but a light sweater.

We did bring one small bar of soap for our personal use, but not enough for doing laundry. Mother had become a wizard at improvising during our restricted lifestyle. Washing clothes was reduced to running icy water over a garment, hoping to release some of the superficial dirt. We did wash our underwear and, by doing it before going to sleep, we could hope that it would dry in the cool mountain air by morning.

For three weeks my body escaped the rigors of a bath. Even washing our hands and face was a major task, considering the sole fountain in the courtyard had to serve more than 1,500 people. I had no problem skipping a bath, although not taking one was only a slight departure from what we had finally adapted to in Ospedaletto for many months.

"I cannot tolerate being dirty," Mother said. And almost every morning she left the room before anyone had awakened to get to that fountain and brave the icy mountain water running down her partially naked torso. I, not as bold or as concerned with my own cleanliness, chose to remain dirty and in bed rather than expose myself to snooping eyes or endure the water's chill.

Most people had fled without food, and food stores did not exist on this mountain spot. The two small stands peddling dried chestnuts and roasted hazelnuts that had been there on our arrival had soon disappeared when their merchandise was depleted.

On the fourth morning, Mother took me by the hand and together we walked to the monks' dining room. It was an immense hall, with very long, bare wooden tables and benches instead of chairs. Mamma asked for the friar in charge, marched up to the man and, with authority in her voice that fear often creates, spoke to him. "I don't care about myself, but you must give my son something to eat."

His arms folded inside the brown vestment sleeves, the monk explained why they could not provide food for me. "*Signora*, it's just not possible to feed 2,000 people. We don't have enough for ourselves."

But the explanation did not impress my mother and, because she refused to accept no for an answer, beginning that evening and for the remainder of our three-week stay, two Jews, Mamma and I, sat with seventy Catholic priests, grateful to secretly partake in their prayers and a small bowl of warm beans.

We did not have breakfast in the mornings except on rare occasions when someone shared their food with us. More than 1,500 people found refuge within the walls of Montevergine and, without regard to their own needs and misfortunes, when social status had lost all meaning, almost everyone displayed that generosity of spirit which is so much part of the Italian nature.

The bombing of Avellino had ceased, but the intense fighting could still be heard in the distance beyond the mountains toward

Salerno. We felt cut off from the rest of the world. The occasional arrival of new refugees brought confusing news of what was happening elsewhere. Adding a kind of black humor to the very tragic events, everyone had a different version of the same facts. Then we heard the unimaginable. Ten days after the bombing, thousands of bodies were still decaying on the streets of Avellino.

During our first week on the mountain, the superficial calm was disrupted by the clamorous arrival of a German half-track, which stopped outside the monastery gate. No one seemed to know what to make of it. The children milled around the military vehicle while the adults kept their distance. One soldier jumped out the rear and attempted to speak with the onlookers. He spoke German and, as he approached them, people stepped backward. Some women even ran away screaming.

"*Deutsch sprechen?*" the soldier shouted.

Realizing no one else could understand what he wanted and forgetting the fear German soldiers had engendered less than a month before, I called out, "*Ya! Ich spreche Deutsch.*" As those words popped from my mouth, panic set in. How could I have done such a stupid thing?

"This kid speaks German!" the man said. I even saw a smile on his face. He had walked back from the small crowd and was talking to the men inside the vehicle. From the stripes on his sleeve I guessed he was either a corporal or a sergeant.

He approached me and placed his hand on my shoulder. "We need to set up an observation post. Can you help me find a good spot?"

Why was he asking me? Did he really think I would know the requirements for an observation post? "I'm not sure where," I said. "Perhaps a little farther up. I've only been here a few days." I should never have spoken to him. Why did I always get myself into trouble? I was so nervous.

The soldier invited me to join him and his three men on the half-track. "Come with us." What an alluring thought: Me inside a half-track. How could I even think about doing it? Going with German soldiers? Was I totally insane? Then I looked around to see if *Mutti* was anywhere in sight. The man must have sensed my hesitation. "It's all right. We'll bring you right back."

Mother was nowhere to be seen and so, ignoring my inner conflict, I allowed my fascination with the military and curiosity to prevail. With the helping hand of the soldier in charge, I climbed onto the German vehicle. For a fleeting moment I even hoped that they might let me shoot the machine gun. Benedetti did. I looked outside, certain to be the envy of every boy in the square when horror, Mother was there in full view. Even from a distance I could see her face was ashen white. I shut my eyes and prayed that the color was caused by fear and not rage.

We rode up the small stretch of road, about one hundred or more meters, to where it came to an end. Beyond lay a vast expanse of grassy fields, where, during the season, women from Ospedaletto would pick wild strawberries.

"What do these stripes mean?" I asked the soldier who had spoken to me.

He was a sergeant, he told me. When we stopped, the sergeant took a fast look around and decided to relieve himself behind a tree, after which he ordered his man to drive him back down.

When we reached the main gate unsure of what to expect, I said, "I must get off now."

The vehicle was rolling quite rapidly down the hill and had just passed the monastery. Mother was standing there.

"Sure, sure," the sergeant said. He ordered his driver to back up to the gate. "*Geh zurück!*"

I said a short goodbye, jumped off and ran to my mother. There was no doubt. Fear was not the only emotion that had created pallor on her face. It was mostly anger. A great deal of anger. As the half-track pulled away, clumsily swaying down the uneven road, the sergeant called out in German, "You must come to visit me!"

My mother grabbed my arm and gave it a snap. "I just died a million deaths," she shouted under her breath. "Do you realize that? We came here to escape the Germans and you jump on their tank and leave me standing here not knowing where they were taking you!"

"It's not a tank, *Mutti*. It's a half-track."

My mother's face changed from white to crimson red. "A tank, a half, whatever. I should beat the daylights out of you, and if you correct me again, I might still do it."

For the rest of the day I kept quiet and stayed out of Mother's way. I had gotten in enough trouble for one day.

The next morning I went for a walk down the main road with a secret hope to see my German friend. I never told my mother where I was going for I was certain of her reaction. The unit had set up an observation post a few hundred yards down the road. I spied the vehicle parked on the edge of the cliff, a tall antenna planted in the ground and a tent erected to one side. I lay on the ground and, hidden by a thick bush, watched the men's activities. For a time I remained unnoticed, torn about what to do. These were my enemies, the people who, I came to realize, were our curse, the cause of our having to leave Vienna and to live like vagabonds for the past sixty-six months. My father, my dear *Omama*, my Aunt Stefi, my grandparents, everyone I loved might still be prisoners and forced to work on some farm for them. I remembered what Aunt Stefi had written from Germany. Why did I want to be with these people?

With conflicting emotions and against my own better judgment, I walked down the dusty footpath, twice crossed the serpentine road, until I came up to the armored vehicle.

The sergeant saw me first. "Hello! What a nice surprise." He jumped down on the soft terrain, giving me a big smile and a pat on my shoulder. "Hey, look who is here!" He shouted to his men inside the vehicle. Two turned around, looked with disinterest and went back to their work.

He clasped his arm around me. I shuddered. What was he going to do? "I'm so happy you've come. Would you like something?"

"No, thank you," I replied.

"I know. Chocolate." Without waiting for my reaction, he hopped into the half-track and returned with two bars of chocolate and a canned chicken.

I could not remember how long it had been since I last tasted real chocolate. Must have been at least two long years or maybe more. The man must have sensed my reluctance. He pushed the candy toward me. "*Ach du lieber*! Take it. It will not bite you. It's good German chocolate." Seduced by the sight of the candy, I took it from the man, tore open the wrapper and enthusiastically sank my teeth into it.

He laughed. "Take it easy. I can get you more." He seemed to enjoy watching me eat the candy as much as I enjoyed pushing it into my mouth.

Without asking me, he lifted me inside the jam-packed cabin and showed me the radios. He hopped up and came alongside. "These are shortwave transmitters. They allow us to communicate with our head-quarters. From up here we can observe what the Americans are doing and we radio to our command." He seemed pleased to share this information with me. "I don't even know your name. What is it?"

I was happy to be there but at the same time intimidated and tongue-tied.

"Well, what is your name?"

I gave him the Italian and German version of my name. "*Enrico. Nein, Erich.*"

"My name is Gerhard." Then turning to the men inside, he introduced me. "Ludwig, this is Erich. And this is Karl and this is Hans." Each man nodded and turned back to his task.

I pointed to a large contraption mounted on a tripod alongside the truck. It resembled a strange animal with two gigantic ears.

"What's that?" I asked.

"It's a periscope." Gerhard jumped off the vehicle and, holding his arms outstretched, he invited me to jump into them. I felt relaxed and allowed his strong arms to catch me in midair. For a long moment he held me close. The empty stare in his eyes looking through me suggested his thoughts were somewhere else. Side by side we walked down the poorly graded and unsurfaced road. "These Italians don't do anything right. Not even the roads are good. How old are you?"

"Thirteen."

"How is it that you speak such good German?"

"I was born in Vienna." I trembled, worrying what might follow.

"I'm from Munich. I have a son. He is eleven." The look in his eyes was the same look I had seen moments before. "I often wonder what he is doing and if he will ever see his papa again."

I instinctively knew I could trust this nostalgic man. "I haven't seen my papa in almost five years."

"Where is he?" Gerhard asked.

"I don't know. He was in Poland the last time we heard from him."

"What division is he in?"

"What division? I don't know what you mean."

"Is he in infantry, Panzer Corps, air force?"

I did not understand his question right away. "Oh no, he is with his parents."

He looked at his watch. "I have to go back. Come again tomorrow. You remind me so much of my boy."

Mentioning my father saddened me, just as I sensed my presence seemed to have saddened the sergeant. I liked Gerhard. He was a gentle man and did not even closely resemble the soldiers in the Vienna terminal. Somewhat depressed, on my way back to the monastery I removed my shirt and wrapped the precious booty in it, fearful that, if someone had seen the food, they might attack me.

Mother was in the room alone. I took a fast look around and dumped the remaining chocolate and the large can on my bunk. She did not need to ask where it all came from. "You really are wishing for my death. Don't you know these people are murderers?"

I was incensed that she could say such a thing about that kind man. "Gerhard is not a murderer."

"You're a know-it-all. Because he gave you a lousy piece of chocolate, now he is no longer a murderer?"

"No, *Mutti*. He's a good man who has an eleven-year-old son in Germany and I remind him of his son."

"Sure, sure." Then she posed the question I should have asked my German friend. "How are you going to open this can?"

We stood there in silence. "First, let's hide it. Then we'll think of a way to open the can," I said.

That afternoon I explored the caverns surrounding the dormitory we called home. I found nothing except a new way to get to the monk's inner quarters. The passages proved to be of no help toward opening our treasured canned chicken. Disheartened, I returned to the room. I found Mother all smiles. She was pointing to our Neapolitan neighbor. "This gentleman was so kind to open the can for us."

That evening we enjoyed the best meal during our stay in Montevergine. In fact, I thought it was the best ever, or so it seemed at the time. Cold chicken soup and a small piece of chicken, some of which we shared with our roommates.

That evening Mother implored me again. "Please, Erich, stay away from them."

I ignored my mother's pleading and went to see my German friend every day for two weeks. He had become a real friend. For the time being he could even be the father my papa was or Pietro had become. Gerhard liked me. He allowed me to enter the cabin where his men talked with other German units. The soldiers had become friendlier. During that period when hunger was a major problem for us, these soldiers assured me of at least one good meal a day.

One morning, as Gerhard saw me coming down the road, he jumped out of the cabin and motioned for me to follow him. Once out of earshot of his men, he stopped and looked me in the eyes. "I know you are Jewish, but you have nothing to fear. *Nicht alle Deutsche sind gleich.*"

I should have been reassured to know there were decent Germans and that Gerhard was one, but, at that moment, those words caused me to shudder and the more I thought of what to say, the greater I felt the tightening in my chest. I had experienced that same terror twice before when that big, ugly, and mean Nazi woman searched my naked body at the railroad station and then when I heard the Germans were looking for Jews in Ospedaletto. Never should I have befriended this man. Never! Now I was angry with myself. I should have listened to my mother.

"Oh no, only my grandmother was Jewish," I lied.

He added not one word, only a compassionate look. I was scared and wanted to run away while I was still alive. He sensed my turmoil.

"Please, don't be afraid." A sad pleading tone rang in his voice, as though he was asking forgiveness. "Believe me. I will not harm you."

Though his words would become embedded in my memory, the upheaval I felt at that moment surpassed any of the terrifying moments I had already known. The Nazi threat loomed and I felt closer to death than ever before. This was the man I had befriended, for whom I had developed such warm feelings. A gentle man, a caring father figure just like Pietro. Now he knew of my Jewishness and everything his uniform stood for made us enemies. Thus, while part of me screamed "Run away," another part wanted to stay. I wanted him to show me that knowing I was a Jew had not changed his feelings for me.

"I have to go now," I said.

"Please don't be angry with me. Nothing has changed the way I feel about you."

"I know, but I have to go."

"Can we at least shake hands?"

I couldn't say no to the man who had hugged me every day and in whose eyes I saw tears at that moment. Although no words were exchanged as we shook hands, it was a sad goodbye. I so much wanted to remain his friend but dared not.

Up the steep hill I ran back to my room at the monastery to bury my face in the clothes lying on my cot. How I hated the war!

For the next few days I watched Gerhard from a distance until one morning, from my hidden observation post, I saw the soldiers hastily preparing to leave. The antenna had been dismantled, the tent was gone. They had thrown everything inside the vehicle. Then the noisy rumble of the engine cut through the trees. As I stared at the half-track rolling down the mountain road, I felt the choking in my throat. I had not even said goodbye. I wanted to call out, "Stop! Stop!" Gerhard had never given me his full name and I wondered if he would get back to his son and if we would ever meet again.

27

The Battle for Salerno

Soon after my friend Gerhard's departure, an uneasy stillness settled in on the mountain. The sounds of battle in the valley below had ceased and so had the familiar din of airplanes. For almost two weeks we had not seen a new refugee, and no one at the monastery knew what was going on down below. Nerves were tense and the unnatural calm made everyone more jittery. Strangely, we had become accustomed to the incessant rumbles and booms of war and now the total silence had become ominous.

Mother did not sleep for two nights. Nor did she wash at the fountain or eat. Each morning, in a tremulous voice, she asked the same question, "Has anyone heard what is going on?" Confined to our tiny cubicle, she moved about restlessly. She never sat for more than a few minutes before moving around again. "I can't go on like this. Not knowing what is happening is going to drive me crazy."

No one had news to share. Except for a few echoing steps, the sounds made by small children running, the long hallway was deserted. Everyone waited for something to happen.

Three days after the Germans left, just as we were reaching the breaking point of our mental exhaustion, four American soldiers, displaying the 5th Army emblem on their shoulders, arrived in an open car, which I later learned was a Jeep. The Allied forces had won the battle of Salerno and liberated the valley and the surrounding villages below. Cautiously, as people came out of their cubicles, an explosion of human voices filled the courtyard. The soldiers, in their early twenties or perhaps only late teens, looked bewildered. They sat in their open vehicle stopped before the church's staircase as they were greeted by a sudden burst of frenzied enthusiasm.

Soon, as reality set in and Mother realized what really had happened, she became delirious. She frightened me for a few moments, for I had never seen my mother dance, sing, and shout in such an uncontrollable fashion, but soon I too, became infected by her actions. Realizing we were finally free, we were anxious to touch those brave soldiers and speak to them. But, under such emotional stress, neither one of us could put together more than a few words in English, so we just stood and stared.

The four young men, mobbed by a cheering crowd, struggled to step out of their Jeep. When they finally did, they left their gear in the open car and started up the steps to the sanctuary. Through gestures, people in the crowd tried to tell them not to leave their equipment unguarded. The soldiers looked at each other. "What's he saying?" one asked. I understood the question but how could I tell them their bags and rifles could be stolen? I tried to create a sentence to convey the message but to no avail. In the end, people stopped them from going up the stairs and, with sign language, let them know they might not find their belongings when they returned.

And so, with guns over their shoulders and backpacks in hand, the Americans climbed the steps and walked into the church with me and others in tow. Their young faces showed the strain and fatigue brought on by war. Must not have slept in days. They knelt by the last row of pews, made the sign of the cross and, unable to hold back their tears, those four battle-hardened men cried openly. And so did I.

When I came out of the church, I rejoined Mother in the courtyard.

"*Erichl*, I can't believe it," she cried out loud. "Do you know what this means? It means we can leave. We are no longer prisoners. We're free!" She clutched me tightly, covering my face with kisses and tears.

All around us people were celebrating. The Italians were rejoicing in being liberated by men who for three years had been their country's enemy. Liberated from Fascism and the German presence, friends and strangers hugged and kissed. I was caught up by this exuberance, even if not quite certain what it all meant. Only days before I had cried watching my German friend leave, now I was cheering the arrival of the Americans. As I sorted things out, the realization of what had happened began to sink in. For us, the war was over and I finally understood what Mother had been saying.

Before noon, I ran to say goodbye to the monks I had befriended. Mamma went to bid farewell to the people we had met and then, with what little we had in hand, we left our refuge and made a fast descent from the mountain. I could not believe how rapidly Mother skipped down that stony path. Keeping up with her was a struggle.

"What's your hurry?" I asked.

Instead of answering, she hummed a Viennese waltz. This was my mother of old. I heard her shriek every so often, cry out loud, and speak to shadows, leaving me somewhat perplexed. This was a side of her I had never seen. Had she lost her mind? I couldn't ask my mother that. Yet, she was doing things I would do, like kicking stones and jumping from shadow to shadow.

"Come here," she called out. "Dance with me." *Mutti* sang and we danced to the tune of the "Blue Danube."

Some refugees caught up with us. They, too, were returning to their homes. "*Cche bella cosa na iurnata e sole.*" They had interrupted our music with "*O sole mio.*"

"*É veramente una bella giornata,*" Mamma shouted.

Our apartment in Ospedaletto was just as we had left it. The Germans were gone, leaving behind three fallen soldiers and a number of dead mules and horses. From the shallow graves by the side of the main road, it was obvious the dead men had been buried in great haste. A gun had been planted near the grave with a helmet hanging from it and a poorly made wooden sign identifying the fallen soldier's name had been laid on the ground.

I stopped to look for Gerhard's name and was relieved not to find it, but felt pity for those three Germans who never received a proper burial. Surely they had family and children who would never see them again. The dead animals remained belly-up in the fields for days as a reminder of the battle that had been. I shuddered thinking of what could have been and was grateful my mother and I were alive.

We had just settled in when torrential autumn rains started as though wanting to deprive us of our newly acquired freedom. The dusty roads turned into mud had become impossible to maneuver. For two days Mother attempted to go outside but was held back by the incessant downpour. By the third day she announced, "I'm going to the Howells'. I don't care how wet I get."

Together we ran and splashed in the muddy puddles. Although the Howells lived less than one hundred yards away, we arrived soaked to the bones. Mrs. Howell helped us dry, prepared a pot of tea and filled us in on what they knew. All the internees were safe and, thanks to the courage of Don Pepe, who had refused to furnish the list of Jewish internees to the German officer, none of the Jews had fallen into

German hands. The Kamplers, who escaped the midnight raid and had also taken refuge in Montevergine, were back safe and sound. This bit of news came as a surprise, because during our three-week stay in Montevergine, we had not run into them.

Mother's old spirit had come back. She was cheerful and was once again the *Mutti* I knew and that had a great effect on how I felt. I was such a lucky young man to have her as my mamma! Now that the Germans were gone, we could begin the life we had left behind in San Remo or perhaps even return to Vienna. Papa would come back to be with us soon and Pietro was sure to join us, too. I wasn't quite sure how that would work, but I wished it so much that the thought seemed perfectly logical.

It took a few days to readjust to the new life in our old surroundings. No longer in the charge of local authorities, we were on our own and responsible for our own lives.

"What are we going to do?" I asked. "Do you have any money left?"

"*Pupo* was very good and with one of his letters he sent us money. I hope we get some news from him soon."

"I never hear you say that you want news from Papa. How about *Omama* and *Tante* Stefi? How about *Opapa*? Whom can we ask about them?"

Mother had a sad look in her eyes. "I don't know. Perhaps soon we will be able to find out what happened."

Similar questions were raised by other internees. No one had news from family or their hometown. The war was not yet over and we were still separated from the rest of Europe. After these many months without a newspaper, we still did not have one. And because electricity had not been restored, the radio too was denied us.

As soon as the rains slowed, we stopped at Dora's new home. Mother had not seen her little Lello in nearly a month. We found everyone alive and well. Although we were recent friends who had been separated for just a few weeks, our ecstatic embraces were like those of close relatives who had not seen one another for years.

As we were preparing to leave, Dora handed us a pillowcase half-filled with homemade pasta and a round loaf of bread she had saved in her cellar, which she kept fresh by covering it with ashes. "I want the pillowcase back," she said.

Mother kissed her again. "Dora, how I love you."

We also visited our landlords downstairs to salute the new era. Even Don Antonio, the devoted Fascist who, of all people, I never thought could be happy with the turn of events, rejoiced with us. We kissed Filomena, but, when Mother exuberantly hugged Don Antonio, his wife had a shocked expression on her face.

American troops had arrived en mass and were now encamped in the woods where Germans once had been. They had set up a battery of heavy guns and hurled their explosive loads over the mountain. During the first few days, the Allied gunners had trouble with their aim, regularly hitting the mountain peak and filling the air with the unbearable noise of whistles and explosions. How this jarred our still-frazzled nerves! The gunners, busy day and night, did little to help us catch up on lost sleep.

Three weeks had passed since we joined the exodus to walk up the mountain and, with the exception of the pasta and bread Dora had given us, we had nothing else in the house to eat. Mamma and I went through the village and found most stores closed and the few open ones with bare shelves.

We also needed water. Not everyone was where they used to be. Many villagers had gone to stay elsewhere but, after much searching, I finally found a girl willing to fetch us water from the fountain.

The American soldiers were our real salvation. Somehow they learned that foreign internees lived in the village and soon began searching for some who may have needed help. One morning, Mother spotted a Star of David hanging from a soldier's neck. "*A Yid?*" she called out in Yiddish.

The man looked perplexed. "You speak Yiddish? In this little village?"

Mamma had not conversed in that language for many years. "*Ain bissle.*" Her voice choked up as a flood of words rushed out. She asked his name, where he was from. Oh, yes, she was also of Polish descent. What city? No. She was born in a small town, a *shtetl.*

Immediately she invited the soldier to Friday supper. "*Die willst ein Shabbes essen?*"

It was Thursday. Mother, struggling between English, German, and Yiddish, made the man understand that she would do the cooking if he brought the food. "*Die kennst andere Yidden?*" Mother asked.

"I know lots of Jewish soldiers. You do not want me to bring every Jew I know."

"You bring two, three. Not more than four." With great effort, Mother created a sentence.

"Okay, you got a deal."

"I got what?" Mother asked.

"You got a deal. It's an American expression. It means . . . ." He hesitated. "It means it is a fair exchange."

Later that afternoon, the soldier returned. He dropped two cardboard boxes on the kitchen floor with a big thud. "I brought you some food," he said. He had a broad smile of satisfaction.

Mother looked in disbelief. "This is very much."

"That's okay. You'll use it later. There is plenty where this came from. I've got to go. I'll see you tomorrow."

He had brought enough food for several days, maybe even several weeks: cans of gefilte fish, canned ham, loaves of white bread, butter, and cans of chicken soup as well as cartons of cigarettes and soap. We found items we had never seen before, such as margarine and canned fruit. Mother never even looked to the bottom of the large cartons.

"I have enough to share with others," *Mutti* said.

Our homemade lamp had run out of oil several days before and we hadn't been able to find a candle in the apartment. But at the bottom of the carton, we found that our American friend had included a dozen candles.

Mother began early on Friday and cooked all day so she could get finished before darkness set in. I helped by starting the stove and fanning it to keep it burning and because we used both burners, I had to ask Filomena for extra wood so Mamma could finish her cooking.

"Erich, this is going to be a dinner fit for a king."

Friday night, our American friend showed up with four buddies. Our kitchen turned into a Tower of Babel. Communication between Mother, the American soldiers, and me was a comedy of errors. Two of the guys spoke Yiddish, or so they said, and their translation of what we were saying, judging from the other soldiers' expressions, often was far removed from what had transpired. We laughed ourselves silly, and the dinner, which was the first home cooked meal these men had eaten in a long time, was an overall success.

There was a break in the rain, so, wanting to see what a bombed city looked like up close, I ventured down to Avellino alone. I had no idea what was awaiting me or I would certainly not have gone. At the outskirts of the city I found smoldering dead bodies piled up high on street corners. What a horror! The stench of burning flesh stung my nostrils and the sight of smoking human limbs made me nauseous. More than three weeks had elapsed since the air attacks I had witnessed from the mountain peak and most of the victims were still on the streets where they had died.

"Too many bodies," a bystander said. "Just couldn't bury them." He told me how Allied soldiers had poured gasoline over the corpses and set them on fire.

I never made it to the center of town. The gruesome sights, worse than anything my eyes had seen during all the war years, made me retreat and turn around to climb the four miles back home. For days I did not tell my mother what I had seen.

We stayed in Ospedaletto one more month, but now life was somehow different. Even though we no longer had reasons to fear, people had trouble adjusting. What had been no longer was and a new lifestyle had not yet filled in its place.

The *confinati* were preoccupied with their individual options. Mother spoke with those to whom she had grown close and, when she came home, she looked puzzled.

"No one seems to know what they'll be doing. Only the Howells and Clara will be going back to Naples as soon as the city is liberated, but the Kamplers don't know. Neither does Paula nor the Weils. I wish I knew where Pietro was."

The rains kept coming and didn't stop for days. Never before in the twenty-nine months we had been in Ospedaletto had it been so wet for so long. Nature seemed to be making an attempt at keeping us there.

"I have waited long enough," Mamma said.

While I remained home, she hitched a ride to Avellino on an American army Jeep. She went looking for a place to stay, found a furnished room and came right back thoroughly soaked. "I don't care that I'm drenched. I want out of this *verstunkenes* village. We'll move to Avellino and wait there until we hear from Pietro."

In early November, when we had planned to move, a downpour descended upon us and turned roads into beds of mud. Armed with her usual resourcefulness, Mother stood on the main road with umbrella in hand and commandeered a passing army truck to move us, baggage and all, to Avellino. The truck belonged to the new Italian army, a shiny new vehicle driven by soldiers wearing brand-new uniforms. I was struck by how fast, only two months since the armistice, these men had made the transition from enemy to ally. But they were truly a new breed and appeared delighted to help victims of their former government.

Sixty-seven months, more than 2,000 days, had passed since that ill-fated Sunday in March 1938, when Hitler's troops had invaded Austria and turned us into nomads. Sixty-seven long months of running, hiding, trying to stay alive and maintaining our sanity. We had survived and were free from fear at last.

28

Normalizing Our Lives

My mother's very first act, after getting to Avellino and dropping our belongings with the new landlord, was to find a public bath. The furnished room *Mutti* had secured for us had a toilet but not a tub or a shower. Three years had elapsed since we had sunk into a bathtub of hot water and, although bathing had never been my most favorite pastime, stretching out in that delicious, clear, warm water this time was most enjoyable.

We stayed in Avellino for three months until Pietro was able to communicate with us through Dora and make arrangements to meet us in Naples. Mamma and I sought out the men from the Palestinian Brigade, soldiers we had befriended during our stay in Avellino and, with their most valuable help, moved to Naples with our limited belongings.

Within days, after we left Avellino, Pietro rented a car with a driver for his trip to Naples. The slightly more than five-hundred-mile trip from his hometown of Mazara del Vallo, in Sicily, over the war-torn roads, took one night and day of nonstop driving.

When Pietro rang the house bell, I ran downstairs and fell right into his arms. I could not get my eyes off the car. Never had I seen anything so overloaded. Four suitcases were tied to the roof and all sorts of other packages were crammed inside. There was hardly space for the two men. But for our Pietro, a Sicilian, flour and olive oil, the main ingredients that filled the car, were life's necessities.

My *Pupo* looked tired and haggard, but he again filled our lives with his smile, his warmth and his overwhelming love.

We had survived the ferocity of war and were together at last. In a few weeks, living in a furnished apartment with the luxury of a full bathroom, our lives in Naples normalized. I started school and, thanks to all the tutoring my wonderful mother had forced upon me, was able to complete the final four months of the last year of junior high without difficulty.

German planes sporadically bombed Naples several times after their retreat from the city. But our ordeal was over and we, like the brave people of London, were not about to be defeated by a few bombs.

On May 8, 1945, Germany surrendered and the war in Europe came to an end. With little time to savor peace, we were soon exposed to and traumatized by pictures of the Nazi extermination camps. Newspapers, magazines, and newsreels were filled with the specter of what was left of a people. We may not have been exterminated in a Nazi camp, but we died slowly with every picture we saw and article we read.

Although old enough to realize that my father, my grandparents, my *Omama*, my Aunt Stefi, and all the relatives I had known could have been massacred, I rebelled against that thought. In no way was I going to accept that all those I loved so dearly had perished.

"*Mutti*, tell me it's not true."

"Who knows? I keep hoping for a miracle."

Mr. and Mrs. Rozental and Runia Kleinerman in Naples, 1945.

The synagogue in Naples was hidden on the second floor of an old building buried behind some antique structures, possibly why the Germans never made an attempt to destroy it. It was a small place of worship, but large enough for a portion of the Neapolitan Jewish community that at most totaled four hundred.

True to her Jewish heritage and in honor of our family, which may no longer have been alive, my mother had arranged for my Hebrew studies with the rabbi, and that same month of May, fifteen years old and wrapped in a new prayer shawl, I was called to the *bima*, where, with pride, I read the Torah and became Bar Mitzvah.

Throughout 1945, we heard nothing from my father nor from any of our relatives and in 1946, seven years after my papa's last letter, long enough to satisfy Italian law, a court declared my dad legally dead. I was devastated, not yet able or willing to come to grips with that possibility. That Raffaele's father was dead I could accept, for he had died before my very eyes. But my papa dead? That was something else. How could some judge, who did not know my dad, who had not seen him die, just write on a piece of paper "Deceased"?

Shortly after the war's end, we were able to contact the Wovsis' sons in Milan. They had terrible news. Soon after their parents had returned home, they had been arrested by the Gestapo and shipped to a concentration camp. They never returned. I asked myself, was it fate or the sadistic delight of some supernatural creature, cynically toying with the lives of so many innocent human beings? What had passed me by when I was eleven now, five years later, made a profound impression as I tried to absorb all that had happened since our escape from Vienna.

In the late fall of 1946, while I was attending boarding school near Florence to repeat the year of high school I had failed, a miracle happened. Through my mother's niece, Toni Hübner, who had lived in Tel Aviv since before the war and was our only relative not to have moved, we received a postcard with the astonishing and unbelievable news that Papa was alive and searching for us.

Giorgio Kleinerman, on furlough, with his mother at the fountain in Naples in February 1945.

Mother made contact with my father, then wrote to tell me he would be visiting me at school. From the moment I received her note, my behavior radically changed. I became restless and unable to concentrate on my studies. It had been eight interminably long years since I had last seen my papa, and now I looked forward to picking up where we had been forced to leave off. What good fortune! Despite the death and destruction that had engulfed Europe, at least my immediate family had remained alive. True, Pietro had assumed a very important place in my life. I respected him and loved him more than I could have loved anyone. He had acted as my father for four years. Except now, I was about to be reunited with my real father. And if my papa was alive, I was optimistic that the rest of my family might be alive too.

I knew it all along. That judge had been wrong. But now what? Mother had set up house with Pietro and was known as Mrs. Russo. Would all that change? I did not know then that my father had already visited with Mother and learned what for him must have been a painful truth. His wife was in love with another man and no longer willing to reunite with him.

On the day my father was to arrive, I was given permission to leave school to meet him at the railroad station. From the moment I awoke, before the 6:00 wake-up bell, my emotions were out of control. I must have looked at my watch a hundred times. In class I was unable to sit still or pay attention and was reprimanded a few times until I told the teacher the reason for my agitation.

Thirty minutes before the train's scheduled arrival, wearing the compulsory boarding school uniform, I entered the station to wait for the man whose face I remembered so well. The Prato station was a small terminal. The platform, short and set between two tracks, served both for arriving and departing passengers. Many trains sped by and with each sound of a locomotive's whistle, my heart picked up its beat. But very few trains stopped. I so wished *Mutti* had been with me. This could have been such a fantastic family reunion. What about *Pupo* now that my papa was alive? Mother had not said anything about her plans in her letter to me.

I waited and paced on the narrow concrete strip for the longest time. Several trains stopped, passengers stepped off, others departed. So many thoughts rushed through my head. At sixteen, I had been without my papa for half of my life! An eternity! Would he even recognize me? I was a little kid the last time he saw me.

Another train slowed and came to a full stop. People got off. With accelerated breathing I scrutinized every man's face. I witnessed happy reunions of men embracing women and children hugging parents. I envisioned Papa rushing to put his arms around me, trying to pick me up, as he had done eight years before. "I'm too heavy, Papa," I would say. But there was no sight of my father. One by one, the people disappeared down the stairway. Watching the last person leave, my heart lost its beat and hope had vanished. All alone, I did not know what to do.

One person was still on the platform. I had not seen him get off the train. An older man, stooped over, walking with a cane. I paid no attention until I heard a faint call: "Erich?" A cold chill ran through my whole being. That voice. I knew that voice. With calculated steps, we moved toward each other. I saw the man, a broken-down human being, dragging a poorly healed leg and showing the remaining effects of starvation. His hair was combed back tightly as it had been in years past, but it was not the dark, lustrous hair I remembered so well. His face was gaunt and drawn, its red blood vessels visible through the concave cheeks. The suit, too large for his diminished frame, did not resemble any of the dapper clothes he had worn years before. The dream of my father, as I had seen him last at the train station in Milan, the dream I had kept alive all those years in France, San Remo, Ospedaletto, and Naples, crumbled. The elegant picture of my father, the image I had jealously preserved for so many difficult years, was destroyed in a few, short seconds on that railroad platform in Prato.

Eric's father after his return in Siberia in 1946.

"Is this my little *Erichl*?" the stranger asked. His voice lacked the assurance I remembered. "Let me look at you." The words sounded apologetic. He embraced me with caution. I was too shocked to hug him back, as I had so hopefully fantasized I would. He clung to me and I, very slowly, tried to cling to him.

When we let go, stepped back and looked at each other, the questions poured forth.

"What did you do during the war? Did you have enough to eat?" he asked in an old voice. Much older than his forty-nine years.

He described how he had escaped Lwow after the German invasion of Poland only to be caught by the Russians and sent to a concentration camp in Siberia. There he came close to dying of starvation and broke his leg in an accident. He knew nothing of his parents or the other members of the family.

We sat on a wooden bench and talked for about two hours. I know we cried a lot, but possibly, because these details were so painful to hear and my disillusionment so profound, I was incapable or perhaps unwilling to remember most of that event in my conscious memory.

Papa inquired about Signor Russo. Did I like living with him? Was he nice to me? I knew then that my parents had already spoken and Dad knew of my mother's final decision. At that instant, in spite of the pain that wrenched my soul, listening to the sadness in his voice and looking at the shadow of the man I had once known, I realized that nothing that had happened to me could compare with the pain and suffering that had befallen him.

My only solace was that my papa was not dead. He was seated next to me, although he was not the man I remembered. In his eyes was that same melancholic look I had seen at the Milan railroad station on the day *Mutti* and I departed for France.

My own feelings of disappointment gave way to the pity I now felt for my own father. I had never asked myself to choose which man I wanted for my papa. I loved Pietro more than a child could love a parent, but I loved my father, too. Sitting on that bare, wooden bench, older and more knowledgeable, I came to the painful realization that both men could not be part of my daily life.

Papa was going back to a refugee camp in Austria. His train arrived and, once again in a railroad station, we found ourselves bidding each other goodbye. We held hands for a long time and kissed. But by then, I didn't want to let go.

I had lost my relatives and my youth. The train, which I had hoped would never come, was on the tracks. Papa slowly dragged his poorly healed leg to the open door of the third-class cabin. He grasped the handle and with great effort pulled himself up the four high steps. From the platform he stopped and turned to look at me. The shrill locomotive whistle intensified my pain. Through swollen eyes I saw Papa's arm waving and, as the train diminished from view, I realized the painful truth: I was losing my father once again.

When I returned home to Naples in the summer of 1947, I tried to speak to Mother about my father. She told me it was strictly between the two of them and there was nothing to discuss.

Being home, I began to appreciate the relationship that existed between Mamma and Pietro. Their friends talked about it. *Pupo* idolized my mother and carried her on a pedestal. In all the years we lived together I never heard him utter a harsh word to her. Never would Pietro leave or return home without kissing Mother and me, a warm practice we enjoyed all the years we were together, one I continue with my own family. Perhaps my mother was the stronger of the two, but Pietro gave in to her not out of weakness but out of love. I rejoiced in the atmosphere of their mutual adoration. Mamma had finally found her well-deserved happiness.

At seventeen I reexamined what life had been when we lived with my father. Arguments had been more numerous and the criticisms my mother expressed about my father all suggested that their marriage was not as solid as I had wanted to believe. Mother's falling in love with Pietro was a natural outcome.

By 1946, life in Italy had normalized. The war had become an ugly memory. Goods were plentiful and the stores were full of merchandise, theaters competed with dazzling vaudeville shows, people were working and the horrors of the war were slowly being put aside. That year we made our first visit to Sicily. We traveled by boat to Palermo and from there boarded a *rapido* train to Mazara del Vallo. The Russo family was at the station to welcome us. It was a large family. Pietro had six siblings living in Sicily and they were all there. The reception was overwhelming. The warmth of the island was not only in the air but in part of every Sicilian's temperament.

Summer was a period of intense activity on the island. It was harvest time—grapes and wheat and the Russo family had plenty of both.

Every day I enjoyed riding the horse-drawn buggy with Pietro to one of several of their farms. Lunch, the big meal of the day, we ate together with the more than twenty-five workers. The huge table, with retaining ledges to prevent food from falling off, served as a gigantic communal platter for the mountain of homemade pasta prepared for all to enjoy. What an experience! No plates, just loads of pasta.

Our one-month stay in Sicily was a true delight. We met many of Pietro's friends and every day was a different occasion for celebration. We liked the family and they liked us.

But all was not smooth. During our stay, Pietro's family learned of our Jewishness. To people who lived by the teachings of the Catholic church in a small Sicilian town, the idea of a Jewish woman becoming part of their family was inconceivable. From childhood they had been taught to believe that Jews were the killers of Christ. How could Pietro think of marrying a woman who had yet not been redeemed in the eyes of the church?

I had not been aware of the problem that was brewing between Pietro and his family but learned the facts much later. One by one, three of Pietro's siblings traveled to Naples to convince him to abandon his relationship with my mother. This fervently Catholic family was intent on obstructing my mother and me from becoming part of them. But all their attempts at convincing Pietro failed and only helped to create a schism between Pietro and his siblings, one of the reasons we eventually would leave Europe.

Years later I asked *Pupo* if everyone in his family was against him marrying Mother. "What about your mother?" I asked.

"My mother is the sweetest person in the world," he replied. "I would have her blessing no matter what I did. That is what she told me the first time we all went to Sicily."

We returned to Sicily several more times. Everyone was always cordial, but that cloud always seemed to hang over us.

We had lived in Naples for almost six years when, toward the end of 1949, just as I had started my studies of engineering at the university, Mamma announced we were going to America. None of our friends could understand why we would leave such a comfortable lifestyle to seek who-knows-what in the New World.

The villa, our home for more than three years, included our own three-tier garden filled with a variety of flowers and thirty-three fruit trees. But more than its size was its idyllic location, the envy of most who came to visit. Located on winding Via Agnello Falcone, halfway between the town below and Il Vomero, the district at the top of the hill, we faced the gulf of Naples and had a clear view of Capri and Mount Vesuvius.

Pietro had built up a successful wholesale food business, and Mother, after managing a bottling business for the Allied forces, had begun to enjoy the type of social life she had known in Vienna. Both my parents had a large circle of friends and dinner parties at our home were at least a weekly occurrence. Judging from our lifestyle—the vacations, the full-time housekeeper, and the luxury car with our own chauffeur, I had to assume that Pietro's business was doing well. Nevertheless, my mother had made her decision.

"Why are we leaving Naples?" I asked.

Mamma explained the reason. Not having been born in Italy precluded me from ever applying for citizenship. "I don't want you to live in a country where you will always be a foreigner."

With a heavy heart I accepted my mother's explanation and plans for our departure began in earnest.

During the last few months in Naples, our home became a beehive of social activities. Friends came for lunch and for dinner. It seemed that Mother never left the kitchen, but she loved that. Several times I overheard close friends question her decision to leave. "You have everything you want. Anything. A man who adores you and would reach for the moon if you asked him to." Mother had many reasons, but I never heard her say that one of them was Pietro's family.

As the time of our departure drew closer, I began feeling the pain of parting from friends, from my dog and my cat. I had grown up in Naples during my most important formative years. I had many friends and *Pupo* had bought me a motor scooter for graduation, giving me the freedom to move around. It was a comfortable life, finally without the fears we had faced for many years before. The war was behind us, so why leave this heavenly land? Why should I care if I could not become a citizen? But in the end I never revealed my true feelings.

Two weeks before our planned departure, leaving the housekeeper to take care of the pets and home, we moved from our villa to a small hotel and the day before our sailing, I went back to the house to bid my pets a final goodbye. They knew I was leaving them. I had been away on trips before, yet they had never displayed the kind of behavior they did on that day. The cat saw me and ran away, while the dog allowed me to pick her up. She soon wiggled out of my arms to slowly climb up the stairs of the garden. I called her name several times, but Dianina never as much as stopped or turned her head. This little dog, who would jump at the sound of my voice, had to know I was abandoning her.

29

Life in America

Our ship, the SS *Atlantic*, sailed from Naples on February 2, 1950, and landed in New York in the midst of a snowstorm on February 16. Only Mother and I had sailed. Pietro, who had to settle some matters in Naples and Sicily, would follow us a few months later.

During the trip I realized the irony of it all. My whole family— Mother, Father, and I—were supposed to have emigrated together before the war if not for the difficulty of obtaining an American visa.

We stayed in New York, living in a hotel on 103rd Street off Broadway. The hotel and the neighborhood were crowded with immigrants, so much so that I wondered if the entire city was made up of transplanted Europeans. We knew we were not going to set up house in New York. We had been told so by HIAS, the Jewish sponsoring organization that had facilitated our immigration to the United States. So we stayed only long enough to decide where to go and for HIAS to make the necessary arrangements.

During our six months' stay, Mother made contact with several of her old European friends. It was almost like going back in time, except that living in a hotel room made it impossible for Mother to entertain as she would have liked.

I started to work, a new experience. On my first job I learned to box macaroons, earning seventy-five cents an hour. From there I graduated to waiting on tables, which paid forty dollars per week.

One afternoon, soon after our arrival, Mother and I walked into Eclair's, a Viennese coffee shop on New York's Upper West Side. From a table in the rear, a woman let out a shriek. "Lotte!"

I had heard that shriek before. Mother immediately realized it was Bertl, and the two women repeated the performance I had witnessed on the streets of Nice eleven years earlier. Mother began crying, something she was doing more frequently as of late. They hugged and kissed.

"Bertl, *du bist so dick geworden.*"

"*Du auch,*" Bertl said. They were both shouting, referring to their added weight.

"Erich, *ich muss dich anschauen,*" Bertl said. Holding me at arm's length, she wanted to look at me. "*Ich hätte dich nicht erkannt.*" Then she kissed me and pulled me to her abundant bosom.

I would have recognized her anywhere. There was a short applause from the patrons for a scene that repeated itself almost daily in those postwar years.

Under pressure from HIAS, we moved to Philadelphia on July 3, where a nice furnished room had been arranged for us.

Within days Mother made friends with a family living across the street from our rented room and soon that family, with its many members scattered across town, became our family. Overnight I was adopted by this generous and warm group of people and acquired new aunts and uncles and a most wonderful grandmother.

Neither my mother nor I allowed for the world to pass us by and, while Mom looked for an apartment and some furnishings, I looked for a job, any job. My English had improved enough so that I could hold a simple conversation. Within days we both succeeded.

In October, Pietro followed us, but his landing turned out anything but smooth. To bypass the Italian immigration quota, my dad arrived on a tourist visa but only purchased a one-way ticket, never thinking this might create a problem. But it did. In fact, he was detained at Ellis Island for five days and the indignity of living in that large hall with hundreds of other detainees without any privacy engendered in him a negative feeling toward America. Eventually we posted a cash bond to secure his return to Italy and release.

When Pietro was able to join us in Philadelphia, he found us in a furnished one-bedroom apartment surrounded by a large extended family, all of whom immediately adopted him, too. Despite language difficulties—Pietro did not speak a word of English—he impressed everyone as a most unusual person. His warmth, his friendliness, but mostly the affection and love he held for my mother needed no language to be expressed.

Evelyn and Lou Maximon had adopted Mother as their sister and a very close relationship developed between us. On April 1, 1951, they planned and paid for my parents to be married officially. The happy event took place at the Inn in Princeton, New Jersey, with half of our new extended family attending.

Because I was already working, Pietro, a university graduate who had never worked for anyone, decided he too should find a job. To him it was unacceptable to have his son support the family. He considered that his responsibility. A new acquaintance suggested that, because of the language difficulty, he contact the Italian community to seek employment. There he did find a job in a cheese factory where he had to endure standing in water for most of his working hours. Soon after he was offered a job at a bakery, where he reported to work before midnight and stayed until early morning. Our conflicting hours disrupted family life, so Pietro sought another job. Months later, through people in the Italian community, he landed one as a presser with a clothing manufacturer.

For more than two years, while Mother was able to get his tourist visa extended, *Pupo* endured these low-level jobs, which crushed the spirit of this cultured and refined man. The menial work, the only type my dad had been able to find, reinforced his negative feelings about his future in the United States.

The residency problem needed to be resolved. Mother had been advised at the time of the visa extension that another one would not be granted. Pietro needed to obtain a permanent residence status, which required a congressional bill or return to Italy. Never to be deterred, Mother made a connection with a Philadelphia congressman, who agreed to introduce a bill to grant Pietro an immigration visa. There remained one additional hitch. United States immigration laws required anyone who became a permanent resident through such a special congressional bill to exit the country and re-enter it under the new visa.

Rather than return to Italy, Pietro chose to go to Mexico, a closer destination. He traveled by bus from Philadelphia, partially to save money but also because other modes of transportation were not readily available in those days. This was 1952.

On his second day in Mexico, my dad met Ernesto Segre, a Jewish doctor of Italian origin. It was the meeting that would change my family's future. The two men formed an immediate bond, and through Ernesto, Pietro was introduced to members of an Italian community who welcomed him and immediately made him feel comfortable and at home. He wired Mother that he had found the land where he wanted to spend the rest of his life and asked her to prepare for the move. Pietro did return to Philadelphia for a short stay, long enough to convince my mother to make the move permanent, which they did in 1953.

In Mexico my parents adapted easily. They soon met a large contingent of European immigrants, which offered them a continental lifestyle such as the one they had left back in Naples. My mother even met a branch of my real father's family that stemmed from his uncle, Max Lifschütz, my *Opapa's* brother. When Mother wrote to me about her encounter, it was exciting news since I remembered that in Vienna, when I was only five, I had seen Uncle Max's two young daughters, Martha and Edith.

I visited my parents often and met many of their friends, who were unanimous in feeling that my parents were two unusual and unique human beings. The love they felt for one another served as an example and admiration for all who knew them, a love that would last for thirty more years.

In Mexico my mother, for the third time in her life, at the age of sixty-four, exhibited her ability as a remarkable entrepreneur. In Vienna she had opened a vegetarian restaurant. In Naples she succeeded in the wine-bottling business and now her apple strudel helped launch a wholesale bakery that, after two years, could boast of more than two hundred employees.

My parents lived in Mexico City until my mother's Parkinson's disease became hard to manage at home. In 1972, she entered the Jewish retirement home in Cuernavaca. Pietro, after several stints in his own business, had gone to work for a close friend. When Mother moved to Cuernavaca, Pietro remained in the city during the week but spent every weekend with his beloved Lotte. In the true spirit of their marriage vows, his life was devoted to his wife "in sickness and in health."

Anyone to whom I spoke marveled at the devotion this man showed for his ill wife. Not one weekend would go by without his traveling to Cuernavaca.

"Mamma needs me and waits for me," he said when I tried to convince him that he needed a life of his own. It was at a point when *Mutti* was no longer fully aware of her surroundings, but Pietro was as stubborn as he was good. For him Lotte was his whole life and he wanted to spend his weekends with her.

From the time he joined us in Naples in February of 1944, Pietro remained Lotte's friend, companion, and husband for the next thirty-nine years. Earlier, while still in Ospedaletto, he had taken on the role of my father and I have always referred to him as such. He was the best parent any son could hope for. He set the highest example of morality, rectitude, and integrity for me. In the midst of our time as *internati*, during the low period in our lives, Pietro was the greatest gift Mussolini could have given us. The effect this gentle and sensitive man had on people prompted an acquaintance in Mexico to say, after asking me whether Dr. Russo was my father, "You should be proud to have a father like him." Indeed I was.

My adored *Pupo* succumbed to a heart attack on July 31, 1983, while traveling through a small village in Mexico. He was buried there until December 1996, when, with help of a Mexican friend, I had his body exhumed and cremated. With great love, on my next trip to Italy, I carried him to Mazara del Vallo, his beloved land, to rest next to his own mother.

My dear mother never learned of Pietro's death. She left me two years later, on February 17, 1985, and was laid to rest in the Jewish cemetery in Mexico City. Because Pietro was not Jewish, he had been denied his earned right to be next to her.

Epilogue

$\mathbf{M}$any of the internees had settled in Naples, although some did so only temporarily. Clara Gattegno and the Howells returned to their former homes. We ran into Runia, her son Giorgio, and her parents, as well as the Spaechts, the Kamplers, and the few others with whom we had never grown close.

We heard that Paula Alster had joined one of her brothers in Milan and later moved to Chile. The Michelagnoli family settled in Venice, where Alfredo found a position as a reporter for a local newspaper. Gaby Perutz married Cesare Meneghini, her Italian aviator, while Giorgio Kleinerman enlisted in the Polish brigade attached to the British Eighth Army. He saw heavy fighting up the Italian boot and with luck came through unscathed.

One by one we found several of the other internees. Clara Gattegno eventually emigrated to Palestine before I had an opportunity to see her. Through her uncle, Beppe Gattegno, whom we had befriended, we learned that she married there and, against her physician's advice, became pregnant, causing her untimely death.

Eric with his mother and step-father in the public gardens on Via Caracciolo in Naples in 1945.

Gusti Kampler met an American soldier who was born in the same German town and with whom she had gone to grammar school. They fell in love and were married in 1945 in Naples with many of the internees and some friends from Ospedaletto attending.

From my papa I learned what happened to his two brothers and his parents. There was an unconfirmed report from a neighbor that my loving *Opapa*, my grandfather, had been shot on the street and left to die in front of his home in Lwow. My dear grandmother succumbed in a Nazi extermination camp. My father's two brothers, one cousin (who was hidden by a Christian friend in her closet in the basement), and Uncle Maximilian's immediate family were my only relatives to survive the Holocaust. None of the other eighty members did.

Papa also told me how, that first week in September of 1939, after the German army had overrun Poland, he and his two brothers fled on foot in different directions. Uncle Norman, wearing two suits and two heavy overcoats, proceeded south. Years later he told me how he walked through Rumania, the Balkans, Turkey, and Syria before reaching

Palestine. From there, in 1942, at the height of the war, he boarded an American cargo ship to join his wife, Sally, in New York. There he practiced medicine until his death in 1987. They had one daughter, Ettie.

At the end of the war my father was able to leave the Siberian camp. Partially on foot he returned to Vienna from where he took the train to meet with me. His brother Oswald, my Uncle Osi, showed up in Palestine. In 1950, Uncle Osi traveled to Vancouver to seek the woman he had married before the war. (He had not followed her to Canada at that time.) She had obtained an annulment, remarried, and given birth to two children. Heartbroken, he returned to Israel for a short time where he shared an apartment with my father. Osi eventually returned to Vienna, where he remarried years later. Although he never recovered from the war years nor from the breakup of his first marriage, he lived a productive life, becoming president of an insurance company and head of the Vienna Jewish Community until his death in 1979.

Eric with his mother, stepfather, and others in the public gardens on Via Caracciolo in Naples in 1945.

Soon after our reunion at the lonely rail terminal, my father emigrated to Israel. In Tel Aviv he encountered the woman to whom he had been engaged in Vienna before he met my mother. They took up the relationship they had broken up some twenty years earlier and spent the rest of their lives together. I stayed in regular contact with my father and shared a short telephone call to him each month until his death on December 4, 1975, at the age of seventy-eight.

Five months before my father's death, fate smiled upon us for a wink of time. Papa's heart had failed but rapid intervention at the hospital in Tel Aviv brought him back to life, giving me the chance to fly to Israel and see him one final time since our sad meeting at the Prato railroad station twenty-nine years earlier.

Ettore Costa went back to Rome where he had lived before his years of internment. He no longer wrote, but devoted his talent to painting. Already blind in one eye and with less than 10 percent vision in the other, he astounded Roman art critics by creating some of his best oil paintings. He became known as the "Blind Painter" and a book was written about him. I greatly treasure my copy as well as the one original oil painting in my possession.

A twenty-five-year difference existed between me and this exuberant, fascinating, intellectual man, who honored me with his friendship for more than two decades. Ettore and I kept in touch through the years following the war. I visited him several times in Rome, where he delighted in playing Cicerone and showing me the magnificence of the Eternal City. From the intimate chapels to the grandiose monuments, never has there been a better guide—not in Rome, not anywhere. After I settled in the United States, we corresponded often. He expressed a desire to visit me and meet my family. In a letter dated February 15, 1965, he categorically stated that "nothing will interfere from my coming to New York in June." Nothing except death, which snatched him on a street in Rome in April of that year. He was not yet sixty.

After the war, I visited Vienna several times. Each time I struggled to find that small flat near the Prater where my dear *Omama* had lived. She was among my dearest and most beloved relatives. I revisited many landmarks in my native city but the name of the street where Grandma had lived kept escaping me. After Uncle Osi's death, his wife handed me two envelopes. They contained a picture of *Opapa*, my grandfather in Poland, and some documents, one of which was my parents' marriage certificate, listing my grandmother's Vienna address. My wife and I hurried across town, asked a stranger for directions and soon, breathless, found ourselves before the large, old entrance of 6 Ybbs Strasse. My heart was pounding. My eyes were glazed. I tried to read the tablet over the portal. "This building was destroyed by Allied bombing and rebuilt in 1946," I translated to my American wife.

I had no interest in visiting a rebuilt edifice and, giving full freedom to the tears that had swelled my eyes, we left the site.

My wife and I were back at 6 Ybbs Strasse the following year. The intensity of my emotions of the previous year now quieted, I reread the tablet. The building had been "damaged" and not destroyed, the inscription read. Without hesitation, I pushed open the smaller door inside the heavy portal, crossed the metal threshold and entered the poorly lit ground-floor foyer. I found the caretaker's flat. A young woman answered my knock.

"Is there anyone who has lived here since before the war?" I asked.

In a marked Viennese dialect and without catching her breath, she replied, "Oh yes, apartment number nine."

My wife close behind, I ran up the circular staircase. The apartment was on the third floor, at the end of the hallway, where the little water fountain, built into the wall around the corner from the landing, awoke old memories. I knocked on the door.

An old woman unlocked her door. Three chains stopped it from opening more than a fraction. "Would you remember where a Frau Brandwein lived before the war?" I asked.

"She lived right here," she replied, without a moment's hesitation, then removed the three chains and invited us in.

Oh yes! This was *Omama's* place. I recognized the cupboard where she kept my prune jam, the tiny kitchen, the bedroom where I had taken many naps. Only my dear *Omama* was missing. We stayed to talk a while. I was aware of what the Nazis had done with Jewish homes and properties. This woman had taken over what once had belonged to *Omama*, yet I could not find hate or resentment for her.

Whenever I go to Vienna, I pass by 6 Ybbs Strasse. Perhaps *Omama* knows I am visiting her.

Jimmy Howell and I have gotten together on many occasions and have been in regular telephone contact for many years.

After almost fifty years, I was successful in finding Giorgio (now George) Kleinerman and Davide (now David) Kampler. I have spent some memorable days with both, looking back at the times spent in Ospedaletto d'Alpinolo and remembering many of the other *confinati*. Sadly, George Kleinerman passed away in July 2004.

Gusti Kampler, who married the American soldier she knew from kindergarten, lives alone in California, having lost her husband shortly after their golden anniversary.

After much searching, I located one of the Perutz daughters, Ciocca. She was not well. I spoke to her several times but never got to see her. She told me about her family. Her parents were dead as were her sister who passed on very young and her husband. Ciocca had an emergency surgery in 2008 and died on the operating table.

Eric and Eric's wife Cookie (Judith), the first one on the left, with Giorgio Kleinerman and his wife at their fiftieth anniversary reunion, 1997.

In March 2008, I was summoned to Ospedaletto d'Alpinolo by the town's mayor. With great fanfare and celebration, I was awarded the town's honorary citizenship. Much has changed in that backward village. I visited the apartment we occupied during our stay. At that time there was no running water nor a toilet, except for the outhouse attached at the end of the corridor. This time we found a magnificent modern bathroom, including a bidet and gold-plated fixtures and in the various rooms, instead of a singular light bulb, I saw displayed gorgeous Murano chandeliers.

Every home that we visited had one or more modern bathrooms, central heat, washing machines, and lots of marbles.

Children now have an opportunity to attend the school of their choice, aided by the buses that come to the village to transport them to the provincial city of Avellino. Many are the college graduates I encountered during my visit and just about everyone seems to have completed high school.

During that stopover I also met the boy, a senior now, who back in 1943 had purchased my bicycle.

In April 2010, I was invited by the Austrian Federal Chancellery to spend one week in Vienna as their guest. It was a trip with mixed emotions: nostalgia, sadness, and gratification.

The manager of the Jewish Community's Registry was able to locate the records of my aunt, my mother's sister, whose name I was unable to recall. He searched through a number of old books and by matching witnesses on my parents' marriage certificate, he found my aunt's name, her marriage date, and the date of her divorce. From the record book, I learned her full name: Tauba Ruchel Schif, who I mentioned in this book as Aunt Stefi, the only named I recalled. He also furnished me with the gruesome details surrounding her deportation to Auschwitz on July 17, two days before her forty-ninth birthday.

After graduating high school in Naples in 1949 and after our emigration to the United States, my life followed a new trail quite diverse from what I would have experienced in Italy. My mother and I first settled in Philadelphia, while my step-dad followed a few months later. My first ambition was to study and become an opera singer. I took piano and voice lessons, but my mother, the eternal pragmatist, suggested I follow a career in popular music, ignoring that her son was more of a dreamer.

While devoting some time to studying music, I obtained work with an engineering firm and at the same time, enrolled at Drexel Institute of Technology to continue my academic studies. At the end of the first year, after realizing that work in an office was not suited for my personality, I dropped out of college and resigned from my job. I was supporting my mother at that time, and people thought I was insane to give up a job that paid $10,000 a year. That was in 1952, when the minimum wage was the great sum of 75 cents per hour and a $2,500 annual income was considered a living wage. I accepted a job as a salesman without guarantee of income but in less than a month, my earning equaled what I had recently given up.

I also discovered I had managerial skills and soon ventured into my own business. In Mexico, where I went to visit my parents, I made contacts to import lady's garments and so began my importing business. Two friends offered financial support and off I was as an entrepreneur. I soon expanded the enterprise to include European giftware making my task of selling, packing, and shipping a greater selection of items much more demanding. For four years I struggled, until good judgment dictated that I should close shop and return my friend's money.

Fortunately the company that originally had hired me as a salesman and where I set a record of earning offered me the opportunity to take over the direction of their New York branch. It had been losing money and was doomed to be shut down. I devoted six months to reorganize both the sales and office staff, while trying to overcome the objection of the outgoing manager who kept reminding me that "We don't do things this way in New York." After hearing his remark several times, I finally suggested that he go home and wait there for his severance pay.

Before the end of the first year, I succeeded in turning a profit for the branch. But after two years, my free spirit induced me to try a hand at my own business once again. Soon thereafter, to satisfy my wife's desire, I sold the business and we moved to Miami Beach, where I faced new challenges. Our marriage was on the rocks and lasted less than one more year. The break-up was a financial disaster and compelled me to earn enough to support two households including two small children.

Having freed myself from an unhappy marital life, I embarked once more on a new venture. This time I opened a real estate office. Two years later I expanded into other fields, allowing the company to deal with commercial accounts, which led us to launch a national collection agency. The business flourished for two decades, at its peak employing about one hundred people. In 1992, after hurricane Andrew partially destroyed our home, I decided to retire and devote myself to writing and singing my favorite music: opera and Neapolitan songs.

Sad to say that my business successes were not matched by two of my marital experiences. That, however, is not true of my third marriage to my current spouse, Judith K., known as Cookie, to whom I have been wed twenty-nine tumultuously happy years.

At the age of eighty, I feel no older than I felt at forty. I enjoy racing a road bike and do so some thirty-five miles a week, I play tennis, and occasionally like to go skiing. I also prefer walking up the stairways unless the building is more than five stories high.

Time and time again I have been asked what effect the war years and the circumstances under which I grew up had on me. Often I have examined myself to reach an honest answer. Growing up among mature and intellectual people guided my young malleable mind to grasp philosophical theories and to develop psychological understandings that in later years might not have been easy to absorb. Much of what I learned in those early years, many people do not learn until many years later in life and with much greater effort.

It is true I lost most of my childhood, but many, who know me, will tell you that I regained it in my adult years, gauging from my tendency to often act as a youngster. The deprivations I suffered as a child, in spite of my mother's effort to spare me much of that, evolved into many positive traits in my later years. Without question I adapt more easily to negative aspects of life. Often I have been on a financial roller coaster realizing how truly little it affected me when compared to the emotions of others close to me or perhaps even party to it.

I find it easy to shed everyday problems. Very little is so important that it makes me sad or even angry. But I do look for the humor that surrounds us every day and try to laugh at that hoping to dispel the excessive seriousness that people insist on making part of their lives.

Glossary

Ach Du lieber (German): idiomatic expression meaning "dear one."

a danke Gott (Yiddish): thank the Lord.

A kholeriye oyf dir. (Yiddish): you should be struck by cholera.

ain bissle (Yiddish and German): a little.

Alle Deutsche sind nicht gleich. (German): all Germans are not alike.

arrivederci (Italian): so long.

a suo favore (Italian): at your pleasure.

Auflauf (German): dumplings.

auguri (Italian): best wishes.

a yid (Yiddish): a Jew.

Bellissimo. Fatto in Inghilterra. Per bacco! (Italian): very beautiful. Made in England. My goodness!

bello (Italian): nice, beautiful.

Bello, molto Bello. (Italian): Beautiful, very beautiful.

bene (Italian): good.

bima (Hebrew): platform where the Rabbi or reader stands to read the holy scriptures.

Black Shirts (English): synonymous with "Fascists" and signifying those who used the black shirt as a uniform.

bono o bellissimo (Neapolitan dialect): good or very beautiful.

briscola (Italian): old card game played with special playing cards.

bubbe mayse (Yiddish): a grandmother's tale.

buon giorno e benvenuti (Italian): good day and welcome.

buon giorno (Italian): good day.

Camicie Nere (Italian): Black Shirts; Fascist paramilitary groups supporting Mussolini.

camionette (Italian): pick-up trucks.

carabiniere; pl., *carabinieri* (Italian): policeman, at one time the Royal Guard.

caserma dei carabinieri (Italian): police station.

Cche bella cosa na iurnata e sole. (Neapolitan dialect): how nice to have a sunny day is. First line of "O, Sole mio."

centesimi (Italian): fraction of the Italian currency, the lira.

centime (French): one hundredth of French franc.

certainement (French): certainly.

Certo, padrone. (Italian): Certainly, master.

C'est formidable (French): This is terrific.

chaserai (Yiddish): filth, garbage.

Che cazzo ne saccio? (Local Italian dialect): Literally, "What do I know about dicks?"

Che lo pozzino ammazzare, qual benedetto Mussolini. (Italian and local Italian dialect): Literally, "May they kill that blessed Mussolini." "Blessed" is used ironically and here signifies damned.

Che vulite? (Local Italian dialect): What do you want?

Cicerone (Italian): a tour guide who is well informed of the area.

Claruccia (Italian): endearing diminutive of Clara.

commissario (Italian): superintendent or police chief.

confinati politici (Italian): political internees.

cosi sia (Italian): equivalent to "Amen."

cummare (Neapolitan dialect): has many meanings, such as best friend, godfather, best man at a wedding.

Curten spieler (Yiddish): a card player.

Dass ist incredibile. (German and Italian): This is incredible. *Dass ist* is German *incredibile* is Italian.

Dass kann dir nicht weh tun. (German): This cannot hurt you.

De gustibus non disputandam est. (Latin): There is no disputing taste.

Deutsch sprechen? (German): Do you speak German?

Die kennst andere Yidden? (Yiddish): Do you know other Jews.

Die willst ein Shabbes essen? (Yiddish): Do you want a holiday meal?

Dobusch (German): a Viennese twenty-layer cake with glazed sugar topping.

Du auch. (German): You too.

Du bist so dick geworden. (German): You've gained so much weight.

Eccoci. È tempo per un pó di tè. (Italian): Here we are. Time for some tea.

ein bissle (German): a little.

Einlauf (German): enema.

Enricuccio (Italian): an endearing diminutive of Enrico.

Erich. Ich muss dich anschauen (German): Eric, I must look at you.

Er redt auf di menschen man siht von oiben (Yiddish): he's talking about the people you see from the top of the hill.

Eych zoll azoy wissen fon tzures! (Yiddish): I should know so much about trouble!

eyn curten spieler (Yiddish): a card player.

Eyn glik hot mik getrofen! (Yiddish): Good fortune has met with me!

Eyn stick dreck. (Yiddish): A piece of filth.

E veramente una bella giornata. (Italian): It is truly a beautiful day.

fasce (Italian): bandages; strips of cloth, usually from old sheets.

feldmarschall (German): field marshall.

figli di puttana (Italian): sons of whores; sons of bitches.

galleria (Italian): gallery; refers to a cross-like structure, generally with a domed roof and filled with eating places and shops.

geh zurück (German): go back.

geschmat (Yiddish): conversion to Catholicism or other religion.

Gesu Cristo mio (Italian): My Jesus Christ.

goldenes (German): golden.

Groschen (German): fraction of Austrian currency: the Schilling

Hasele (German): little rabbit

Ich haette dich nicht erkannt (German): I would not have recognized.

il commerciante (Italian): the businessman.

Il Duce (Italian): the leader; epithet given to Benito Mussolini.

il portinaio (Italian): the janitor.

Inferno (Italian): underworld. The first book of Dante's *Divina Commedia*.

internati (Italian): internees.

joie de vivre (French): joy of life.

Kaddish (Hebrew): traditional Jewish prayer for the dead.

kasche (Hebrew): question typically asked at the Pesach Seder by the youngest member at the table.

Katzele (Yiddish): little kitten; term of endearment.

Kennst du das Land woh die Zitronen bluehn? (German): Do you know the land where the citrus blooms?

Kol Nidre (Hebrew): the special chant which opens the Yom Kippur services.

La Domenica del Corriere (Italian): an Italian weekly magazine with artist renditions, in lieu of photographs, to show world events. Popular during the war years.

l'shana tova (Hebrew): the customary good wish for the Jewish new year.

ma cher (French): my dear.

Madonna mia (Italian): My Holy Mary.

mammina (Italian): diminutive of mamma.

maresciallo (Italian): sergeant.

Maronna mia! Hanno ammazzato Peppino! (Local Italian dialect): Holy Mary! They've killed Peppino!

mein (German): my, mine.

Mensch (Yiddish and German): a human with great sensitivity and feeling for others.

mercato nero (Italian): black market; contraband.

merci (French): thank you.

mon ami (French): my friend.

merveilleux (French): marvelous.

meshuge (Yiddish): crazy.

mia cara signora (Italian): my dear lady.

milanese (Italian): veal cutlet similar to a *Wiener Schnitzel*.

miny'n (Hebrew): required number of men, ten, to perform Jewish religious services.

mio caro signore (Italian): my dear sir.

Mischa (Yiddish): the name my mother called my papa.

mishegas (Yiddish): craziness.

MSM (*metri sul mare*) (Italian): meters above sea level.

Mutti (German): derivative from Mutter. Generally the name used for "Mother" will denote the language the characters are speaking. Thus, *Mutti* denotes German and *mamma* or *mammina* denotes Italian.

natürlich (German): naturally; of course.

nein (German): no.

Nicht alle Deutsche sind gleich. (German): Not all Germans are alike.

niente (Italian): nothing.

Non voglio. (Italian): I don't want to.

Non so, ma ci dovremo adattare. (Italian): I don't know, we will just have to adapt.

Nous parlerons français. (French): We shall speak French.

Geshmat (Yiddish): conversion to Catholicism or other religion.

O, Madonna mia (Italian): Oh, Holy Mary.

opera buffa (Italian): comic opera.

orzo (Italian): barley.

padrone (Italian): master (term of respect).

palatchinka (Hungarian): a Viennese/ Hungarian version of a French crepe, usually filled with jam, cottage cheese, or chocolate cream.

Paludi Pontine (Italian): a very large, mosquito-infested swamp in the vicinity of Rome.

pardon (French): pardon [me].

Peppino (Italian): man's name; diminutive of Giuseppe (Giuseppino).

Perdete ogni speranza—O voi che entrate.—Queste parole di colore oscure . . . (Italian): Abandon all hope oh Ye who enter. These dark words I found written at the entrance . . . (from *Dante's Inferno*).

Pesach (Hebrew): Passover.

piano secondo (Italian): second floor.

Podestà (Italian): Mayor, out of use.

portiere (Italian): concierge or janitor.

povedl (Polish?): prune preserve.

pronto (Italian): ready.

prosche (Polish): please.

pupo (Italian): doll; term of endearment.

puppale (German): little doll; term of endearment.

Quel benedetto Mussolini! (Italian): That blessed Mussolini! Phrase used sardonically to signify the opposite of its literal meaning.

raconteuse (French): storyteller (feminine).

rapido (Italian): an express train, making few stops.

Roma. Bellissima! *La Città Eterna*! (Italian): Rome. Very beautiful! The eternal city!

Rosh Hashanah (Hebrew): the Jewish New Year.

s'accomodi (Italian): make yourself comfortable.

Sai sha (Yiddish): Be quiet.

Schatzele (German): little treasure; term of endearment.

schnell (German): fast.

Schnell! Schnell! Ich kann nicht auf die Juden Schweine warten! (German): Fast, fast. I can't wait for these Jewish swine.

scopa (Italian): old card game played with special playing cards.

Se avanzo seguitemi, se indietreggio uccidetemi. (Italian): If I advance, follow me. If I retreat, kill me!

Seder (Hebrew): traditional meal eaten the first and second night of Pesach.

Sei nela terra fredda, sei nella terra negra, ne il sol piu ti rallegra, ne ti risveglia amor. (Italian): You lie in the cold ground, you lie in the dark ground, nor does the sun cheer you nor wake you up my love.

Shana Tova (Hebrew): Customary good wish for the Jewish New Year.

sheytl (Yiddish): traditional hairpiece worn by orthodox woman after her head was shaven.

shmatte (Yiddish): rag.

shofar (Hebrew): the ram's horn blown during religious services.

shtetl (Yiddish): small village where Jewish communities lived.

Signor maresciallo, sonon arrivati I nuovi internati. (Italian): Sergeant, the new internees have arrived.

Signor podestà (Italian): Mister mayor. Nolonger in use.

Signora, posso? (Italian): May I, Madam?

Simmu arrivate ad Ospidaletto e a Maronna cce Stan rimpetto. (Local Italian dialect) We have arrived in Ospedaletto and the Holy Mary is before us.

Simmu arrivate a Summonte e a Maronna cce Stanin fronte. (Local Italian dialect): We have arrived in Summonte and the Holy Mary is before us.

simpatico (Italian): charismatic, with charm.

Si na bestia. (Local Italian dialect): You're an animal.

Sotto la caserma mi metto ad aspettar. (Italian version): "Under the barracks I will wait for you." The song "Lilli Marlene" was sung by the German army and spread to Italian, American, and British soldiers.

Stück gold (German): piece of gold; term of endearment.

takke meshuge (Yiddish): really crazy.

Tante (German): aunt.

Tatale (Yiddish): little daddy; term of endearment.

Tfilin (Hebrew): phylacteries.

Totonno (Neapolitan dialect): a contraction of Antonio.

très bien (French): very well.

Trinacra: a three-legged woman, representing Sicily because of its triangular shape. This was the antique name given to the island and attributed to the Greeks.

tsetses (Hebrew): braided, fringed ritual undergarment.

Umen (Yiddish): Amen.

un minuto (Italian): one minute.

un momento (Italian): one moment.

Upim (Italian): the Italian version of the American five-and-dime store.

venite (Italian): come in.

verstunkenes (Yiddish and German): stinking, lousy.

vieni qui! (Italian): come here!

vieni su (Italian): come upstairs.

Viri Napule e po mori (Local Italian dialect): see Naples, then die; a common Neapolitan expression.

Voulez-vous manger avec nous? (French): Would you like to eat with us?

Wie heist dass? (German): What do you call this?

Ya! Ich spreche Deutsch. (German): Yes, I speak German.

Yeshiva (Hebrew): Jewish parochial school.

Yom Kippur (Hebrew): the Day of Atonement.

Zey zindt keyn fleysh un keyn fish. (Yiddish): they are neither flesh nor fish.

zoccoli (Italian): wooden shoes, similar to Dutch wooden shoes.

People Interned in Ospedaletto

Maria Carmen Dias, Giovanni Howell, Carina Pirinolo, Alfonso Carmine, Jovenne Bernard, Giorgio Cook, Angela Cook, Germaine Duwal, Rute Gillen, Margherita Laicok, Ester Chiappini, Costanza Wooder, Matilde Chale, Marcel De Rappard, Elisabette De Rappard, Ottavia Zingoni, Giulia Grazielly, Maria Penhard, Vera Hartung, Carlo Ravel, Edidia Cesan, Kristin Bjorndottia, Agnese Caine, Minnie Eldred, Francesca Peterson, Mira Gilbert, Geltrude Long, Pinklas Rozenthal, Liba Klinkowstin, Sara Kleinerman, Alice Mabel, Betty Lange, Hildegard Wolff, Mary Dowlimg, Doraty Anna Longod, Sehma Sara Lewin, Tommaso Perutz, Alessandra De Korlowska, Gabriella Perutz, Arturo Specht, Kamilla Sara Lustig Specht, Ettore Costa, Amalia Liebenthal, Michelina Krzesiukska, Elvira Noro, Paola Holloschultz, Yeanna Grillot, Anna Cavallaro, Maurizia Bedos, Carlotte Brandvei, Clara Grafegna, Rungre Ahnanda, Anna Crince, Genoveffa Robilland, Germaine Romastin, Salvatore Vellucci, Salvatore Guidone, Gusti Rosa Kampler, Agata Moglie Accolti, Giacomo Howell, Giorgio Kleinerman, Susanna Specht, Benita Perutz, Enrico Lifschust, Walter Robilland, Vittorio Romastin, David Klamper, Carlo Willy Weil, Guglielmo Weil, Carol Peirce, Aldredo Michelagnoli, Liberta' Moglie Spina, Tatiana Michelagnoli, Mirella Michelagnoli, Attone Micassi, Lucio Servadio, Hildegard Kleptar, Ottorina Crippa, Maria Crippa, Romano Karemar, Remo Garosci, Ferdinando Nikelsbacher, Cornelia Nikelsbacher, Teodoro Rena, William Fratello Pierce, Agata Howell, Pietro Padre Russo, Paula Alster, Karel Weil, Fam. Wovsi, Flora Rotschild, Isidor Gruner.